Lecture Notes of the Institute for Computer Sciences, Social Informatics and Telecommunications Engineering 311

More information about this series at http://www.springer.com/series/8197

Rafik Zitouni · Max Agueh ·
Pélagie Houngue · Hénoc Soude (Eds.)

e-Infrastructure and e-Services for Developing Countries

11th EAI International Conference, AFRICOMM 2019
Porto-Novo, Benin, December 3–4, 2019
Proceedings

Springer

Editors
Rafik Zitouni 🔟
ECE Paris Graduate School of Engineering
Paris, France

Max Agueh
EFREI Paris
Paris, France

Pélagie Houngue
Institut de Mathématiques et de Sciences
Physiques (IMSP)
Porto-Novo, Benin

Hénoc Soude
Institut de Mathématiques et de Sciences
Physiques (IMSP)
Porto-Novo, Benin

ISSN 1867-8211   ISSN 1867-822X (electronic)
Lecture Notes of the Institute for Computer Sciences, Social Informatics
and Telecommunications Engineering
ISBN 978-3-030-41592-1   ISBN 978-3-030-41593-8 (eBook)
https://doi.org/10.1007/978-3-030-41593-8

This Springer imprint is published by the registered company Springer Nature Switzerland AG
The registered company address is: Gewerbestrasse 11, 6330 Cham, Switzerland

Preface

We are delighted to introduce the proceedings of the 11th edition of the 2019 European Alliance for Innovation (EAI) International Conference on e-Infrastructure and e-Services for Developing Countries (AFRICOMM 2019). This conference has brought together researchers, developers, and practitioners who are leveraging and developing new technologies such as cloud computing, IoT, data analytics, green computing, etc. in developing countries. Deploying efficient and effective infrastructures and solutions when limited resources are available is a challenging task and a key-enabler for the diffusion of Information and Communication Technologies (TCT) in developing countries. The aim of this conference is to bring together international researchers, students, engineers, policy makers, and practitioners in ICT to discuss issues and trends, recent research, innovation advances, and on-the-field experiences related to e-Governance, e-Infrastructure, and e-Business with a focus on developing countries.

The technical program of AFRICOMM 2019 received 49 submissions, including full and short papers. 18 papers were accepted as full papers. Authors were from different countries including Benin, Tunisia, South Africa, Senegal, Italy, Burkina Faso, Ivory Coast, Germany, Namibia, etc. Some contributions were also joint between several institutions and countries.

The accepted papers cover several topics related to emerging technologies and their use in developing countries in particular, and in rural areas in general. These topics span different infrastructures, technologies and paradigms, and application fields. Examples include targeted infrastructures, Internet of Things (IoT), Wireless and Mobile Networks, Intelligent Transportation Systems (ITS), Software and Network Security, Cloud and Virtualization, Data Analytics, Machine Learning, etc. The conference tracks were as follows: Track 1 – Software and Network Security; Track 2 – Smart Cities; Track 3 – Internet of Things (IoT); and Track 4 – Data Management and IT Applications. Aside from the high-quality technical paper presentations, the technical program also featured two keynote speeches and an AFRICATEK workshop. The two keynote speakers were Mr. Pierre Dandjinou Icann (Vice President of Stakeholder Engagement in Africa, Benin) and Mr. Colombiano Kedowide (Consultant and IT expert, Canada). The AFRICATEK workshop focused on African's personal data security issues and on an Artificial Intelligence (AI) based prediction system, which improves student academic performances.

Coordination with the steering chairs was essential for the success of the conference. We sincerely appreciated their constant support and guidance. It was also a great pleasure to work with such an excellent Organizing Committee and we thank the team for their hard work in organizing and supporting the conference. In particular, the Technical Program Committee (TPC), led by our TPC Co-Chairs, Dr. Pélagie Houngue and Dr. Henoc Soude, completed the peer-review process of technical papers and made a high-quality technical program. We are also grateful to conference manager,

Kristina Lappyova, for her support as well as all the authors who submitted their papers to the AFRICOMM 2019 conference and workshop.

We strongly believe that the AFRICOMM 2019 conference provided a good forum for all researcher, developers, and practitioners to discuss all science and technology aspects that are relevant to smart grids. We also expect that the future AFRICOMM conference will be as successful and stimulating, as indicated by the contributions presented in this volume.

December 2019

Rafik Zitouni
Max Agueh
Pélagie Houngue
Hénoc Soude

Organization

Steering Committee

Imrich Chlamtac   University of Trento, Italy
Max Agueh   ESIEE Paris, France

Organizing Committee

General Chair

Max Agueh   ESIEE Paris, France

General Co-chairs

Pélagie Houngue   IMSP Porto-Novo, Benin
Soude Hénoc   IMSP Porto-Novo, Benin

TPC Chair and Co-chairs

Rafik Zitouni   ECE Paris, France
Max Agueh   ESIEE Paris, France

Local Chairs

Pélagie Houngue   IMSP, Université d'Abomey-Calavi, Benin
Hénoc Soude   IMSP, Université d'Abomey-Calavi, Benin
Jules Degila   IMSP, Université d'Abomey-Calavi, Benin

Workshop Chair

Arnaud Ahouandjinou   IFRI, Université d'Abomey-Calavi, Benin

Publications Chair

Rafik Zitouni   ECE Paris, France

Posters and PhD Track Chair

Aghiles Djoudi   ECE Paris, France

Demos Chair

Stefan Ataman   ELI-NP, Romania

Tutorials Chairs

Pierre Courbin   ESILV, France
Frederic Fauberteau   ESILV, France

Technical Program Committee

Max Agueh	ESIEE Paris, France
Pélagie Houngue	IMSP, Université d'Abomey-Calavi, Benin
Soude Hénoc	IMSP, Université d'Abomey-Calavi, Benin
Rafik Zitouni	ECE Paris, France
Carlyna Bondiombouy	ECE Paris, France
Patrick Valduriez	Inria, France
Muhammad Ijaz	University of Manchester, UK
Bouziane Brik	Eurecom, France
Ahmed Kora	ESMT, Senegal
Marco Zennaro	ICTP, Italy
Eugene C. Ezin	UAC, Benin
Hamid Harroud	Alakhawayn University, Morocco
Christian Attiogbe	Université de Nantes, France
Jonathan Ouoba	VTT, Finland
Karl Jonas	H-BRS, Germany
Kokou Yetongnon	Université de Bourgogne, France
Pierre Courbin	ESILV, France
Stefan Ataman	ELI-NP, Romania
Idris Rai	University of Zanzibar, Tanzania
Tayeb Lemlouma	IRISA, France
Benaoumeur Senouci	ECE Paris, France
Fréderic Faubertea	ESILV, France
Taha Ridene	RTIT, France
Sihem Zitouni	Université de Bejaïa, Algeria
Hakim Badis	Université Paris Est, France
Joel Hounsou	IMSP, Université d'Abomey-Calavi, Benin
Sanda Tidjani	IMSP, Université d'Abomey-Calavi, Benin
Arnaud Ahouandjinou	IFRI, Université d'Abomey-Calavi, Benin
Romaric Sagbo	IMSP, Université d'Abomey-Calavi, Benin
Victor Odumuyiwa	University of Lagos, Nigeria
Aghiles Djoudi	ECE Paris, France
Laurent George	ESIEE Paris, France
Nadir Bouchama	CERIST Research Center, Algeria
Houda Chihi	Sup'Com, Tunisia
Yassine Boufeneche	USTHB, Algeria
Kyung-Hyune Rhee	KIISCn, South Korea
Bo Jing	Baidu Technology, China
Na Inseop	Chosun University, South Korea
Balint Kiss	Budapest University, Hungary

Contents

Internet of Things

Data Management and IT Applications

Software Security

Analysis of the Impact of Permissions on the Vulnerability of Mobile Applications

Gouayon Koala[✉], Didier Bassolé, Aminata Zerbo/Sabané,
Tegawendé F. Bissyandé, and Oumarou Sié

Laboratoire de Mathématiques et d'Informatique, Université Joseph Ki-Zerbo,
Ouagadougou, Burkina Faso
gouayonkoala1@gmail.com, dbassole@gmail.com, aminata.sabane@gmail.com,
tegawende.bissyande@fasolabs.org, oumarou.sie@gmail.com
http://www.univ-ouaga.bf

Abstract. In this paper, we explored the potential risks of authorizations unexplained by benign apps in order to maintain the confidentiality and availability of personal data. More precisely, we focused on the mechanisms for managing risk permissions under Android to limit the impact of these permissions on vulnerability vectors. We analyzed a sample of forty (40) apps developed in Burkina Faso and identified abuses of dangerous authorizations in several apps in relation to their functional needs. We also discovered combinations of dangerous permissions because it exposes the confidentiality of the data. This analysis allowed us to establish a link between permissions and vulnerabilities, as a source of risk of data security. These risks facilitate exploits of privileges that should be reduced. We have therefore proposed the need to coordinate resolution mechanisms to the administrators, developers, users to better guide the required permissions by benign apps on Android.

Keywords: Permission abuse · Vulnerability · Privilege exploit · Security

1 Introduction

The availability of many apps and features for smartphones and tablets has attracted a large number of users, which in turn has generated interest for growing number of malware authors [22]. The latter benefit from access to sensitive resources to conduct their business despite existing detection and protection efforts [14]. To this end, we are studying the security of a sample of forty (40) apps developed in Burkina Faso, with an emphasis on analyzing the risks associated with permissions.

We have particularly worked on the Android platform which dominates the mobile OS market with more than 81% users [13]. This popularity of Android makes it the most widespread mobile operating system in the world and therefore

R. Zitouni et al. (Eds.): AFRICOMM 2019, LNICST 311, pp. 3–14, 2020.
https://doi.org/10.1007/978-3-030-41593-8_1

the preferred target of attacks. Although the existing studies have proposed several mobile data protection alternatives, they have not focused on permission management, which remains an important issue. We propose to analyze the potential risks of permissions in order to propose mechanisms to ensure the security of data stored on Android.

The rest of this document is organized as follows: the Sect. 2 presents the context and motivations of this study. In the Sect. 3, we present some existing related work before explaining in the Sect. 4 our analytical methodology adopted to achieve our objectives. The Sect. 5 is devoted to the presentation of results followed by proposals to improve the protection of user data. In the Sect. 6, we conclude by reviewing our analyses with our contributions and also present future work.

2   Context

The use of smartphones and tablets with increasing technological characteristics, combined with the multitude of diversified apps, has led to a recent explosion in their market [23]. In 2018 alone, more than 1.55 billion smartphones sold worldwide accounted for 85.7% billion of total sales, compared to less than 260 million computers sold, according to Gartner's report [26,27].

This use of mobile phones leads to a continuous growth of sensitive data on these devices. In 2015, more than 16.2% of the files downloaded through file sharing services contained sensitive data [8]. This sensitive data includes conference call numbers, passwords, credit card or bank account numbers, alarm codes and secure corporate offices, names and phone numbers, multimedia content, etc. [11] and reveals a personal nature. With users having so much personal data on their devices, the confidentiality and availability of this data becomes an imperative [5,9,10]. Mobile OS are becoming more and more like computer operating systems. As a result, the data protection challenges in these mobile devices are becoming similar to the challenges of computer platforms.

Android dominates the market and therefore attracts authors of malware and researchers [12,14]. This market domination makes it a privileged target for pirates. Friedman et al. [7] presented a taxonomy of threats such as malware, phishing and social engineering, direct attack by hackers, communication data (interception and spoofing), loss and theft of removable storage devices or media, malicious insider actions and user policy violations.

3   Related Works

The work of Shewale et al. [11] and Jimenez et al. [12] have revealed that, despite Android's patch efforts, the number of vulnerabilities continues to grow. These vulnerabilities cause denial of service attacks (KillingInTheNameOf [19]), privilege escalations (GingerBreak [11]), code execution and non-authenticated access (Master Key), sniffing with clear text sending of connection information and the middle man with monitoring user activity on the Android browser.

Figures 1 and 2 show the evolution of the vulnerabilities extracted from the Common Vulnerabilities Exposures (CVE) site [25]. Vulnerabilities with a score between 9.3 and 10 are critical because they expose more data.

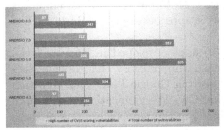

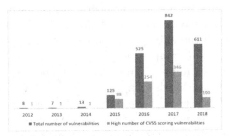

x-axis: number of vulnerabilities
y-axis: Android version

x-axis: years
y-axis: number of vulnerabilities

Fig. 1. Vulnerabilities by version

Fig. 2. Vulnerabilities per year

Among the attacks against Android, malware represents the largest part and is the most recurrent [13–15,24]. Thanh [2] has grouped these malware into families with malicious activities and areas where searches have been conducted. He selected the recognizable features of ordinary users and concluded that 99% was designed for Android. The most common malicious objects on smartphones Android are computer viruses, worms, adware, spyware, ransomware, botnets, rootkits, Trojans and bugs [8,19,21]. Also, more than 86% of malware is piggybacked apps [3]. Unfortunately, the mechanisms for detecting and blocking these attacks remain insufficient. Several tools based on static or dynamic analysis [1–3,20] have been developed for securing mobile data. FlowDroid [16], developed by Arzt et al. allows to determine the flows for sensitive Android sources. Avdiienko et al. have developed the MudFlow tool [17], which uses several classifiers, trained on the data flow of benign apps, to automatically identify apps with suspicious features. Chin et al. [18], designed *ComDroid*, for vulnerability detection in app communication systems. However, these tools cannot verify the existence of attacks or fixes for vulnerabilities found in the app design. Some characteristics are resistant to obsufcation. Thus, Sawadogo [4] proposed an extraction technique based on graph partitioning. This involves using the INFOMAP algorithm to extract community-related characteristics in order to use supervised learning to detect associated risks. The work of He et al. [1] is helping to detect and reduce malware threats. In [6], Gilbert et al. [6] proposed *AppInspector*, a cloud-based approach to monitoring suspicious behaviour of certain resources. This approach makes it possible to identify the risks related to the confidentiality of data stored in mobile applications.

4   Analytical Methodology

4.1   Characteristics of the Analyzed Apps

Studies in some countries have identified security breaches of data stored via mobile apps [2]. Thus, through this study, we wish to put a particular emphasis on the degree of data exposure with the use of apps developed in Burkina Faso with the habits of developers.

Our sample includes a total of forty (40) apps developed in Burkina Faso. This sample includes at least one app in each app category that Google Play offers. All these apps have been downloaded from Google Play. This approach allows us to have apps that have undergone Google's verification tests before being published on its site. We were interested in the number of users of these apps as a criterion. On the one hand, we have chosen the apps that are most downloaded from the Google Play website. On the other hand, we were interested in the different categories of activities (see Fig. 3). We have apps in all sectors of activity such as tourism, news, health, education, financial transactions, justice, culture, religion, job search, history, geolocation services and entertainment.

Fig. 3. Analyzed apps

The objective of this analysis is to evaluate the risks of attacks related to data confidentiality, availability and integrity. This consists in verifying the management of access authorizations, code vulnerability, intellectual property protection (the piggybacking) of mobile apps developed in Burkina Faso. Our analysis therefore focused on the functionalities of the app, the resource requirements of these features, the necessary permissions for these features, the required permission abuses, the communication between apps and the integration of advertising libraries considered dangerous.

4.2   Analysis Tools

For the analysis of our apps, we used the static approach. Our technique is based on analyses based on comparisons. The choice of this approach to analyze our apps is linked to the following advantages:

- it allows to inspect the source code of an app, because the semantic information, methods and structure of an app are contained in its file manifest;
- is an approach that is not influenced by the continuous evolution of Android environments;
- it allows to analyze the characteristics of a normal app and that of its app piggybacked;
- it allows to check the interactions of an app with the system;
- reveals potential security threats and privacy breaches by examining of code;
- some malicious apps do not activate immediately when performing dynamic detection analysis.

The current method used by static analysis is reverse engineering. Before you can inspect the source code of an Android app, you must decompress its apk. We used the Apktool decompression tool (version Apktool 2.2.2) (Fig. 4).

Fig. 4. Tools and procedure for decompiling/recompiling an apk.

Apktool is used to disassemble (or reassemble) the file *class.dex* in the apk and get the bytecode of the file *.dex*. It is used with the tools smali and baksmali (smali-2.2.5 and baksmali-2.2.5). smali allows you to have the files in a more human-readable format and also to compile the file if you have made changes. baksmali is used to decompile the files *class.dex*.

5   Results of the Analysis

One of the disadvantages of the Android security model is the permissions management [17]. Android has approximately one hundred and thirty (130) permissions, including permissions that are at risk with respect to their access to sensitive and personal information. Some permissions are new and more exploited by malware authors [14].

5.1   Impacts of Permissions

Developers of malware exploit the weaknesses of permissions management at several levels. Figure 5 presents cases of privileges granted, by inheriting permissions from dangerous libraries (Scenario 1) or by reusing the code (Scenario 2). Libraries being integrated into the host apps that use them, they essentially form a symbiotic relationship. A library can effectively take advantage of and naturally inherit all the authorizations that a user can grant to an app, thus compromising the confidentiality, availability and integrity of sensitive data. For the inheritance of permissions by piggybacked apps, the pirate may, after modification of the code of the benign app, add dangerous permissions or libraries to the initial permissions to compromise the confidentiality and availability of the data and grant themselves additional privileges.

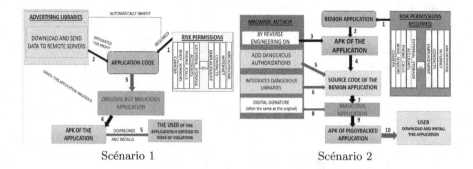

Scénario 1   Scénario 2

Fig. 5. Inheritance of dangerous permissions

The consequences of these scenarios are the exploitation of privileges granted through dangerous permissions, the probable collection of private information, the risk of confidentiality violations and data availability, an app identical to the original that the user will use unsuspectingly and that will expose his data. The Fig. 6 (Scenario 3) presents the exploitation of data residue privileges after data recovery from an uninstalled app. These are data residue attacks. When a

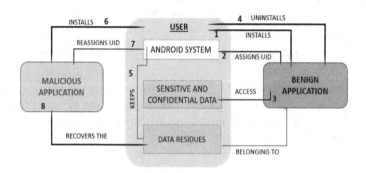

Fig. 6. Scenario 3

user installs an app, the system assigns an identifier called a User ID (UID). It is with this ID that the app can access the resources it needs. If this app has privileges to access sensitive data (such as access to accounts), this data is stored in several components accessible with the UID. If this app is uninstalled, this data is stored in several forms as data residue. If the user installs a new app of the same type, the system can assign the UID of the uninstalled app to the user and the new app therefore inherits all the privileges of the uninstalled app.

These three scenarios show that the permissions granted are vectors of exposure of sensitive data and constitute a weakness that makes these resources vulnerable.

5.2   Results

Our analysis allowed us to determine the most requested resources across apps requiring the same authorization. To determine the permissions granted in each app, we represented the set of app permissions request data as a binary matrix with N as the number of apps, and T as the total number of permissions, $x \in \{0,1\}^{N*T}$. The entry $x_{it} = 1$ means that the i app requests permission t. The line $x_{i*} \in \{0,1\}^T$ represents all the required permissions of the app i. And for each app analyzed, we have the required dangerous authorizations, all the permissions granted and the permissions necessary for the app's functional needs. Figure 7 associates to each permission the number of apps having this authorization while Fig. 8 associates to each app its number of permissions.

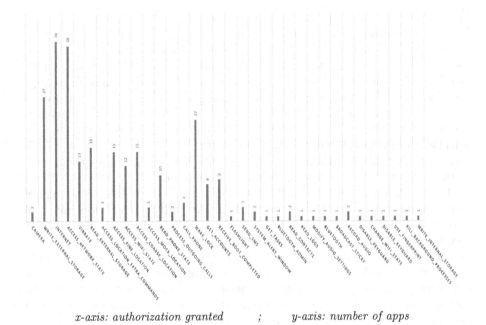

x-axis: authorization granted   ;   y-axis: number of apps

Fig. 7. Number of apps per permission

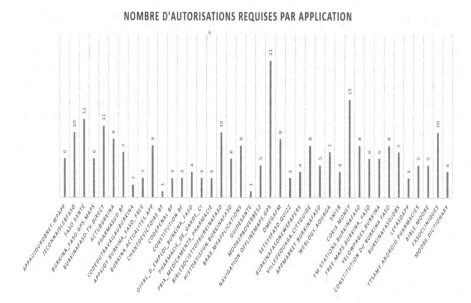

x-axis: app   ;   y-axis: number of permissions

Fig. 8. Number of permissions per app

5.3 Discussion of the Results

Among the forty (40) apps analyzed, only ten (10), or 25%, have normal (risk-free) authorizations. These authorizations do not provide access to sensitive information, although some of these apps have access to the Internet. Moreover, there is only one app that does not provide Internet access. The other thirty (30) apps (i.e. 75%) provide access to various sensitive resources. Each of these apps requires at least one risky permission and thus grants access to the corresponding sensitive data. We found that 17.5% of the apps have only one dangerous permission including access to the SD card (READ_EXTERNAL_STORAGE or WRITE_EXTERNAL_STORAGE). Access to the SD card for writing is 67.5% (27 apps) that grant authorization against 40% (16 apps) for reading access to the SD card. 20% of apps grant access to accounts (GET_ACCOUNTS or GET_ACCOUNTS_PRIVILEGED). Only half of these apps (the 10%) require these permissions for their functionality. The other half therefore does not need these authorizations due to their functionalities. 7.5% of the apps allow abusive access to the messaging system (sending, receiving or reading SMS messages).

The results of this analysis show that twenty-seven (27) apps (or 67.5%) only require the authorizations necessary for their operation, compared to thirteen (13) apps (or 32.5%) that have authorization abuses that can compromise data confidentiality, integrity and even availability. Also, seven (7) apps (or 17.5%) have integrated high-risk advertising libraries.

Permission Management

Authorization management has evolved with fixes to the latest versions of Android. Since Android 6.0 (Marshmallow), permissions are required to install the app. Users ability to revoke the individual authorizations of an app via the app settings interface. However, with Android 5.1 (Lollipop) and earlier versions, the app permissions are all required for installation. Users have no choice, they must accept all the permissions of the app or refuse them all. Authorizations giving access to sensitive resources expose these resources to malware threats. The need to find alternatives is essential for the protection of sensitive resources. Also, in most of the analyzed apps, there is no expression of hardware aspects to use technical capabilities.

Permissions-Risk Link for Using an App

Two permissions can each be harmless but granted together, the risk of exposing confidentiality can increase considerably. For example, permissions INTERNET and READ_SMS, may seem harmless each, but combined we have an app that can read SMS and send content to a third party. There are several combinations of permissions that carry significant risks but are not presented as such to the user. In our analysis, the permission INTERNET_ACCESS was used by thirty-nine (39) apps of which thirty-eight (38) also have permission ACCESS_NETWORK_STATE. These two common permissions take control of the device's hardware and help the user connect to the Internet and maintain a constant connection to the network properties of the devices. Also, the permission ACCESS_FINE_LOCATION has been used by fifteen (15) apps as well as the permission ACCESS_COARSE_LOCATION. These two permissions are used simultaneously by twelve (12) apps. These two permissions provide access to user information and allow the user's location to be determined, whether it is an approximate or precise location. Therefore, the combination of permissions that control the device hardware and permissions that access user information makes the app more vulnerable to the risks of malicious attacks.

5.4 Proposals for Solutions

After analyzing apps and identifying potential threats to mobile data, we propose various preventive measures to prevent malware from infecting smartphones. The recommendations we make are intended to reduce the risks discovered from the scenarios cited and the related work.

As the main service provider, the administrator is the regulator of apps and services on mobile devices. It must therefore add to its security policy:

- extend the permission management policy to verify the need for permission by each app to limit malicious or unknown actions;
- block potentially dangerous combinations of permissions. In our case, having the permissions "INTERNET_ACCESS or ACCESS_NETWORK_STATE" and "ACCESS_COARSE_LOCATION or ACCESS_FINE_LOCATION" in the same app increases the risk of data leakage;

- improve its User-ID (UID) allocation system to prevent any reuse. Thus, he could associate the app life cycle with his UID;
- have only one signature per app to avoid its reuse by piggybacked app's developers;
- ensure that apps that offer the same features use the same permissions or permissions groups;
- have appropriate mechanisms in place to approve third-party libraries used in app development;
- have a file *manifest* containing the necessary permission group for each app category based on functionality and avoid modifying this file that developers will exploit.

The developer is primarily responsible for granting permissions through the declaration of the resources to be accessed. To reduce the risk of privacy breaches, it should respect certain principles:

- inquire about or comply with the good practices provided by Android in order to make apps less sensitive to security issues and reduce security vulnerabilities that can be exploited by malware;
- use approved libraries;
- ask for permissions related to the app's features;
- add comments on the app and its features with permissions.

The user, by accepting these permissions, will have access to different functions of his device. However, he may not understand the potential danger associated with each permission or how combinations of permissions can expose his data to attacks. The choice of authorizations for the installation is up to them in addition to being the first to be concerned by the consequences of the attacks. We offer a number of precautions for the user:

- the user must check the risks for each combination of permissions to avoid making his data vulnerable;
- it must be careful in approving dangerous permissions during the installation of apps;
- the system simply tells the user which permission groups the app needs, not individual permissions, hence the need to review the permissions granted to prevent vulnerabilities.
- the user must stop apps that access sensitive resources and also have access to the Internet to limit the leakage of their data to remote sites;
- it must disable networking features such as WiFi or Bluetooth if they are not used, to prevent smartphones from being infected by malware;
- make the updates taking into account the possible added permissions.

6   Conclusion and Future Work

In this paper, we focused on the management of permissions granted in Android; an aspect that has not been developed by this existing work. This orientation has led to the discovery of permission abuses and the establishment of three privilege exploitation scenarios. We have discovered cases of abuse of permissions exposing confidential data. In addition, there are threats of violations through the integration, in certain apps, of ad libraries that inherit permissions from host apps. Our results can be used to reduce the threat vectors of malicious apps through improved vulnerability management policy. By focusing our approach on permission abuse and the integration of dangerous advertising libraries, we have been able to highlight that the high level of use of dangerous permissions is a risk indicator. We have therefore established a link between the permissions granted and the risk of attacks. We also identified the habits of Android app developers in Burkina Faso. For data protection, we have proposed measures for the user, developer and administrator.

Following the various security issues related to the use of identified mobile services and apps, proposals have been made to improve mobile data protection. Thus, in future work, we will address some studies that we have not been able to deepen. It is about:

- analyze a sample of apps developed in Africa to broadly study the habits of developers in Africa and the risks faced by users of these apps;
- develop a tool to warn and guide the user or administrator when an app requires a dangerous authorization or a combination of authorizations that will expose the user's data. The warning will occur during the publication of the app at the administrator's and during the installation at the user's;
- put more emphasis on data residue attacks.

References

1. He, D., Chan, S., Guizani, M.: Mobile application security: malware threats and defenses. IEEE Wirel. Commun. **22**, 138–144 (2015)
2. Thanh, H.L.: Analysis of malware families on android mobiles: detection characteristics recognizable by ordinary phone users and how to fix it. J. Inf. Secur. **4**, 213–224 (2013)
3. Wang, Y., Alshboul, Y.: Mobile security testing approaches and challenges. In: Conference Paper, February 2015
4. Sawadogo, S.: Partitionnement de Graphes: Application à l'identification de malwares, master 2, mai 2015
5. Mishra, R.: Mobile application security: building security into the development process (2015)
6. Gilbert, P., Chun, B.-G.: Vision: automated security validation of mobile apps at app markets (2011)
7. Friedman, J., Hoffman, D.V.: Protecting data on mobile devices: a taxonomy of security threats to mobile computing and review of applicable defenses. Inf. Knowl. Syst. Manag. **7**, 159–180 (2008)
8. Rezaie, S.: Mobile security education with android labs. Ph.D. thesis, The Faculty of California Polytechnic State University, March 2018
9. Zonouz, S., Houmansadr, A., Berthier, R., Borisov, N., Sanders, W.: Secloud: a cloud-based comprehensive and lightweight security solution for smartphones. Comput. Secur. **37**, 215–227 (2013)

10. Lindorfer, M., Neugschwandtner, M., Platzer, C.: MARVIN: efficient and comprehensive mobile app classification through static and dynamic analysis. In: 2015 IEEE 39th Annual Computer Software and Applications Conference, vol. 2, pp. 422–433 (2015)
11. Shewale, H., Patil, S., Deshmukh, V., Singh, P.: Analysis of android vulnerabilities and modern exploitation techniques, March 2014
12. Jimenez, M., Papadakis, M., Bissyandé, T.F., Klein, J.: Profiling android vulnerabilities (2014)
13. Mobile Threats Report, Juniper Networks Third Annual, March 2012 through March 2013
14. Li, L., et al.: Understanding android app piggybacking: a systematic study of malicious code grafting (2016)
15. Li, L., et al.: On locating malicious code in piggybacked android apps. October 2017
16. Arzt, S., et al.: FlowDroid: precise context, flow, field, object-sensitive and lifecycle-aware taint analysis for Android apps. In: Proceedings of the 35th ACM SIGPLAN Conference on Programming Language Design and Implementation, PLDI 2014, New York, pp. 259–269 (2014)
17. Avdiienko, V., et al.: Mining apps for abnormal usage of sensitive data. In: 2015 IEEE/ACM 37th IEEE International Conference on Software Engineering, May 2015, vol. 1, pp. 426–436 (2015)
18. Chin, E., Felt, A.P., Greenwood, K., Wagner, D.: Analyzing inter-application communication in Android. In: Proceedings of the 9th International Conference on Mobile Systems, Applications, and Services - MobiSys 2011, pp. 239–252. ACM (2011)
19. Ratsisahanana, R.A.: Caractérisation et détection de malware Android basées sur les flux d'information. Autre, Supélec (2014)
20. Calvet, J.: Analyse Dynamique de Logiciels Malveillants. Cryptographie et sécurité [cs.CR]. Université de Lorraine (2013)
21. Sang, F.L.: Protection des systèmes informatiques contre les attaques par entrées-sorties. Cryptographie et sécurité [cs.CR]. INSA de Toulouse, pp. 9–10 (2012)
22. Grace, M., Zhou, W., Sadeghi, A-R., Jiang, X.: Unsafe exposure analysis of mobile in-app advertisements (2012)
23. Dinh, H.T., Lee, C., Niyato, D., Wang, P.: A survey of mobile cloud computing: architecture, applications, and approaches, October 2011
24. Symantec, 19 August 2013. https://www.symantec.com/security-center/writeup/2013-081914-5637-99. Accessed 18 Dec 2018
25. Vulnerabilities of Android. https://www.cvedetails.com/product/19997/Google-Android.html?vendor_id=1224. Accessed 18 Jan 2019
26. Gartner: Preliminary Worldwide PC Vendor Unit Shipment Estimates for 2018, January 2019. https://www.gartner.com/en/newsroom/press-releases/2019-01-10-gartner-says-worldwide-pc-shipments-declined-4-3-perc. Accessed 22 Apr 2019
27. Gartner: Worldwide Smartphone Sales to End Users by Vendor in 2018, February 2019. https://www.gartner.com/en/newsroom/press-releases/2019-02-21-gartner-says-global-smartphone-sales-stalled-in-the-fourth-quart. Accessed 28 Apr 2019

On the Relevance of Using Multi-layered Security in the Opportunistic Internet-of-Things

Antoine Bagula[1,2($\boxtimes$)], Lutando Ngaqwazai[2], Claude Lubamba Kakoko[2], and Olasupo Ajayi[1,2]

[1] ISAT Laboratory, University of the Western Cape, Cape Town 7535, South Africa
abagula@uwc.ac.za, 3944991@myuwc.ac.za
[2] Department of Computer Science, University of the Western Cape,
Cape Town 7535, South Africa

Abstract. Wireless Sensor Networks (WSNs) have recently gained more importance as key building blocks for the Internet of Things (IoT); a network infrastructure which has greatly increased in number of connected objects with instantaneous communication, data processing and pervasive access to the objects that we manipulate daily. However, WSNs may sometimes need to be deployed in an opportunistic fashion when there is no network with stable power supply available to support the dissemination of the sensor readings from their collection points to a gateway. For such deployments, traditional networking paradigms may fall short to secure the WSNs since most of the well-known security algorithms have been designed for the traditional high quality of service and fully connected networks. Building around some of the security algorithms and protocols which have been developed in the context of Delay Tolerant Networking, this paper presents a multi-layered security model for the opportunistic IoT. The model combines a hash based message authentication code (HMAC) algorithm implemented at the application layer of the IEEE 802.15.4 stack and an Access Control List (ACL) based identity based encryption algorithm used by the IEEE 802.15.4 MAC layer as a new and novel method of signing and authenticating data which is stored and forwarded on an opportunistic Internet of Things (IoT) infrastructure.

Keywords: Multi-layered security · Internet-of-Things · Wireless sensor networks · Opportunistic networking

1 Introduction

Recently, Wireless Sensor Networks (WSNs) have gained more significance as key building blocks for the Internet of Things (IoT). As a network infrastructure, it has seen a great increase in the number of connected objects with instantaneous

© ICST Institute for Computer Sciences, Social Informatics and Telecommunications Engineering 2020
Published by Springer Nature Switzerland AG 2020. All Rights Reserved
R. Zitouni et al. (Eds.): AFRICOMM 2019, LNICST 311, pp. 15–29, 2020.
https://doi.org/10.1007/978-3-030-41593-8_2

communication, data processing and pervasive access to objects that we manipulate daily at "anytime", from "anywhere" and using "anything". Next generation wireless sensor networks are predicted to deployed on the *Internet-of-the-Things (IoT)* paradigm, connecting islands of ubiquitous sensor networks (USNs). Some of these USNs would follow an opportunistic communication model where the sensor motes are provided the capability of communicating with each other even in the absence of established route(s) between them. This is achieved by building communication pathways "on-the-fly" by having each message finding its next-hop to a gateway opportunistically, with the expectation of bringing the message closer to its USN gateway. When deployed in the harsh environments of the developing world where grid power supply is intermittent or energy is harvested through solar, wind or other energy scavenging methods, these islands of USNs provide a great opportunity to positively impact different daily life activities and bridge the digital divide as they are built around low cost, cheap-to-maintain devices; making it easy to construct networks that can be deployed unattended in thousands of nodes. A typical opportunistic IoT networking scenario is depicted in Fig. 1, where pollution sensing devices are deployed in a city with the need to measure different types of pollution. There is the need to have different settings for the sensing node in order to accurately measure the pollution levels at various areas of the city. In essence thee is the need to form a pollution monitoring network with settings tuned for the particular application area viz.: industrial pollution network in industrial settings, education pollution network in educational settings, residential pollution network in residential settings and traffic pollution network on roads. In such networks, buses, humans and bikes can be used as mobile gateways collecting data opportunistically from the pollution sensors when they are within communication range of these sensors. A similar scenario can be considered in rural deployment where a rural sensor mesh network can benefit from a mobile network of humans, buses and bikes playing the role of data collectors for the sensor network. These scenarios illustrate typical opportunistic IoT deployments in both developed and developing regions when reliable end-to-end network solutions are either financially not feasible or unavailable, and would possible not be in the foreseeable future, due to problems not limited to unsustainable power supply and/or poor local infrastructure. As suggested by the authors in [1], opportunistic networking is more general than delay tolerance, although both terms are often used interchangeably. While opportunistic networking systems are a viable low entrance solution to connecting devices over vast distances, they are still a green field in terms of field readiness and for research in the security field. Figure 2 reveals the interactions between the data mules and the IoT network infrastructure.

1.1 Related Work

Research works on opportunistic networks' security have mostly been conducted in the context of delay tolerant networks. Kate *et al.* [12] showed that security and anonymity are critical in many delay tolerant network implementations and

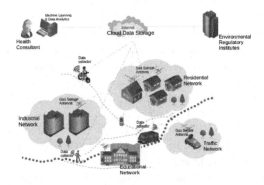

Fig. 1. The opportunistic IoT network infrastructure

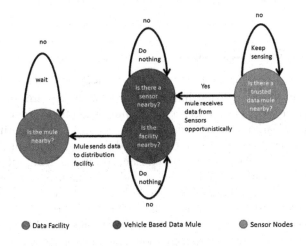

Fig. 2. The mule-infrastructure interaction model

revealed that due to the very low quality of service nature of delay tolerant networks, traditional security implementations based on public key cryptography and infrastructure are not suitable for these intermittent networks. They also showed how maintaining anonymity in delay tolerant networks is not applicable either and demonstrated how identity-based security (IBS) can be used as a security architecture suitable for such network implementations. While their work made a deep analysis of key revocation and generation, our work falls beyond the scope of such security mechanisms. In [13], Seth *et al.* addressed the challenges for securing data communications in delay tolerant networks by making various valid points about how traditional public key infrastructure (PKI) based approaches are not suitable for such networks. In a PKI, a user authenticates another user's public key by using a certificate signed by a certificate authority. In highly intermittent network infrastructures like a delay tolerant network, gaining instant access to a trusted third party certificate authority can prove to be infeasible due to the disconnected nature of the network. PKIs also do not work because key revocation cannot be enforced in an instance. This results in a situation where nodes with compromised keys or outdated keys cannot be forcefully removed from self authenticating them. In a book on delay tolerant networking written by Farrell and Cahill [14], the use of IBS in a delay tolerant network is heavily criticized for not having a valid key management solution as it falls short of providing proper authenticity. This is exemplified by the fact that in DTN environments, it would be very hard to discern between two "Bobs" as the second bob may be an attacker or intruder. This problem can be overcome by using IP or MAC addresses in conjunction with a unique device identifier as the device identity. This however, does not stop an attacker from assuming a name which is the same as another node on the network by using IP/MAC spoofing. Farrell and Cahill also believe that IBC-based security is not scalable as the user must know the public parameters of all the private key generators (PKGs).

1.2   Contributions and Outline

This paper's main contribution is to propose and assess the relevance of using a multi-layered security model that harnesses some of the features of the existing 802.15.4 mac layer security and uses a novel application layer security algorithm to secure communication over a wireless sensor network. The security approach adopted in this paper combines a Hash-based Message Authentication Code (HMAC) algorithm with an Identity Based Encryption (IBE) algorithm to secure an opportunistic network of wireless sensor nodes. Using prototyping, the model was implemented on an arduino-based wireless sensor device as a new and novel method of signing and authenticating data which is stored and forwarded on the opportunistic network. This method involves using the MAC layer security features in the IEEE 802.15.4 specification and an application layer security implementation. The method proposed in this paper has been designed to secure healthcare networks in the context of a CyberHealthcare project described in [5–8] and [9,10]. The project aims at collecting pollution data in areas of interest and correlating the data to health issues in these areas.

The remainder of this paper is organized as follows. Section 2 presents the proposed multi-layered security model. The results of the cyberhealthcare field readiness experiments in the city of Cape Town are presented in Sect. 3 while Sect. 4 contains our conclusions.

2   The Multi-layered Security Model

Some of the main goals of a security model are to provide data integrity and authenticity and data confidentiality. These goals have been used to guide the design and implementation of the multi-layer security model. It involves utilizing the existing technologies contained in 802.15.4 and other features resulting from security requirements that cannot be met by using the security features of the standard only. These include application layer cryptography and message

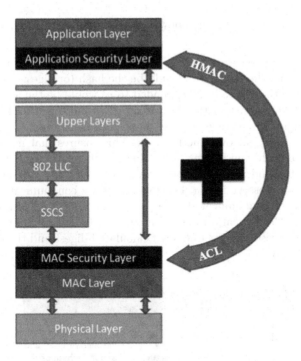

Fig. 3. The multi-layered security model

authentication codes which need to be implemented to add additional security safeguards against spoofing, forgery and service attacks on the delay tolerant network. As depicted by Fig. 3, the multi-layered architecture reveals different layers of a typical 802.15.4/ZigBee protocol but also highlights the two layers where the proposed multi-layer model is implemented, that is: (a) at the MAC security layer where access control lists are used to enable only authorized data mules to interact with the system and (b) at the application security layer where encryption/decryption mechanisms are implemented to secure data.

2.1 Data Integrity and Authenticity

Cryptographic hash functions are usually used for data integrity and authenticity. A cryptographic hash function is an algorithm which takes an arbitrarily sized block of data (usually called the message), and returns a fixed size fingerprint or signature of the data (usually called the digest) [2,3]. Cryptographic hash functions are characterized by the following key features:

– Modifying the message without changing the hash is not feasible.
– The hashing of a message is easy.
– Reversing the hash process is not feasible.
– Two different messages must not hash to the same digest.

The hash function itself is publicly known, thus allows for any mote to implement and use it.

Integrity check: When a message is sent within the network, it will usually arrives in two parts, the first n bits would be the hash (or digest) of the original message [2], while the last m bits (appended to n) would be the actual message. To check that the integrity of the data is intact, a mote will hash the original message, and compare the digest of the message which the mote calculated, to the digest which was sent over the network. This ensures that no tampering of the data was done while in transmission. Such an integrity check can safeguard against man-in-the-middle attacks, and can also be used as a rudimentary error-detection method. Observe in Fig. 4, if two motes are communicating and mote A sends mote B the communicated data (which contains the digest and message appended to it), Mote B can calculate the digest of the message bit string and do a bitwise comparison between its own calculated digest and the digest which was sent by mote A.

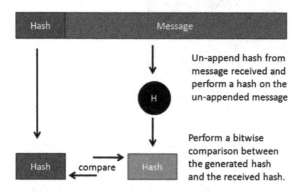

Fig. 4. Integrity check illustration

Hash-Based Message Authentication Code (HMAC): A hash-based message authentication code is a type of cryptographic construct which allows the calculation of a message authentication code using a cryptographic hash function [2]. To generate an HMAC, two pieces of data are requires - a key and the message itself. HMAC is commonly used to verify the authenticity of data and at the same time serves as a data integrity check mechanism (message error check). HMAC generation is defined by:

$$HMAC(K, m) = H((K \oplus o_pad) \,\|\, H((K \oplus i_pad) \,\|\, m)) \tag{1}$$

where o_pad and i_pad are the outer padding and inner padding respectively.

2.2 Data Confidentiality

802.15.4 is an IEEE standard which offers functionality of the lower layers of the OSI network model. It is a very lightweight Wireless Personal Area Network

(WPAN) specification which ensures that the cost of producing an 802.15.4 radio is cheap. 802.15.4 is slow (250 kb/s) and covers low range (10 m), though the range can be increased by tweaking various power output values of the radio transceiver. Collision avoidance follows the CSMA/CA scheme. The 802.15.4 secure communication works mainly on the media access control (MAC) sub layer which offers protection of the payload using AES 128 encryption. Rudimentary integrity and code error checking is also performed when communication is being done.

Security Modes. The 802.15.4 allows for various modes of communication. These modes of communication are typically set by the application utilizing the medium access layer protocol. There are a multitude of modes and they will be discussed. The media access control layer consults or sets the flag field in the packet to determine or set the security mode which must be applied to the communication transaction. If no security flag is set, then the packet is passed onto the application layer as is. If there is a security flag checked, then the media access control layer will conform to a protocol which discerns what type of security methods should be employed for that particular communications security flag [18].

No Flag Set: This is the simplest setting that you can have on 802.15.4. It does not perform any additional security functionality and provides zero security guarantees [11].

AES-CTR: This security mode provides confidentiality using AES with counter mode. Basically the sender partitions the plaintext packet into 16-byte blocks. For every plaintext packet, there is an equivalent cipher text packet.

AES-CBC-MAC: This security mode provides integrity assurances using CBC-MAC. The sender can compute a MAC using a CBC-MAC algorithm. The MAC can only be computed by parties with the same symmetric key. The MAC basically encapsulates packet headers and the data payload (which comes from the application). The sender appends the plaintext data with the MAC, and the recipient verifies the MAC by re-computing the MAC by reconstructing the packet and computing the MAC again against the sent MAC [18].

AES-CCM: This security mode uses CCM mode for encryption and authentication. It initially applies integrity protection over the header and data payload using the CBC-MAC algorithm, it then encrypts the data payload and MAC using the AES-CTR mode. One can think of AES-CCM as the combination of CBC-MAC and AES-CTR modes [18].

Security in IEEE 802.15.4: Payload encryption and access control lists are discussed in this section as 802.15.4 security mechanisms.

Payload Encryption: The payload (or message) can be encrypted in three different ways, depending on your network configuration and network requirements. The payload can be encrypted using AES-CTR scheme, which is just an encryption on the payload but the frame counter sets a unique message ID. The AES-CBC-MAC scheme is when the message authenticity code (MAC) is appended to the data payload. This adds authentication and integrity checks at the medium access control layer. And then there is AES- CCM, which is a combination of the two previously stated schemes.

Access Control Lists (ACLs): The Access Control List (ACL) is a list of "trusted devices" along with the security policy that each of the devices have. Each node must have an ACL. An ACL is a table containing the nodes address (IP and MAC address pair), the encryption algorithm allowed by that node (AES-CTR, AES-CCM etc.) and the Replay Counter field, which is used to avoid replay attacks. When a node wants to send or receive a packet to or from a specific device, it checks the packet, to see if it from/to a node in the ACL of the source/destination. If the device is a trusted unit, an authentication process will take place.

2.3 The Proposed Security Solution

With only 8 KB of usable primary memory, the Wasp Mote is a low power sensor device running an 8-bit CPU and a 16-bit ALU clocked at 8 MHz. It uses a radio transceiver which conforms to the IEE 802.15.4 specification. This specification mandates that 802.15.4 radios have AES-128b and error checking capabilities. It also requires hardware managed Symmetric-key key cryptography, which can be set to either pair- or group-wise. The radios also have a feature called access control lists allowing devices with only certain MAC addresses to be permitted on the network.

2.4 The Key Exchange Algorithm

As presented in Fig. 4 and discussed above, the key exchange algorithm works similarly to that which is present in today's world of digital signatures. Basically if two entities on the network wish to communicate, then both of the entities need to assure themselves that both of the nodes are infact authorized nodes within the network. Public key cryptography presents the best option for entities on the network to mutually authenticate each other. However, since public key cryptography could not be implemented, a different approach using Access Control List (ACL) model had to be taken. This way, each node has to make sure that they are on each other's ACL. The ACL is defined before network deployment, and can be updated over the air. If the nodes are mutually trusted devices then shared key exchange can take place using a key agreement scheme called the symmetric-key key exchange. This algorithm is depicted in Fig. 5.

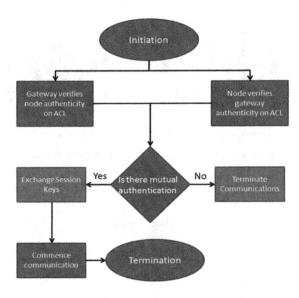

Fig. 5. The key exchange algorithm

3   Performance Evaluation

Different experiments were conducted to assess the field readiness of opportunistic networks when considering the distance between communicating nodes and the security features implemented using the multi-layer security model.

3.1   Opportunistic Contacts

Opportunistic contacts define moments when two devices (mobile nodes) of an IoT network can exchange messages with mesh router at acceptable signal strength and throughput. To assess the field-readiness of the oppotunistic IoT scenario described in this paper, we conducted a number of experiments to determine how the communication range and the speed of the mobile node can impact the opportunistic contacts. The results presented in Fig. 6 reveal that:

- both the RSSI and throughput decrease as distance increases.
- while the throughput for different modes seem not significant, the RSSI may have a different impact on the quality of signal received as these values are expressed in dBm.

Further investigations are being conducted to assess the quality of the opportunistic contacts for cars and UAV drones, and to comparing obtained results from these, with those presented in this paper.

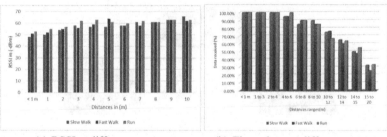

(a) RSSI at different ranges.   (b) Throughput at different ranges.

Fig. 6. Opportunistic contacts.

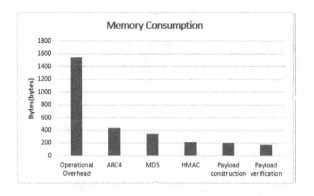

Fig. 7. Memory usage

3.2   Impact of Security on Memory Usage

Figure 7 reveals that the secondary memory footprint of the application security layer did not exceed 2 KB. Typically, devices using 802.15.4 as a means of communication hardly have over 24 KB of capacity on the programmable EEPROM. In terms of primary memory, the application security layer did not exceed 2 KB in usage although it occupied 1.5 KB of the device's RAM. The operational overhead was lower because not all items in memory were explicitly implemented and it was measured at the beginning of each loop. These operational overheads usually include processes which handle the API subroutines, interrupt management or allocated hardware memory allocation. Arduino uses both memory mapped I/O and bus/hardware mapped I/O. The ARC4 algorithm used the most amounts of bytes in memory, consuming about 446 bytes. A large chunk of the bytes can be attributed to the permutation array "S" which is of the size 256 bytes. The rest can be attributed to the cipher text array (The cipher text array is the exact same size as the plaintext array) The MD5 algorithm consumed about 326 bytes of memory. MD5 characteristically chunks a message or plaintext into chunks of 64 bytes (pads the message with zeros to make it naturally "chunk-able" by 64 bytes). The other byte consumed can be attributed to other arrays like the message digest context. The HMAC algorithm uses 224 bytes. This measurement was obtained by subtracting the MD5 byte usage from the total HMAC byte usage. The HMAC uses a few memcopy calls to store the key outer and inner padding arrays. Payload Construction is the routine which is responsible for allocating memory space enough to append a 32 byte hash to a payload of 60 bytes (give or take) and then encrypt it using the ARC4 stream cipher. The ARC4 stream cipher text is double the size of the plaintext since hexadecimal encoding is used to encode bytes and two hexadecimal values are needed to encode a single byte.

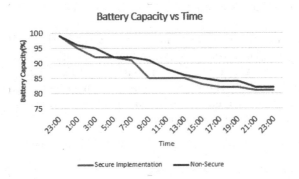

Fig. 8. Battery usage

3.3 Impact of Security on Battery Usage

The power overhead for securing communications can be seen in graph depicted in Fig. 8. This data shows that the power drain resulting from our multi-layered model is slightly higher compared to a non-secure implementation of 802.15.4 communications. The battery usage test was conducted over a 24 h period. Libelium have lauded their devices' minimal power requirements and have openly marketed that their product can be battery powered for up to 1 year with the correct hibernation and sleep programming practices. This experiment was conducted by having a Wasp Mote using 802.15.4 send arbitrary packets to a gateway node approximately 3 m away from it. The experiment was conducted by using the deep sleep method. Each time the wasp mote woke up, it would send a Comma Separated Value (CSV) of its current battery to the gateway. CSV was used in order to make plotting the data easy on tools such as MS Excel. This battery test was done for two cases, the first involved sending data to the gateway using the security methods; while in the second case, data was sent in plaintext.

3.4   Impact of Security on Processing Time

As shown by Fig. 9, the processing time is lower for the MD5 security encryption while payload construction consumes more processing time followed by payload verification. It can be observed that the processor is always at 100% usage. This is in agreement with most Arduino boards because they are typically 95%–100% in use at all times as a result of the processor itself having a very low clock speed. Even if the device had minimal code flashed onto it (The Hello World example code) the processor usage rarely drops below 95%. The Arduino community at large has unanimously experienced this. The graph in Fig. 9 details the processing times of the various routines which make up the bulk of the security methods. The data input size was the maximum allowed data payload allowable by the 802.15.4 specification (96 bytes). The payload construction and payload verification routines often make use of the HMAC-MD5 and ARC4 algorithms, this explains their relatively higher execution times. However, it should be noted that ARC4 only takes about 20 ms to encrypt a payload of size 96 bytes. We noticed that the payload construction is high because it requires the device to do dynamic memory allocation many more times than the Payload verification algorithm would need to do.

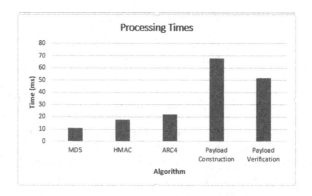

Fig. 9. Processing time

3.5   Impact of Security on Hash Function Overheads

Figure 10 depicts the hash function overheads in terms of execution time of the hash function and the HMAC routine. The results reveal that the HMAC-MD5 model outperforms the others in terms of processing time. The stand alone MD5 function is known to be a cryptographically insecure algorithm, and has thus lost its appeal as a hash function. SHA-1 is generally regarded as being a safer solution. However, in this work it was combined with the HMAC therefore making it safer and less susceptible to attacks. MD5 was chosen as the underlying HMAC function because it is the lightest hash function known.

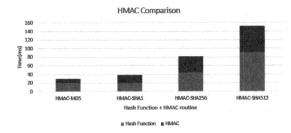

Fig. 10. Hash function overheads

Figure 10 shows the relative difference in execution time between the HMAC portion and the the underlying hash function. It reveals that HMAC-MD5 is indeed very light weight. When the other hash functions were run on the wasp motes, they all required more execution time. This is due to the fact that MD5 (used in HMAC-MD5) produces the smallest hash and works on the smallest block size. Of significant note, is that MD5 is not necessarily a compromise as far as hash functions in HMACs are concerned, as it is secure enough as a means of achieving message authentication and integrity checks.

4 Conclusion and Future Work

This paper has shown that a solution which satisfies security requirements for delay tolerant network of light-weight devices is an achievable goal. This paper also shows how lightweight cryptographic methods can be used to secure a delay tolerant network and revealed how two different protocol layers can be used to achieve network security. The multi-layered approach shows that coupling the security features in 802.15.4 and current lightweight cryptography is a great way to secure a network. The results extracted from a number of experiments conducted around the city of Cape Town to test the field readiness of a cyberhealth-care network infrastructure reveal that our multi-layered security algorithm is a viable security solution that ensures (1) data confidentiality, authenticity and integrity and (2) a lightweight implementation solution which is suitable for the low processing and memory footprint of the low powered sensor devices. The proposed solution had minimal impact on the device's primary memory as it only used a total of just below 1 KB of memory (out of 8 KB) and used a minimal amount of secondary memory (12 KB out of 128 KB).

The results presented in this paper also show that implementing this solution on lightweight devices imposes minimal memory, low processing footprint but requires marginally more battery power.

The management of the opportunistic IoT infrastructure is a key parameter that may require redesigning existent network management techniques to efficiently engineer the cyber-healthcare system. When redesigned in the context of opportunistic networking, the multipath routing techniques such as presented in [15,16] may be used to support QoS by having different forms of health-care data propagated over different paths form a source to a destination. These methods can be combined with the redesign of the cost-based traffic engineering techniques proposed in [17,18] to balance traffic over the cyber-healthcare communication platform and thus increase throughput and reduce communication delays. Extending the reach of an opportunistic IoT infrastructure over a long distance wireless mesh sensor network is another key issue that needs to be addressed that needs to be addressed to support cyber-healthcare network deployment in the rural settings of the developing world. These management techniques are an avenue for future research work.

References

1. Pelusi, L., Passarella, A., Conti, M.: Opportunistic networking: data forwarding in disconnected mobile ad hoc networks. IEEE Commun. Mag. **44**(11), 134–141 (2006)
2. Kaps, J.-P.: Cryptography for ultra-low power devices, Ph.D. thesis, Worcester Polytechnic Institute (2006)
3. Aumasson, J.P., Henzen, L., Meier, W., Naya-Plasencia, M.: Quark: a lightweight hash. J. Cryptol. **26**(2), 313–339 (2013)
4. Padmavathi, G.: A survey of attacks, security mechanisms and challenges in wireless sensor. Networks **4**(1), 1–9 (2009)
5. Mandava, M., Lubamba, C., Ismail, A., Bagula, H., Bagula, A.: Cyber-healthcare for public healthcare in the developing world. In: Proceedings of the 2016 IEEE Symposium on Computers and Communication (ISCC), Messina-Italy, 27–30 June 2016, pp. 14–19 (2016)
6. Bagula, M., Bagula, H., Mandava, M., Kakoko, C., Bagula, A.: Cyber-healthcare kiosks for healthcare support in developing countries. In: Proceedings of the AFRICOMM 2018, Dakar-Senegal, 29–30 November 2018
7. Celesti, A., et al.: How to develop IoT cloud e-health systems based on FIWARE: a lesson learnt. J. Sens. Actuator Netw. **8**(1), 7 (2019)
8. Bagula, A., Mandava, M., Bagula, H.: A framework for healthcare support in the rural and low income areas of the developing world. J. Netw. Comput. Appl. **120**, 17–29 (2018). https://doi.org/10.1016/j.jnca.2018.06.010
9. Bagula, A., Lubamba, C., Mandava, M., Bagula, H., Zennaro, M., Pietrosemoli, E.: Cloud based patient prioritization as service in public health care. In: 2016 ITU Kaleidoscope: ICTs for a Sustainable World (ITU WT), pp. 1–8. IEEE (2016)
10. Lubamba, C., Bagula, A.: Cyber-healthcare cloud computing interoperability using the HL7-CDA standard. In: 2017 IEEE Symposium on Computers and Communications (ISCC), pp. 105–110. IEEE, July 2017
11. Murillo, M.J., Aukin, M.: Application of wireless sensor nodes to a delay-tolerant health and environmental data communication system in remote communities. In: Proceedings of the 2011 IEEE Global Humanitarian Technology Conference, pp. 383–392, October 2011
12. Kate, A., Zaverucha, G.M., Hengartner, U.: Anonymity and security in delay tolerant networks. In: Proceedings of the 2007 Third International Conference on Security and Privacy in Communications Networks and the Workshops - SecureComm 2007, pp. 504–513 (2007)

13. Seth, A., Keshav, S.: Practical security for disconnected nodes. In: Proceedings of the 1st IEEE ICNP Workshop on Secure Network Protocols, pp. 31–36 (2005)
14. Sastry, N., Wagner, D.: Security considerations for IEEE 802.15.4 networks. In: Proceedings of the 2004 ACM Workshop on Wireless security - WiSe 2004 (2004)
15. Bagula, A.B.: Modelling and implementation of QoS in wireless sensor networks: a multi-constrained traffic engineering model. EURASIP J. Wirel. Commun. Netw. **1**, 1–14 (2010)
16. Bagula, A.B.: Hybrid traffic engineering: the least path interference algorithm. In: Proceedings of the 2004 Annual Research Conference of the South African Institute of Computer Scientists and Information Technologists on IT Research in Developing Countries, pp. 89–96, South African Institute of Computer Scientists and Information Technologists (2004)
17. Bagula, A.B.: Hybrid routing in next generation IP networks. Comput. Commun. **29**(7), 879–892 (2006)
18. Bagula, A.B.: On achieveing bandwidth-aware LSP/LambdaSP multiplexing/separation in multi-layer networks. IEEE J. Sel. Areas Commun. **25**, 987–1000 (2007)

Analysis of Software Vulnerabilities Using Machine Learning Techniques

Doffou Jerome Diako[1]([⊠]), Odilon Yapo M. Achiepo[2],
and Edoete Patrice Mensah[3]

[1] EDP, INPHB Yamoussoukro, Yamoussoukro, Côte d'Ivoire
kingdjako@gmail.com
[2] Peleforo Gon Coulibaly University, Korhogo, Côte d'Ivoire
[3] INPHB Yamoussoukro, Yamoussoukro, Côte d'Ivoire

Abstract. With the increasing development of software technologies, we see that software vulnerabilities are a very critical issue of IT security. Because of their serious impacts, many different approaches have been proposed in recent decades to mitigate the damage caused by software vulnerabilities. Machine learning is also part of an approach to solve this problem. The main objective of this document is to provide three supervised machine to predict software vulnerabilities from a dataset of 6670 observations from national vulnerabilities database (NVD). The effectiveness of the proposed models has been evaluated with several performance indicators including Accuracy.

Keywords: Machine learning · Vulnerabilities · Naive Bayes · Support vectors machines · CVSS

1 Introduction

The use of computer software has now become part of everyone's daily life. There are different forms of software ranging from simple applications to sophisticated distributed platforms. These softwares are developed with many different methodologies, based on a wide variety of technologies. The recurring problem with these software is the discovery of vulnerabilities. In the context of software security, "vulnerabilities are specific flaws or omissions in software that allow attackers to perform malicious tasks, expose or modify sensitive information, disrupt or destroy a system, or take control of a computer system or program" [1]. Many approaches have been proposed in recent decades to reduce the damage caused by software vulnerabilities. Machine learning is one of the new approaches to solving this problem. The main objective of this article is to propose three approaches based on supervised learning to effectively predict software vulnerabilities based on a dataset of 6670 observations.

2 Methods for Analyzing Software Vulnerabilities

Several approaches have been proposed and studied by researchers and practitioners to analyze vulnerabilities in the context of software security. The programs are implemented in a variety of languages and contain serious vulnerabilities that can be

R. Zitouni et al. (Eds.): AFRICOMM 2019, LNICST 311, pp. 30–37, 2020.
https://doi.org/10.1007/978-3-030-41593-8_3

exploited to cause security breaches. A study deepens the analysis methods for reducing software vulnerabilities have been developed by Zulkernine et al. So, they categorized these methods into three categories namely, static analysis, dynamic analysis and Hybrid Analysis [2]. These proposed above approaches are approximate solutions. They lack generally either strength or effectiveness facing the technique of machine learning and data mining.

3 Techniques of Machine Learning and Data Mining

In addition to the approaches outlined above, there are other approaches to analyze software vulnerabilities. This approach is based on data mining by techniques of machine learning. This approach is the focus of increasing attention from the scientific community since 2011 [3].

4 Related Work on the Use of Machine Learning

According to Ghaffarian [4] there are three categories of approaches for analyzing software vulnerabilities by machine learning. Those are: The vulnerability prediction models based on software parameters; The anomaly detection approach; Pattern recognition of vulnerable code. In this study we present the approach of vulnerability prediction models based on software parameters.

4.1 Prediction Vulnerabilities Based on Software Settings

This approach uses knowledge extraction techniques from data to predict the vulnerable software artifacts (source code files, object-oriented classes, binary components, etc.) based on software settings. The models are built from a historical database providing a list of software artifacts that may contain failures to prioritize software testing efforts (Kaner et Bond 2004). Zimmermann et al. [5] investigated the possibility of predicting the existence of vulnerabilities in the vista operating system of Microsoft Windows. Coverage parameters have not produced significant results. Results include a precision of less than 67% and a point below 21%. Meneely and Williams [6] studied the relationship between the parameters of the activity of developers and software vulnerabilities. The authors used the Bayesian network as predictive model, with tenfold cross validation to generate sets of training and validation. According to the authors, the analysis shows that the activity of the developer can be used to predict vulnerable files; however, the precision and recall values are disappointing (accuracy between 12% and 29% and reminders between 32% and 56%). Moshtari et al. [7] proposed a semi-automatic scanning framework to detect software vulnerabilities. Their study examined the prediction of inter-project vulnerabilities based on data collected in five open-source projects. Several classification techniques were used for the experiments. The best inter-project forecasting models achieved a detection rate of about 70%, with about 26% of false positives. Morrison et al. [8] claim that if failure prediction models are adopted by some teams such as Microsoft, this is not the case of prediction models vulnerabilities (PMV). To understand, the authors attempt to reproduce an PMV proposed by Zimmermann et al. [9] for the two most recent versions of Microsoft Windows operating system. The authors reproduced prediction accuracy at the binary level of 75% and a point of 20%; However, binaries are often very large for practical inspection and prediction at the source file is preferred by engineers. Therefore, the authors constructed the same model at the level of granularity of the source file, which gave an accuracy of less than 50% and less than 20% recall. Based on these results, Younis et al. [9] attempting to identify the attributes of the code containing the most likely to be exploitable vulnerabilities. For their efforts they gather 183 vulnerabilities from the Linux kernel and the Apache httpd web server, which includes 82 exploitable vulnerabilities. The authors select eight software settings in four different categories to characterize these vulnerabilities and are using the Welch t test to examine the discriminative power of each parameter. The results of the discriminative power settings are mixed; some parameters have a statistically significant discriminative power and others do not. They also examine whether there is a combination of parameters that can be used as predictors of exploitable vulnerabilities, where three different methods of feature selection and four different classification algorithms are tested. The best performing model is the Random Forest classifier with the selection approach Wrapper Subset, which reaches a F-measure of 84%.

4.2 Note

By observing the work discussed above, it is clear that the area of vulnerability forecasting based on software parameters has not yet reached maturity. This conclusion is explicitly discussed by Morrison et al. [8].

5 Proposed Approach

In addition to the approaches discussed above, there is a new powerful approach to solve the problem of software vulnerabilities. This new approach is the use of the offensive security (Ethical Hacking) and Artificial Intelligence techniques together. Ethical Hacking is a discipline that is to exploit known vulnerabilities to investigate the level of security of computer systems. It is to identify weaknesses in computer systems and propose cons-measures to protect them [10, 11]. It is clear that the field of predicting vulnerability based on software settings has not yet reached maturity, our approach will focus on forecasting software vulnerabilities based on basic metrics Common Vulnerability Scoring System (CVSS). These basic metrics are unique and immutable, it is based on the intrinsic qualities of vulnerability.

5.1   Methodology Approach

Our approach is to provide learning models that allow us to analyze software vulnerabilities. To achieve this, we will: (1) Present rules that must comply with a Ethical Hacker; (2) Building a vulnerability database from 2010 to 2018; (3) Preprocessing and data preparation; (4) Make the treatment of imbalanced classes and standardize the training set; (5) Build different models of vulnerability analysis forecasting the following methods: Naive Bayes, Linear SVM and Polynomial SVM (6) To evaluate these models and to choose the best model that will better forecasting.

5.1.1   Present Rules that Must Comply with an Ethical Hacker
Ethical Hackers must respect the following rules: Obtain authorization written the owner of the system or software before hackers; Protecting the privacy of the organization hacked; Report transparently all the weaknesses identified in the computer system to the organization; Inform the identified weaknesses of the software suppliers.

5.1.2   Building a Vulnerability Database from 2010 to 2018
The data used for modeling are from the NVD database (National Vulnerability Database). This database is created to provide a comprehensive list of software vulnerabilities and a breakdown of the details of a software vulnerability. for our data we have made requests over the year, the publication date, type of vulnerability, CVSS scores, then we removed the redundant information in order to have a final database. Figure 1 below shows the data extraction process and Table 1 which represents the CVSS parameters that will be used for the analysis of software vulnerabilities.

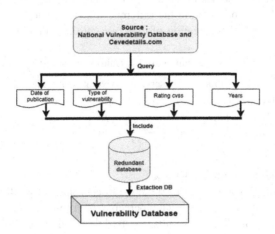

Fig. 1. Acquisition process vulnerabilities databases

Table 1. The CVSS parameters

Characteristics	Description	Values
Access vector	The way with which a vulnerability can be exploited	Local (L) Adjacent Network (AN) Network (N)
Authentication	The level of authentication needed to access the vulnerable system	None (N) Single (S) Multiple (M)
Access complexity	the level of difficulty to exploit the discovered vulnerability...	High (H) Medium (M) Low (L)
Integrity	The impact to the integrity of the affected system	None (N) Partial (P) Complete (C)
Confidentiality impact	The impact to the confidentiality of the affected system	None (N) Partial (P) Complete (C)
Availability impact	The impact to the availability of the affected system	None (N) Partial (P) Complete (C)

5.1.3   Preprocessing and Data Preparation

To pretreatment of the database, we remove unnecessary variables, we have created an "Analysis" variable that will allow us to predict a vulnerability; Then we partition the database into two. 70% for the training set and 30% for the test set. We have transformed the categorical variables into numerical variables by the normalization method and scaled these data to better build the different models (Table 2).

After pretreatment and preparation of data, we get the following information:

Table 2. Noticed the learning base (dbTrain) and the test base (dbTest)

Data	Number of observations	Number of variables
Based	6670	8
dbTrain	4669	20
dbTest	2001	20

5.1.4   Management Unbalanced Data

Having unbalanced data, in our case, we have three values to predict vulnerabilities namely low, medium or high. We can perceive in Table 3. Table 3 presents the unbalanced data, this can skew the results, we used the techniques of oversampling and undersampling to balance the classes. This is illustrated in Tables 4 and 5.

Table 3. Unbalanced data

Vulnerability scanning		
Low	Medium	High
616	2204	1849

Table 4. Training data balanced sub-sampled

Vulnerability scanning		
Low	Medium	High
616	616	616

Table 5. Balanced training data oversampled

Vulnerability scanning		
Low	Medium	High
2204	2204	2204

5.1.5 Building Models

The models we developed will help to solve classification problem. For each new vulnerability entered, these models must be able to predict which category this vulnerability belongs to. Is it a high, medium or low vulnerability? To solve this problem, we use the following algorithms: The Naive Bayes, the Linear and Polynomial SVM. The modelling process can be described by the following pseudo-algorithm (Fig. 2).

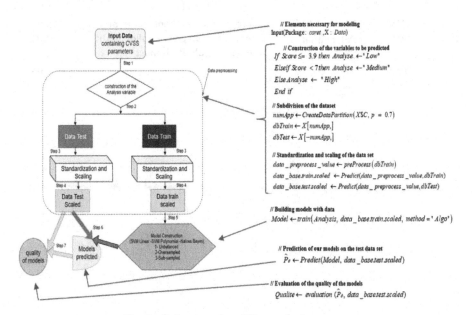

Fig. 2. Software vulnerability analysis process

5.2   Results and Discussion

After the various modeling and evaluations of our models, the optimal model chosen is the one that was performed on oversampled data with CVSS parameters on some supervised learning algorithms such as Linear SVM, polynomial SVM and naive bayes. By comparing it with the previous work mentioned in the state of the art, our model has a good accuracy, as illustrated in the comparative Table 6 and the following Fig. 3.

Table 6. Comparison of results with existing work

Authors	Methods	Parameters	Accuracy
Zimmermann et al. (2010)	The regression binary logistics	Churn rate, complexity, coverage dependency and organization	66%
S. et al. (2011)	Several techniques of classification	Complexity, code confusion and developer activity	70%
Moshtari et al. (2013)	Several techniques of classification	Complexity of the unit, coupling	90%
Mor. et al. (2015)	Semi-automatic	Churn rate, complexity, coverage, dependency, organization	50%
Y. et al. (2016)	Random Forest	Code complexity, information flow, functions, invocations	84%
D. et al. (2019)	**Linear SVM**	**Access vector, authentication access complexity, integrity confidentiality impact availability impact**	**99,80%**
D. et al. (2019)	**Polynomial SVM**		**99,70%**
D. et al. (2019)	**Naive Bayes**		**99,60%**

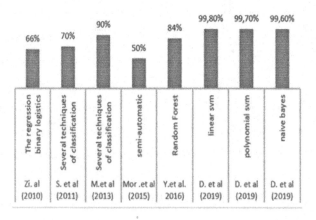

Fig. 3. Graphic illustration of results with existing work

6 Conclusion

In this article, we used the CVSS parameters, unbalanced, oversampled and under-sampled data that we designed and we also used three machine learning based algorithms to effectively analyze software vulnerabilities. After the simulations, the models based on the oversampled data and the following algorithms: Linear SVM, Polynomial SVM and Naive Bayes had very good and therefore optimal accuracy. They can be used to effectively analyze software vulnerabilities in industry and research. In perspective, an unexplored area is the use of deep learning to predict vulnerabilities. This is another promising area for future studies in the area of vulnerability prediction.

References

1. Dowd, M.: The Art of Software Security Assessment: Identifying and Preventing (2007)
2. Zulkernine, M.: Mitigating program security vulnerabilities: approaches and challenges. ACM Comput. Surv. (CSUR), **44**(3), 11 (2012)
3. Cheng, H., Yan, X., Han, J.: Mining graph patterns. In: Aggarwal, Charu C., Han, J. (eds.) Frequent Pattern Mining, pp. 307–338. Springer, Cham (2014). https://doi.org/10.1007/978-3-319-07821-2_13
4. Ghaffarian, S.M., Shahriari, H.R.: Software vulnerability analysis and discovery using machine-learning and data-mining techniques: a survey. ACM Comput. Surv. (CSUR) **50** (4), 1–36 (2017)
5. Zimmermann, T.: Searching for a needle in a haystack: predicting security vulnerabilities for windows vista (2010)
6. Meneely, A., Williams, L.: Strengthening the empirical analysis of the relationship between Linus' Law. In: Proceedings of the ACM/IEEE International Symposium on Empirical Software Engineering and Measurement (ESEM 2010). ACM (2010). Article no. 9
7. Sami, A., Azimi, M., Moshtari, S.: Using complexity metrics to improve software security. Comput. Fraud Secur. **2013**(5), 8–17 (2013)
8. Herzig, K., Murphy, B., Williams, L., Morrison, P.: Challenges with applying vulnerability prediction models. In: Proceedings of the Symposium and Bootcamp on the Science of Security (HotSoS 2015). ACM (2015). Article no. 4
9. Malaiya, Y., Anderson, C., Ray, I., Younis, A.: To fear or not to fear that is the question: code characteristics of a vulnerable function with an existing exploit. In: Proceedings of the 6th ACM Conference on Data and Application Security and Privacy (CODASPY 2016), pp. 97–104. ACM (2016)
10. Ellis, S.R.: Ethical hacking, Chapitre 30. kCura Corporation, Chicago (2017). https://doi.org/10.1016/b978-0-12-803843-7.00030-2
11. Caldwell, T.: Ethical hackers: putting on the white hat-'WhiteHat Website Security Statistics Report', June 2011

Africa's Multilateral Legal Framework on Personal Data Security: What Prospects for the Digital Environment?

Rogers Alunge[✉]

LAST-JD Program, CIRSFID, University of Bologna,
Lungo Dora Siena 100A, Turin, Italy
alungerogers@yahoo.com

Abstract. As the African continent continues to embrace technological innovations and corresponding infrastructures like the Internet of Things, certain concerns have been raised as regards the security risks related to critical ICT network infrastructures in the continent, as well as the safeguarding of the fundamental rights of Africans through the protection of their personal data, especially those shared online. One of such concerns is personal data security, which becomes more crucial as huge amounts of sensitive personal data are increasingly generated across the continent, especially with the proliferation of mobile banking. In response to these developments, African intergovernmental organizations have developed legal frameworks on personal data protection: the Economic Community of West African States (ECOWAS) has adopted a Supplementary Data Protection Act, while the African Union (AU) has adopted a Convention on Cyber Security and Personal Data Protection. However, while other aspects of data protection law are more or less addressed in these instruments, relatively very little focus is put on managing and safeguarding personal data security.

This paper, in an attempt to present a critique of the state of affairs as regards personal data security regulation and online trustworthiness in Africa, strives to show that the above African instruments do not provide a satisfactory response to current personal data security challenges Africa faces. Both instruments can hardly be said to ensure a trustworthy environment for data sharing, as they lack essential pre-breach and post-breach regulation mechanisms, including breach reporting, liability for mismanagement of personal data and available remedies for affected data subjects. The paper concludes by recommending that these deficiencies be addressed in additional protocols to these instruments or in relevant future texts.

Keywords: Personal data protection · Personal data security · Africa · African Union · ECOWAS

1 Introduction

Ever since the beginning of the 21st Century, Africa has had its fair share of ICT penetration, especially in terms of internet and mobile telephony usage. The continent hosted about 453 million internet users by the end of 2017 as opposed to about

R. Zitouni et al. (Eds.): AFRICOMM 2019, LNICST 311, pp. 38–58, 2020.
https://doi.org/10.1007/978-3-030-41593-8_4

4 million by 2000, and the Information Technology Union (ITU) estimates 781 million mobile phone subscriptions in the continent in 2018[1]. Africans are increasingly using the Internet for information society goods and services, ranging from online banking to social networking [1, 2]. Besides being a primary means of communication for most Africans, mobile phones have become a source of significant economic growth and a platform for innovation, especially with the rise of mobile money services: the use of mobile phones to purchase goods or services through funds connected to the user's account [3]. Mobile banking has also been on the rise in the continent for close to a decade now [4], and in 2017, mobile technologies and services generated 7.1% of GDP across Sub-Saharan Africa, a contribution that amounted to $110 billion of economic value added [5]. Mobile application usage for urban transportation is also fairly advanced in some African countries, with, for example, US-based urban transport giants Uber operating in South Africa, Kenya, Nigeria, Tanzania, Uganda, Ghana and Egypt. The so-called Internet of Things[2] is also on the rise, with an estimated 29 billion connected objects by 2022 [6]; objects being reliably connected to each other with the ability 'to auto-organize, share information, data and resources, reacting and acting in face of situations and changes in the environment' [7]. The emergence of 'information ambient environments', is also anticipated, characterised by invisible (i.e., embedded) computational power in everyday appliances and other common physical objects, including mobile and wearable devices where, in essence, people are surrounded with intelligent and intuitive objects capable of recognizing and responding to our presence in a seamless, unobtrusive and even invisible way [8].

As it keeps on embracing ICT usage and internet penetration, and also consequently generating huge amounts of (personal and non-personal) data, the African continent will soon get caught up in this forecasted digital hurricane. This has raised concerns at regional and sub-regional governance forums not only about the safety and security of critical ICT infrastructure and systems which are always vulnerable to cyber attacks [9, 10] but also about protecting the privacy of Africans as regards the personal information which they share over these platforms. The rapid growth of mobile telephony in Africa, for example, has barely been accompanied by appropriate consideration for privacy and security concerns, opening the door for abuse and erosion of the application's utility [11]. Just as was the case in Europe with the advent of computer processing in the 1970s culminating in the adoption of Convention 108 by the Council of Europe on 28 January 1981[3], and later the EU Directive

---

[1] ITU GLOBAL AND REGIONAL ICT DATA, retrieved from https://www.itu.int/en/ITUD/Statistics/Documents/statistics/2018/ITU_Key_2005-2018_ICT_data_with%20LDCs_rev27Nov2018.xls. Accessed 5/5/2019.

[2] Defined by Stuckmann, Peter, and Rainer Zimmermann in: "European research on future internet design." *IEEE Wireless Communications* 16, no. 5 (2009): 14 as a 'world-wide network of uniquely addressable and interconnected objects, based on standard communication protocols". This enables applications involving real-world objects, but also business applications based on network-assisted machine-to-machine interaction.

[3] The Council of Europe's Convention for the Protection of Individuals with regard to Automatic Processing of Personal Data of 28th January 1981.

95/46/EC[4] on October 24, 1995 [12, 13], African leaders, by the end of the first decade of the 21st Century, began identifying the need to protect the privacy and security of personal data of users being processed by service providers using ICTs. The first African multilateral legal framework to directly address personal data privacy protection was the ECOWAS[5] Supplementary Act A/SA./1/01/10 on Personal Data Protection within ECOWAS (hereinafter ECOWAS Data Protection Act), adopted in Abuja on February 16, 2010. This was followed by the African Union Convention on Cybersecurity and Personal Data Protection, adopted in Malabo on June 27, 2014. It should be pointed out that these instruments were being adopted at a time when some African states were also adopting or had already adopted national legislations focused on personal data protection [14] and personal data security. However, national personal data security initiatives are beyond the scope of this paper, which seeks to examine Africa's multilateral legal frameworks on personal data protection with a view of assessing whether they provide a solid basis for efficient personal data security in the face of current technological developments gradually engulfing the continent, and based on which national instruments can conceive adequate laws and policies.

The paper will point out that both the ECOWAS Data Protection Act and the AU Convention on Cyber Security and Personal Data Protection, in relation to contemporary realities of the digital environment or as compared to what obtains in Europe, do not provide a satisfactory legal springboard to guarantee an adequate level of personal information security for African citizens in the face of current data security risks posed by the continent's wide adoption of new technologies. These instruments, however, especially the AU Convention, should nevertheless be lauded for at least providing a commendable basis which could serve as a beginning for those African states which continue to embrace digital and mobile technologies without safeguarding their citizens' fundamental rights with any national framework at all bearing on personal data protection or security.

This introduction shall be followed by a first section briefly discussing the concepts of personal data, personal data protection and personal data security, and a second section briefly discussing the current dangers to personal data security in Africa. A third section shall briefly introduce the ECOWAS and AU Data Protection Conventions, and briefly discuss how they address personal data security. A fourth section identifies and discusses the aspects of personal data security absent from the Act in comparison with the European data protection model, and the fifth and final section features the author's conclusive remarks.

2   Personal Data, Data Protection and Data Security

This section briefly introduces the concepts of personal data protection and personal data security. It shall basically be a rundown of current literature on both concepts.

---

[4] Directive 95/46/EC of the European Parliament and of the Council of 24 October 1995 on the protection of individuals with regard to the processing of personal data and on the free movement of such data.

[5] Economic Community of West African States.

2.1 Personal Data

Personal data is the yolk of personal data protection law; the latter is triggered only if personal data is processed. It is therefore crucial for individuals, their representatives and data processing entities to understand what personal data is exactly, in order to know whether a particular operation or situation falls under the regulatory scope of data protection law.

Personal data, as it is used in Europe and (adopted in) Africa, is also known as personal information or, in the United States, personally identifiable information [15]. The first internationally-established conceptualisation of the term 'personal data' was enshrined in the OECD[6] Guidelines on the Protection of Privacy and Transborder Flows of Personal Data adopted on 23 September 1980. Paragraph 1(b) of the Guidelines defines personal data as 'any information relating to an identified or identifiable individual (data subject)'. The Council of Europe followed suit, adopting the very same definition in its Convention for the Protection of Individuals with regard to Automatic Processing of Personal Data adopted in Strasbourg on 28 January 1981. In the European Union, the General Data Protection Regulation adopts the very same definition, with further clarifications. It states that personal data is *'any information relating to an identified or identifiable natural person ('data subject'); an identifiable natural person is one who can be identified, directly or indirectly, in particular by reference to an identifier such as a name, an identification number, location data, an online identifier or to one or more factors specific to the physical, physiological, genetic, mental, economic, cultural or social identity of that natural person.'*[7] This covers a broad range of data, from the name, date of birth, address, health records, social security numbers, driver's licence data and even the real time location of a person, and beyond. In essence, all data through which an individual is or can be identified. This definition, which also featured almost word-for-word in the repealed 1995 EU Data Protection Directive, has already been criticised for being too broad and could include virtually sort of information. The terms 'any information' and 'relating to' suggest that all sorts of information leading even slightly to a person could be 'personal', especially considering that current and anticipated computer technologies with unprecedented analytical capacities could make use of virtually any piece of information to identify a natural person, hence the risk of making every information personal data [16]. But it has also been defended on grounds that the EU legislator had as mission to provide a high standard of protection for individuals with regard to the processing of their personal information[8].

A very identical definition to the above EU definitions on personal data has been taken up by both the ECOWAS and AU data protection instruments. The ECOWAS Act defines personal data as *'any information relating to an identified individual or*

---

[6] The Organisation for Economic Cooperation and Development.

[7] Article 4(1), Regulation (EU) 2016/679 of the European Parliament and of the Council of 27 April 2016 on the protection of natural persons with regard to the processing of personal data and on the free movement of such data (General Data Protection Regulation (GDPR)).

[8] Article 29 Data Protection Working Party, *Opinion 4/2007 on the Concept of Personal* Data (Adopted on 20th June 2007).

who may be directly or indirectly identifiable by reference to an identification number or one or several elements related to their physical, physiological, genetic, psychological, cultural, social, or economic identity (Article 1), while the AU Convention refers to it as *'any information relating to an identified or identifiable natural person by which this person can be identified, directly or indirectly in particular by reference to an identification number or to one or more factors specific to his/her physical, physiological, mental, economic, cultural or social identity.'* (Article 1). From the terms 'any information' and 'relating to', it appears both instruments appear to reinforce the EU model of covering a broad range of information under the category of personal data which should be protected under the legal mechanism of personal data protection.

2.2 Personal Data Protection

Hustinx posits that personal data protection refers to that set of policies and rules which aim to protect individuals (citizens, consumers, workers, etc.) against unjustified collection, recording, use and dissemination of their personal details [17]. The concept has been particularly trendy in the US and in Europe over the last decades, following the (global) realisation that personal data plays increasingly important role in our economies and is being generated, gathered and processed at alarming rates due to wide range of analytics that can provide comprehensive insights into individuals' movements, interests, and activities[9]. Such use of personal data, if not regulated, could expose individuals to a number of risks ranging from privacy violations to serious injuries like identity theft [18]. In Europe, with the human right to private life (of the home and correspondences)[10] proving increasingly difficult to guarantee with the advent and increased use of ICTs to process personal information, there was the need for a novel regime to introduce safeguards which should be observed by organisations and institutions when processing personal information within the context of an information society [12, 19]. One of such safeguards is the requirement to ensure the security of personal data which these companies or institutions are processing.

In addition to Hustinx's definition above, it should equally be pointed out that contemporary data protection law also targets online trust i.e. making individuals feel confident and safe to share their personal data. Prior to the post-2010 data protection law reforms in the EU and US, the 'notice and consent' model was relied on to protect individuals' privacy by letting them choose, through 'informed, freely given and specific' consent whether or not to allow the processing of their personal information [20]. After 2010, following the established shortcomings of this model, especially considering, inter alia, the processing of data by third parties who were not in any direct relationship with individuals, decision or notice fatigue [21] or the unrealism to always expect data controllers to request consent to process data for purposes other than the original purpose for which it was collected, there was a shift towards equally ensuring

---

[9] See the OECD Privacy Framework. Retrieved from http://www.oecd.org/sti/ieconomy/oecd_privacy_framework.pdf. Accessed 2/11/2019. Page 20.

[10] Article 8 of the European Convention on Human Rights of 4 November 1950.

responsible and trustworthy use of personal data.[11] Considering that data sharing is essential for the exchange of goods and services and economic functioning of any society, data protection is therefore not just about protecting individuals but also about ensuring economic growth. The European Commission, for example, stated that contemporary EU data protection law is poised to 'help stimulate the Digital Single Market in the EU by fostering trust in online services by consumers…'[12] while Lynskey points out that EU data protection law simultaneously pursues dual objectives: economic—to facilitate the establishment of the internal market—and rights-based—to protect fundamental rights when personal data is processed [13]. In this light, and in line with the OECD Guidelines, the following principles were formulated by EU data protection law:

– Principle of lawfulness, fairness, and transparency: personal data shall be processed lawfully, fairly, and in a transparent manner.
– Principle of purpose limitation: personal data shall be collected for specified, explicit, and legitimate purposes.
– Principle of data minimization: Processing of personal data must also be adequate, relevant, and limited to what is necessary.
– Principle of accuracy: Personal data being processed must be accurate and kept up to date.
– Principle of storage limitation: Personal data is to be kept in a form that hinders identification of data subjects for no longer than is necessary for the originated purpose.
– Principle of integrity and confidentiality: Processing should appropriate security personal data.
– Principle of accountability: The data controller (person in charge of processing personal data) should always be ready to demonstrate compliance with all the above principles.[13]

2.3   Personal Data Security

Paragraph 11 of the OECD Privacy Guidelines, titled the Security Safeguards Principle, requires personal data to be '*protected by reasonable security safeguards against such risks as loss or unauthorised access, destruction, use, modification or disclosure of data.*' Personal data security hence refers to the mechanisms undertaken to safeguard of personal information under processing by service-providing companies or institutions from unauthorised access, loss, destruction, alteration or any other circumstance which could negatively affect the processed data.

---

[11] See the White House, 'Executive Office of the President. Big Data: Seizing Opportunities, Preserving Values' (2014). 55–56. http://www.whitehouse.gov/sites/default/files/docs/big_data_privacy_report_may_1_2014.pdf. Accessed 2/11/2019.

[12] European Commission Joint Statement on the final adoption of the new EU rules for personal data protection. (Brussels, 14 April 2016). Available at https://europa.eu/rapid/press-release_STATEMENT-16-1403_de.htm. Accessed on 3/6/2019. Also see Recital 7 of the GDPR.

[13] See Article 5, GDPR.

With personal data being, *prima facie*, information in the first place, consists a subset of the broader concept of information security. The International Standardisation Organisation defines information security as the preservation of the confidentiality, integrity and availability of information, noting that information can take on many forms: it can be printed or written on paper, stored electronically, transmitted by post or electronic means, shown on films, even conveyed in conversation (ISO/IEC 27002, 2005). Arguing that this definition was limited to industry standards and do not consider contemporary information security challenges, Whitman and Mattord [22] add accuracy, authenticity, utility and possession to the list of data security features.

Personal data security thus incorporates the above processed vis-à-vis information which relates to or identifies an individual. This is reflected in the European Commission's definition of personal data security breach as "a breach of security leading to the accidental or unlawful destruction, loss, alteration, unauthorized disclosure of, or access to, personal data transmitted, stored or otherwise processed..."[14]. Conceptually, the term incorporates the procedural engagements taken by organisations to prevent these mishaps from befalling the personal data they process. Such engagement is crucial in any contemporary society, as compromised personal data could be used for a broad range of malpractices including impersonating the individual (identity theft) and making fraudulent transactions, or for abusive marketing, phishing or spying, which could lead to financial loss and emotional distress suffered by the concerned individual [18].

Compared to Europe and the US, personal data protection, though not really a new concept considering the existence of data protection laws in about a score of African countries today [14], is still to receive substantial media attention and legal interpretation in Africa, which is not a comfortable remark considering the continent's adoption of ICTs especially mobile telephony, and hence massive generation of personal data. The continent has generally been slow in adopting a continental privacy policy or culture, which contributes not only to the current lack of national personal data protection initiatives, but could hinder the practical enforcement of national data security legislations based on these instruments. In this light, following section discusses some inherent contextual challenges which could hinder the adequate enforcement of a personal data security framework in Africa.

3 Personal Data Security in Africa: Potential Challenges

This section briefly discusses a number of factors characterizing the African information security context, making a case for the prevalence of an informationally risky environment for African residents.

---

[14] Article 2(i) of Directive 2002/58/EC of the European Parliament and of the Council of 12 July 2002 concerning the processing of personal data and the protection of privacy in the electronic communications sector (Directive on privacy and electronic communications).

3.1 Inadequate Cybersecurity Response

The AU Convention, in its third section bearing on cybersecurity, urges Member States to, inter alia, 'elaborate and implement programmes and initiatives for sensitization on security for systems and networks users' (Article 26(1)(b)). However, many African states suffer from inadequate structures and organs to fight equipment to fight cyber-crime and guarantee cybersecurity. By June 2018, though 40 out of 55 African states have adopted comprehensive cybercrime laws, only 20 States had established national cybersecurity policies, and 18 States had national CERT frameworks[15]. This inade-quate cybersecurity response has eased the infection of a huge number of computers in Africa with malware: reportedly over 80% by 2010 [23]. Also, just as had been predicted almost a decade ago, a huge number of Africans now use mobile phones for mobile banking, accessing the Internet, facilitating commerce, and general communi-cation [11].

Coupled with the inability to guarantee ICT network security, this development implies that there are huge amounts of personal data generated every day in Africa and susceptible to unauthorised access and/or misuse. Securing personal data also involves ensuring information service providers have adequate technical measures in place to safeguard the security of the network or system processing or transmitting such data. As Wayne et al. argue, key steps towards building cyber resilience in Africa should begin with implementation (of the AU Convention) and education [24], but the snail pace of ratifying the Convention so far (only five states by September 2019, since its adoption in 2014) is evidence of the apathy with which African states apparently approach cybersecurity threats and dangers.

3.2 Relatively Weak Privacy Culture in Africa

Privacy as a philosophical or even legal phenomenon has not yet received mainstream attention in Africa [25]. Some commentators even advocating that privacy is of little value in the continent, overshadowed by the togetherness community lifestyle which is dominant in local African communities [26], advocated as one of the principal features of the traditional African philosophy generally referred to as *Ubuntu* [27]. Interestingly, it is not even formally recognised by the continent's most fundamental human rights instrument: the African Charter on Human and People's Rights (ACHPR) of 1981 does not mention a right to privacy in its catalogue of basic human rights. In an effort to justify this omission of the right to privacy in the ACHPR, Olinger et al. purport that 'privacy was simply not seen as a necessary right for Africans to live freely and peaceably' [28]. On her part, Bakibinga contends that Africans generally suffer from 'privacy myopia' which means they underestimate the value of their personal data and the need for its protection [29]. It should be pointed out however that this view is not predominant among scholars: Makulilo [30] for example argues that Western influence

---

[15] See UNCTAD. (2018) *Cybercrime Laws*. [online] Available from: http://www.unctad.org/en/Docs/Cyberlaw/CC.xlsx [Accessed on 6 June 2018]. See ITU. (2018) *Cybersecurity Country Profiles*. [online] Available from: https://www.itu/en/ITU-D/Cybersecurity/Documents/CountryProfiles/ [Accessed 6 June 2019].

and globalization has wrought individualism in African urban areas, and privacy is becoming an evolving concept in the continent. Nevertheless, on the other hand, strong notions of privacy arose in Europe since the end of the Second World War. And while this, since the 1970s, led to advocacy for even stronger personal data protection requirements for companies processing personal data, the absence of a fundamental, continental right to privacy in Africa weakens the grounds for any such advocacy with regard to personal data [11].

This situation is not so static though: most African national constitutions do guarantee a right to privacy[16], and as discussed above, African governments have begun considering privacy protection through personal data protection laws. So far African states have been progressively adopting comprehensive data protection laws which also require security safeguards when processing personal data. These laws in question, however, are fragmented among states, portraying different standards of personal data security safeguards required of data processing organisations [31, 32]. There is also a gaping absence of public interest groups in monitor government behaviour, propose public policy, and promote privacy awareness in relation to privacy [3].

3.3 Potential for Unaccountability by African Governments

One of the core principles of data protection is accountability: personal data processing organisations or companies should always be ready to demonstrate compliance with data protection regulations.[17] Accountability towards their citizens, unfortunately, is generally not a very popular governance option among African governments [33], as many of them demonstrate a willingness to operate outside the rule of law and with little accountability [11]. The absence of a spirit of accountability provides fertile grounds for privacy violations. Contemporary literature has raised these concerns in relation to African governments. A case in point is the ongoing process of African governments in implementing comprehensive electronic ID card schemes (an example being the current 'Uduma Number' scheme by the Kenyan government). Though such initiatives may ease identification and maintain law and order, a worrying factor is that it leads to extensive databases of individuals' personal data, including sensitive and biometric data being kept by governments with virtually no national or regionally-binding personal data privacy obligations of accountability towards their citizens [34]. In the same light, Banisar for example points out that most common ICT privacy issue currently facing African nations is the development of new citizen identification systems, including identity cards and passports [35]. Even more concerning is the fact that the technical development and operation of these ID card schemes are franchised to foreign companies [34, 35] which could make claims against privacy violations difficult in terms of jurisdictional conflict.

Mass surveillance is equally another issue: African governments are extremely reticent to have any accountability or transparency of their interception and surveillance

---

[16] For example Article 12 of the 1996 Constitution of Cameroon, Article 28 of the revised 1992 Constitution of the Republic of Togo, Article 31 of the 2010 Constitution of the Republic of Togo.

[17] Paragraph 14 of the OECD Guidelines on the Protection of Privacy and Transborder Flows of Personal Data (hereinafter the OECD Data Protection Guidelines). Also Article 5(2) of the EU GDPR.

activities [36]. Some of them have even passed laws mandating telecommunication providers to integrate surveillance systems capable of interception of communications. For example, South Africa's Regulation of Interception of Communications and Provision of Communication-related Information Act 2002 requires service providers to incorporate surveillance machinery before they can offer services to the public. Section 9 of Zimbabwe's 2007 Interception of Communications Act similarly requires providers to assist with interception, while Namibia's 2009 Communications Act orders communication companies to build interceptor centres while providing little control as to who can order wiretaps [35]. A point worth noting here is that these legislations were passed to regulate traditional telecommunication systems, which are principally landline and mobile communications, and may not be compatible with the realities of the contemporary ubiquitous digital data processing. The steady advent of the IoT and even information ambient environment where all sorts of data like health, transportation or electricity consumption details can be processed by any object with censors, if not countered by strong data protection legislation, the mass surveillance capacities of African states (and their partner processor companies) on their civilians could grow to alarming levels.

This section illustrates that personal data processing in Africa presents a variety of risks to individuals ranging from unsatisfactory levels of cybersecurity, cultural privacy deficiencies or potential abuse by government or private entities. It was on this basis that African multilateral organisations (in this case ECOWAS and AU) came up with legal responses to introduce, within their respective scopes of competence, guidelines which aim to protect Africans with regard to the processing of their personal information and, in the process, ensure a trustworthy and secure online environment for the flow of personal data.

4 African Multilateral Personal Data Security Instruments

This section presents the selected multilateral instruments addressing personal data protection in Africa: the ECOWAS Data Protection Act and the African Union Convention on Cyber Security and Data Protection. It shall focus briefly on their background, scope and applicability, before discussing their provisions on personal data security.

4.1 The ECOWAS[18] Data Protection Act

ECOWAS is the main interstate organization of Western Africa with fifteen members,[19] established by the Treaty of Lagos on 28th May 1975[20]. Article 3 (2) (a) of the

---

[18] Established by the Treaty of Lagos on 28 May 1975, ECOWAS is the main intergovernmental organization of West Africa currently comprising of 15 sovereign West African States namely: Benin, Burkina Faso, Cape Verde, Cote d'Ivoire, the Gambia, Ghana, Guinea, Guinea-Bissau, Liberia, Mail, Niger, Nigeria, Senegal, Sierra Leone and Togo. (Www.Ecowas.Int).

[19] Benin, Burkina Faso, Cape Verde, Cote d'Ivoire, Gambia, Ghana, Guinea, Guinea Bissau, Liberia, Mali, Niger, Nigeria, Senegal, Sierra Leone and Togo.

[20] Treaty of ECOWAS (28 May 1975) 14 ILM 1200; revised 24 July 1993, 35 ILM 660, (1996).

Treaty states that Member states shall ensure the 'the harmonization and coordination of national policies and the promotion of integration programmes in areas including communications, trade, information, science, technology, services, and legal matters'. It was based on the above provision and the Supplementary Act A/SA.1/01/10 Personal Data Protection within the ECOWAS (ECOWAS Data Protection Act) was adopted during the 37th session of the Authority of ECOWAS Heads of State and Government in Abuja on 16 February 2010.

With this Supplementary Act, ECOWAS is the first and only sub-regional grouping in Africa to develop a concrete framework of personal data protection law; a framework strongly influenced by the 1995 EU Data Protection Directive. It should also be noted that Article 48 of the Act makes it an integral part of the ECOWAS Treaty, thereby making violations of the Act actionable before the ECOWAS Court of Justice. The Act has a dual objective: the protection of privacy and promotion of free movement of information[21]. It equally recognizes that technology advancements greatly ease personal data processing and hence bring about unprecedented problems of personal data protection, and seeks to address the problem through a harmonized legal framework for data protection within the ECOWAS sub-region.[22]

4.2 The African Union Convention on Cybersecurity and Personal Data Protection

Adopted by the 23rd Ordinary Session of the Assembly of Heads of State of the African Union in Malabo on 27 June 2014, the African Union Convention on Cyber Security and Personal Data Protection (the AU Data Protection Convention) provides a legal framework regulating electronic commerce, data Protection and cybersecurity. Its overall objective is to harmonise national legislation in Africa on a number of ICT-related issues; an objective which reiterates the three main AU declarations on harmonisation of ICT and related laws: the Oliver Tambo Declaration Johannesburg 2009, the Abuja Declaration 2010 and the Addis Ababa Declaration 2012 [37]. As regards personal data protection, it seeks to establish a legal framework 'aimed at strengthening fundamental rights and public freedoms, particularly the protection of [personal] data, and punish any violation of privacy without prejudice to the principle of free flow of personal data (Article 8(1) AU Convention) It is set to come into force upon ratification by 15 member states (Article 38). So far (June 2019) though, only four member states (Senegal, Namibia, Guinea and Mauritius) have ratified the Convention. After coming into force, it applies to Member states (which are mostly dualist), however, only upon the individual domestication (by Member states) into the internal law of the state.[23]

The Convention applies *rationae loci* to any automated or non-automated processing of personal data carried out in a territory of an AU Member State (Article 9(1)). However, just like Article 3(2) of the 1995 EU Directive, the Convention does not apply to data processing carried out by an individual in the exclusive framework of

---

[21] Paragraph 10, Preamble, ECOWAS Data Protection Act.

[22] Paragraphs 8–11, Preamble, ECOWAS Data Protection Act.

[23] See for example Section 12 of the Constitution of the Federal Republic of Nigeria.

their personal or domestic activities (Article 9(2)(a)). The Convention also covers processing of personal data for in cases of public security, defence, investigation and prosecution of criminal offences, but subject to the provisions of other existing laws (suggestively regional or national texts operating *lex specialis*) (Article 9(1)(d)).

4.3 Personal Data Security Guarantees Under Both Instruments

Both the ECOWAS Data Protection Act and AU Data Protection Convention provide for means aimed at ensuring that processed personal data is handled securely by data controllers and processors.

4.3.1 Confidentiality and Security of Processing

Firstly, both instruments contain a *Principle of confidentiality and security* when processing personal data (Article 28 ECOWAS Data Protection Act, Article 13 AU Convention), requiring data to be processed confidentially, and protected in particular when processing includes transmission of the data over a [computer] network. This principle is not very explicit under the African data protection regimes, and reference can be made to Convention 108 for a more explicit version of the principle. Article 7 of Convention 108 demands that state parties 'provide that the controller, and, where applicable the processor, takes appropriate security measures against risks such as accidental or unauthorised access to, destruction, loss, use, modification or disclosure of personal data'. Similar obligations are demanded of the data controller and processor under the GDPR.

In Africa, similar to the position of Convention 108, the onus of compliance to this principle falls generally on the data controller, whom the ECOWAS regime expressly puts in charge of ensuring the confidentiality of processing (Article 42) and obliges to "take all necessary precautions in relation to the nature of data, and in particular to ensure that it is not deformed, damaged or accessible to unauthorised third parties." (Article 43). The data controller has got identical responsibilities under the AU Convention (Articles 20 and 21). Both instruments also make the data controller remains the sole responsible entity to guarantee data security, as it is up to the latter, when recruiting a processor, to ensure that the latter is equipped with sufficient guarantees for data security (Article 29 ECOWAS Data Protection Act, Article 13 (b) AU Convention). This, position, it should be noted, is slightly different from what presently obtains in Europe under the GDPR, which provides for the possibility of the processor being individually responsible for processing in the event where it acted outside the processing instructions of the controller (Article 82 GDPR).

4.3.2 The Data Protection Authority

Another data security guarantee finds expression in the wide powers granted by both instruments to the Data Protection Authority (DPA) to promote security compliance and deter non-compliance. Hustinx underlines the importance and uniqueness of the DPA by stating that data protection 'is special in the sense that it is considered to be in need of 'structural support' through the establishment of an independent authority with adequate powers and resources', while pointing out that 'no other fundamental right – except the right to a fair trial – is structurally associated with the role of an independent body to ensure its respect and further development [i.e. Courts]' [38]. In Europe, data protection supervisory authorities have been viewed as 'an element of effective protection of individuals with regard to the processing of their personal information.[24]

Under the African data protection regimes, the DPA is entitled to receive claims and petitions relating to processing of personal data and advice petitioners on the relevant course of action to take (Article 19 (1)(f) ECOWAS Data Protection Act, Article 12(2) (e) AU Convention). He/she can hear claims of data security violations after which, in case of an emergency, he/she may suspend, block or permanently suspend proceedings (Article 19(3) ECOWAS Data Protection Act). He/she can also impose fines on a data controller who is found to be in violation of its personal data security (and, generally, data protection) responsibilities Article 20(3) ECOWAS Data Protection Act, Article 14 (4)(c) AU Convention). Supervisory and enforcement institutions like the DPA will could be particularly useful in terms of creating a trustworthy online environment for data exchange in and among African countries both in terms of sanctioning defaulting data controllers who breach security principles or undermine online trust and ethics and, by virtue of their expertise in data protection law, educating data subjects on their rights towards achieving a trustworthy and secure digital environment for data sharing.

4.3.3 Right of Access and Rectification

Both instruments also provide for a right of access to data processing for individuals (Article 38 (6) and Article 39 ECOWAS Data Protection Act, Article 17 AU Convention) which is basically a right of the individual to request the data controller to present him with his data being processed by the latter as well as any information about the recipients to whom the data has been disclosed. This, at least in theory, gives individuals a chance to ensure their personal data has not been altered, providing them with some level of supervisory powers alongside the data controller. Data alteration being a data security issue in terms of data integrity[25], the right of access actually acts as a complementary security measure.

The above are the main personal data security guarantees under both the ECOWAS Data Protection Act and the AU Data Protection Convention. They admittedly cover some salient aspects in the domain, but these guarantees are quite limited in relation to the contemporary privacy demands of a data-driven society which Africa is slowly but surely becoming.

5 Some Data Security Mechanisms Missing from the Above Instruments

This section reviews the data security weaknesses of the above African multilateral data protection instruments. It shall identify and briefly discuss significant personal data security mechanisms missing from their provisions.

---

[24] Preamble, Additional Protocol to the Council of European Convention for the Protection of Individuals with regard to Automatic Processing of Personal Data regarding supervisory authorities and transborder data flows.

[25] See the EU Article 29 Working Party Opinion 03/2014 on Personal Data Breach Notification (WP213), p. 3.

5.1   Absence of a Security Breach Notification Requirement

Breach notification as a measure of personal data security management has been around for quite a while in data protection legislations, and constitutes an essential tool in ensuring responsible data processing on the part of data controllers. In essence, it requires personal data controllers or processors to inform either the competent Data Protection Authority or data subjects of a security incident which affects or is likely to have affected the personal data being processed. It was first passed into law in the US state of California in 2002 [39], and has been taken up by other states and jurisdictions, including the European Union (first by the e-Privacy Directive[26] in 2002, and later the GDPR in 2016), and is even embodied in Paragraph 15(c) of the OECD Revised Recommendation of the Council governing the Guidelines on the Protection of Privacy and Transborder Flows of Personal Data, adopted on 11 July 2013.

Security breach notification rules have been established to serve three main advantages: 'they provide a systematic feedback about the actual risk and the actual weaknesses of existing security measures; they enable authorities and consumers to assess the relative capabilities of data controllers with respect to data security; they force data controllers to assess and understand their own situation regarding security measures'[27]. In other words, personal data breach reporting serves *ex ante* (shaping the future behaviour of data controllers via deterrence) and *ex post* (mitigating the harm of the breach) objectives [40]. Such mitigation could be very crucial in event of the compromise of highly sensitive data; for example, informing individuals there has been a breach so they can quickly change information like passwords or passcodes to prevent identity theft or other related criminal activity [41]. It also ensures accountability of the data controller in data processing[28] [42].

This measure feature is absent from both the ECOWAS and AU data protection instruments: they do not provide for an obligation for data controllers to inform the DPA or individual data subjects about security incidents which may have led to a loss or unauthorised access by an external body to the personal data they are processing. Though out of the scope of this paper, it should be mentioned here however that among those which have currently adopted personal data protection legislations, data security breach notification requirements currently exist some African states including Chad, Ghana, Lesotho, South Africa and Uganda. Nevertheless, its absence in the main continental instrument on personal data protection remains significant.

---

[26] Directive 2002/58/EC of the European Parliament and of the Council of 12 July 2002 concerning the processing of personal data and the protection of privacy in the electronic communications sector (Directive on privacy and electronic communications).

[27] European Commission, Commission Staff Working Paper SEC (2012) 72 final. Impact Assessment Accompanying the General Data Protection Regulation (2012) p.100.

[28] The principle of accountability requires controllers to be able to actively demonstrate compliance to personal data protection rules without waiting on data subjects or supervisory authorities to point out shortcomings.

5.2   No 'Data Protection by Design' Requirements

Contemporary trends in data protection law, especially as regards data processing using ICT systems, and in order to ensure trustworthy processing, demand that such protection to be considered at the moment of designing the system or product [43]. In the same light, the OECD Revised Recommendations demand that personal data controllers should have in place a 'privacy management program' in charge of ensuring adherence to all the requirements of the Recommendations (Paragraph 15(b)). The EU also has similar provisions, which were in force before the adoption of the ECOWAS and AU data protection instruments.[29]

As Cunningham notes, regulations protecting privacy and personal information simultaneously encourage data security – as well as incentivize those entities that provide data security [44]. And over the years, a number of privacy enhancing technologies (PETs) have been developed in order to achieve information privacy goals especially alongside new technologies such as cloud computing and IoT, and include services like virtual private networks, transport layer security, DNS security extension, or onion routing [45]. These also include techniques like encryption, anonymisation or pseudonymisation [46]. These technologies aim at ensuring the security of communications as well as the preservation of the identity of a user in instances when such information is not required by another party, hence playing an important part in increasing the privacy and security of users and the data transmitted or processed.

Contemporary data protection law, like the EU GDPR (Article 25) for example requires processing systems which process personal information to be conceived around these PETs to guarantee 'automatic' data protection. The ECOWAS and AU data protection instruments are both silent on this aspect, apparently leaving it entirely up to data controllers to determine whether or not to employ the usage of privacy enhancing technologies when processing personal data using ICTs. Nevertheless, this mechanism is provided for by some African national legislations.[30]

5.3   Relatively Vague General Security Standard of Data Processing

Similar to the above point on PETs, the wordings of the ECOWAS and AU data protection instruments set relatively weak data security standards in safeguarding personal data processing, compared to what obtains in Europe, for example. Vaguely requiring that personal data be "processed confidentially and protected", (Article 28 ECOWAS Data Protection Act, Article 13 AU Convention) they appear to leave the methods and level of protection to be determined entirely by the data controllers, giving no guidance as to what technical or administrative measures to take to guarantee security. It could be argued though that, by interpretation, determining whether or not personal data is adequately protected depends on the type of data and the threats such data is likely to be exposed to, hence there could be no further need to stress on the

---

[29] Recital 46 of EU Directive 95/46/EC adopted in 24th October 1995 requires data security measures be taken at the time of designing the processing system as well as during processing itself.

[30] See for example Article 25 of the Ghanaian Data Protection Act 2012 and Article 41 of the Kenyan Data Protection Bill 2019.

measures to take, as the data controller is expected to know the kind of protection appropriate for protecting the data being collected and processed. In other words, how 'secure' a particular processing activity is shall depend on the type of data and risks involved with such processing, data protection having been portrayed by some commentators as a risk-management kind of legal regime [47].

However, this appears to put too much trust in the data controllers, which is risky business because most data processing bodies are privately-owned businesses, and hence are inherently inclined on maximizing profit which could be at the expense of implementing state of the art privacy protection mechanisms. The EU, for example, adopts the same risk-management standard to securing personal data, but goes ahead to lay further guidance as to how a data controller or processor determines if it has put in place adequate security measures. Article 17 of the 1995 Data Protection Directive states that data controllers must "ensure a level of security appropriate to the risks represented by the processing and the nature of the data to be protected…taking into account the state of the art and the costs of their implementation in relation to the risks inherent in the processing and the nature of the data to be protected."[31] Similar to the principle of confidentiality and security of processing discussed in Sect. 3 above, the European approach is much more explicit and lays down guidelines to prove secure processing: state of the art of the security component available on the market, and the cost of its implementation (consideration whether the cost of implementing the security measure is not too superfluous). This provides more explicit guidance to data controllers in knowing what types of security measures to adopt to show compliance.

5.4 No Reference to Certification Schemes

Both African international instruments do not provide for certification schemes through privacy seals. In brief, a privacy seal is a certification mark or a guarantee issued by a certifying entity verifying an organisation's adherence to certain specified privacy standards that aim to promote consumer trust and confidence [48]. Already functional in Europe, privacy certification seals are issued by organisations (known as certification bodies) accredited for such purposes by the competent privacy or data protection authorities. Personal data processing companies wishing to demonstrate compliance to data protection rules can apply to these organisations to be certified under such seals, which could be granted following due review and relevant inspections of their privacy policies in place. Privacy seals permit individuals to quickly assess the privacy or data security levels of the goods and services they subscribe to, as they cannot independently determine the data protection or privacy behaviour of the data controller.

Voluntary privacy certification schemes are encouraged in contemporary privacy legislations[32] as they rapidly demonstrate that certified entity's data protection (and, in parallel, data security) practices meet certain standards to the satisfaction of the certification body. Benefits of privacy seals may also include: generation of privacy and data protection accountability and oversight; enhancement of trust and confidence,

---

[31] Also see Article 32 GDPR.

[32] See Recital 100 GDPR.

reputational, competitive and market advantages to entities using them; generation of privacy awareness; assistance in proving fulfilment of privacy and data protection obligations [49].

5.5   No Direct Data Controller-Data Subject Liability

Another significant setback of the African multilateral response to data security problems is the absence of an established, direct liability relationship between the data controller and the data subject. The provisions of the ECOWAS and AU instruments position the data controller to be answerable solely to the DPA with respect to its data processing obligations; only the DPA can impose sanctions in event of a breach of security obligations. It appears both instruments create a direct liability relationship only between the data controller and DPA, leaving out the individuals whose data is processed and who risk direct harm in event of the compromise of his personal data. Under both instruments, the DPA is charged with receiving data protection violation claims (from individuals) and advising them on the course of action to follow (Article 19 ECOWAS Data Protection Act, Article 12 AU Convention). He appears therefore as an unwavering intermediary who decides a victim's course of action on his behalf. Considering that the very essence of data protection law is the protection of individuals regarding the misuse of their personal information, it appears only rational that data controllers be made directly liable towards them as regards protecting their personal data, so they feel protected during the processing. Leaving individuals out of a liability relationship with the data controller therefore appears a data security omission on the part of the African legislator.

5.6   Lack of a Compensation Scheme for Data Breach Victims

The above-mentioned absence of a direct liability relationship between the data controller and data subject leads to another grey area under African multilateral data protection law: compensation for victims of data security violations. Both the ECOWAS and AU data protection legislations fail to set a legal basis for Member states to enact laws which guarantee compensation for data subjects who are victims of personal data breaches. In the same light as data breach notification, such provisions would serve as an incentive for data controllers and processors to comply with standard security measures of data processing in order to at least ensure compliance. As discussed above, and unlike what obtains in other jurisdictions[33], victims are not provided with a right of direct claim against the data controller.

Also, the only monetary sanction available against the data controller under both data protection instruments is a fine, imposed by the DPA. By nature, fines are generally paid into the state treasury, or could be paid to the office of the DPA, but not to individuals. However, both instruments are silent as to any compensation mechanisms available for victims directly harmed by these security violations, which puts victims in a precarious situation: they cannot bring an action in data protection against the data

---

[33] See for example Recital 55 of the 1995 European Data Protection Directive.

controller, and they cannot lay a claim on a fine paid for a violation in which they suffered injury. It should be pointed out though that nothing appears to prevent victims directly claiming against the data controller on the basis of tort law.

6 Conclusive Remarks

This paper set out to provide an assessment of Africa's multilateral response, as contained in the ECOWAS Data Protection Act and African Union Data Protection Convention, to personal data security threats to which are (or would be) exposed African data subjects as Africa embraces ICTs and other tech-related innovations, occasionally comparing their provisions to European data protection frameworks in the process. Discussions centred in the first place on the notions of personal data, personal data protection and personal data security. Then an overview of the current fertility of African grounds for the adoption and implementation of standard personal data security norms was discussed, illustrating concerns revolving around the continent's weak cybersecurity institutions and fragile privacy culture and unaccountability of its governments in terms of enforcing human rights norms. This was followed by an appraisal of the current AU and ECOWAS data protection instruments, which led to the discovery that though these instruments do feature some provisions which contribute towards ensuring a secure and trustworthy digital African environment like the embodiment of a Security of Processing Principle, existence of a right of access and provision of Data Protection Authorities, they however lack other crucial safeguards to guarantee, at their respective continental and regional levels, an adequately secure and trustworthy environment which seriously limits data processing abuses from public or private entities. The safeguards identified as lacking, which include rules relating to data breach notification or data protection by design, are well guaranteed in European data protection law, and some are embodied as data processing principles in the OECD Privacy Protection Guidelines.

It can therefore be concluded that the adoption of both ECOWAS and AU instruments is an unequivocal indication of the continent's willingness and progress in protecting the personal information of its citizens from security risks related to data processing by public or private entities, and implement online trust. Both instruments do contain a principle of confidentiality and security of data processing, requiring Member States to ensure data controllers implement appropriate security safeguards when processing personal data. However, some significant security mechanisms are missing from both instruments, mechanisms which could be addressed in an additional protocol to these instruments or in future multilateral texts in view of ensuring relatively strong data security standards for African citizens, to promote a trustworthy and safer digital environment.

Acknowledgments. This research is funded by the Erasmus Mundus program LAST-JD (Joint International Ph.D. in Law, Science and Technology) coordinated by the University of Bologna.

References

1. Adesoji, A.: Mobile technology, social media and 180 million people. J. Bus. Adm. Manag. Sci. **6**, 82–85 (2017)
2. Kayisire, D., Wei, J.: ICT adoption and usage in Africa: towards an efficiency assessment. Inf. Technol. Dev. **22**(4), 630–653, 641 (2016)
3. Harris, A., Goodman, S., Traynor, P.: Privacy and security concerns associated with mobile money applications in Africa. Wash. J. Law Technol. Arts **8**, 245–246 (2012)
4. Tchouassi, G.: Can mobile phones really work to extend banking services to the unbanked? Empirical lessons from selected Sub-Saharan Africa Countries. Int. J. Dev. Soc. **1**(2), 70–81 (2012)
5. GSMA: The Mobile Economy Report 2013, p. 3. A.T. Kearney, London, United Kingdom (2013)
6. Ericson Mobility Report, June 2017. https://www.ericsson.com/en/mobility-report/internet-of-things-outlook. Accessed 26 June 2019
7. Madakam, S., Ramaswamy, R., Tripathi, S.: Internet of Things (IoT): a literature review. J. Comput. Commun. **3**(05), 164 (2015)
8. Emiliani, P.L., Stephanidis, C.: Universal access to ambient intelligence environments: opportunities and challenges for people with disabilities. IBM Syst. J. **44**(3), 605–619 (2005)
9. Orji, U.J.: The African union convention on cybersecurity: a regional response towards cyber stability. Masaryk UJL Technol. **12**, 91 (2018)
10. Orji, U.J.: Multilateral legal responses to cyber security in Africa: any hope for effective international cooperation? In: 2015 7th International Conference on Cyber Conflict: Architectures in Cyberspace (CyCon), pp. 105–118. IEEE (2015)
11. Goodman, S., Harris, A.: The coming African tsunami of information insecurity. Commun. ACM **53**(12), 24–27 (2010)
12. Fuster, G.: The Emergence of Personal Data Protection as a Fundamental Right of the EU, vol. 16. Springer, Cham (2014). https://doi.org/10.1007/978-3-319-05023-2
13. Lynskey, O.: The Foundations of EU Data Protection Law. Oxford University Press, Oxford (2015)
14. Rich, C.: Privacy laws in Africa and the Middle East. The Bureau of National Affairs, editor. Privacy and security law report. BNA, Bloomberg (2015)
15. Schwartz, P.M., Solove, D.J.: The PII problem: privacy and a new concept of personally identifiable information. NYUL Rev. **86**, 1814 (2011)
16. Purtova, N.: The law of everything. Broad concept of personal data and future of EU data protection law. Law Innov. Technol. **10**(1), 40–81 (2018)
17. Hustinx, P.: EU data protection law: the review of directive 95/46/EC and the proposed general data protection regulation. Collected courses of the European University Institute's Academy of European Law, 24th Session on European Union Law, pp. 1–12 (2013)
18. Solove, D.J.: The new vulnerability: data security and personal information. In: Chander, A., Gelman, L., Radin, M.J. (eds.) Securing Privacy in the Internet Age. Stanford University Press, Palo Alto (2008)
19. De Hert, P., Gutwirth, S.: Data protection in the case law of Strasbourg and Luxemburg: constitutionalisation in action. In: Gutwirth, S., Poullet, Y., De Hert, P., de Terwangne, C., Nouwt, S. (eds.) Reinventing Data Protection?, pp. 3–44. Springer, Dordrecht (2009). https://doi.org/10.1007/978-1-4020-9498-9_1
20. Mantelero, A.: The future of consumer data protection in the EU Re-thinking the "notice and consent" paradigm in the new era of predictive analytics. Comput. Law Secur. Rev. **30**(6), 643–660 (2014)

21. Soeder, M.O.: Privacy challenges and approaches to the consent dilemma. Masters thesis. SSRN 3442612 (2019)
22. Whitman, M., Mattord, H.: Principles of Information Security. Thompson Course Technology, Boston (2009)
23. Gady, F.: Africa's cyber WMD. Foreign Policy, 24 March 2010
24. Dalton, W., van Vuuren, J.J., Westcott, J.: Building cybersecurity resilience in Africa. In: 12th International Conference on Cyber Warfare and Security 2017 Proceedings, pp. 112–120. Academic Conferences and Publishing International Limited, Reading (2017)
25. Makulilo, A.B.: The Context of Data Privacy in Africa. In: Makulilo, A.B. (ed.) African Data Privacy Laws. LGTS, vol. 33, pp. 3–23. Springer, Cham (2016). https://doi.org/10.1007/978-3-319-47317-8_1. (citing Westin's Privacy and Freedom (1967)
26. Makulilo, A.: Privacy and data protection in Africa: a state of the art. Int. Data Priv. Law 2(3), 163–178 (2012)
27. Kamwangamalu, N.M.: Ubuntu in South Africa: a sociolinguistic perspective to a pan-African concept. Crit. Arts 13(2), 24–41 (1999)
28. Olinger, H.N., Britz, J.J., Olivier, M.S.: Western privacy and/or Ubuntu? Some critical comments on the influences in the forthcoming data privacy bill in South Africa. Int. Inf. Libr. Rev. 39(1), 31–43 (2007)
29. Bakibinga, E.M.: Managing electronic privacy in the telecommunications sub-sector: the Ugandan perspective. In: Africa Electronic Privacy and Public Voice Symposium (2004)
30. Makulilo, A.B.: A person is a person through other persons-a critical analysis of privacy and culture in Africa. Beijing L. Rev. 7, 192 (2016)
31. Rich, C.: Privacy laws in Africa and the Near East. The Bureau of National Affairs, editor. Privacy and security law report. BNA, Bloomberg, September 2017
32. Rich, C.: Privacy laws in Africa and the Middle East. The Bureau of National Affairs, editor. Privacy and security law report. BNA, Bloomberg, June 2015
33. Adejumobi, S.: Engendering accountable governance in Africa. In: International Institute for Democracy and Electoral Assistance (IDEA) and Development Policy Management Forum (DPMF) Regional Conference on "Democracy, Poverty and Social Exclusion": Is Democracy the Missing Link (2000)
34. Abdulrauf, L.A., Fombad, C.M.: The African Union's data protection convention 2014: a possible cause for celebration of human rights in Africa? J. Media Law 8(1), 67–97 (2016)
35. Banisar, D.: Linking ICTs, the right to privacy, freedom of expression and access to information. East Afr. J. Peace Hum. Rights 16(1) (2010)
36. Sutherland, E.: Digital privacy in Africa: cybersecurity, data protection & surveillance. LINK Centre (2018)
37. Makulilo, A.B.: Myth and reality of harmonisation of data privacy policies in Africa. Comput. Law Secur. Rev. 31(1), 78–89 (2015)
38. Hustinx, P.: The role of data protection authorities. In: Gutwirth, S., Poullet, Y., De Hert, P., de Terwangne, C., Nouwt, S. (eds.) Reinventing Data Protection?, pp. 131–137. Springer, Dordrecht (2009). https://doi.org/10.1007/978-1-4020-9498-9_7
39. Stevens, G.M.: Data security breach notification laws. Congressional Research Service (2012)
40. Esayas, S.: Breach notification requirements under the European Union legal framework: convergence, conflicts, and complexity in compliance. John Marshall J. Inf. Technol. Priv. Law 31, 317–368 (2014)
41. Schwartz, P., Janger, E.: Notification of data security breaches. Mich. Law Rev. 105, 913 (2006)
42. Boillat, P., Kjaerum, M.: Handbook on European Data Protection Law, p. 77. Publications Office of the European Union, Luxembourg (2014)

43. See for example Paragraph 44, EU Article 29 Working Party. The future of privacy, WP 168. http://ec.europa.eu/justice/policies/privacy/docs/wpdocs/2009/wp168_en.pdf. Accessed 1 December 2009

44. Cunningham, M.: Privacy in the age of the hacker: balancing global privacy and data security Law. George Wash. Int. Law Rev. **44**, 643 (2012)

45. Weber, R.H.: Internet of things: privacy issues revisited. Comput. Law Secur. Rev. **31**(5), 618–627 (2015)

46. Europa, Privacy Enhancing Technologies (PETs), 2 May 2007. http://europa.eu/rapid/pressrelease_MEMO-07-159_en.htm. Accessed 24 Feb 2019

47. Gellert, R.: We have always managed risks in data protection law: understanding the similarities and differences between the rights-based and the risk-based approaches to data protection. Eur. Data Prot. L. Rev. **2**, 481 (2016)

48. Rodrigues, R., Wright, D., Wadhwa, K.: Developing a privacy seal scheme (that works). Int. Data Priv. Law **3**(2), 100–116 (2013)

49. Rodrigues, R., Barnard-Wills, D., De Hert, P., Papakonstantinou, V.: The future of privacy certification in Europe: an exploration of options under article 42 of the GDPR. Int. Rev. Law Comput. Technol. **30**(3), 248–270 (2016)

Proof of Concept of Blockchain Integration in P2P Lending for Developing Countries

Fatou Ndiaye Mbodji[✉], Gervais Mendy, Ahmath Bamba Mbacke,
and Samuel Ouya

Ecole Supérieure Polytechnique (ESP)/Université Cheikh Anta Diop
de Dakar (UCAD), Dakar, Senegal
{fatou.mbodji,gervais.mendy,ahmathbamba.mbacke}@esp.sn,
samuel.ouya@gmail.com

Abstract. Blockchain is depicted as a promising technology for fintech notably in developing countries. That's why, it's important to be interested in it, so as to know how to realize these probables blockchain's benefits. It presents a diversity of choices that impact on results in various ways. Studies have focused on fintech services business models such as P2P lending, others on the blockchain impact on finance, some even particularized in the case of developing countries. In these areas, a massive penetration of mobile phones is noted. It is in this context that fits this present study. In this paper we study the feasibility of a P2P lending platform based on blockchain and adapted to developing countries. The main contribution made by this article is: we developed a protocol and a business model of Peer-to-Peer (P2P) lending suitable to developing countries and accessible via mobile phone. The protocol integrates a service against the diversion of objectives which is based on smart contract.

Keywords: Blockchain · Fintech · Developing countries · P2P lending · Smart contracts

1 Introduction

In this study, in order to achieve specific objectives, we will have to answer the following questions. Would we be able to settle choices and thus obtain an innovative combination? Would we be able to gauge the combination to identify where and how to act?

Indeed, the blockchain technology used in this study offers various choices combinations, if only for the chosen type, consensus, the content of smart contracts, the choice of blockchain for storage. However, these choices are guided by the expressed needs, it will take exploit its and adapt its to the targets in order to make them pertinent, innovative and ready to challenge the existing. Moreover, many financial sector firms invest in blockchain solutions [1].

© ICST Institute for Computer Sciences, Social Informatics and Telecommunications Engineering 2020
Published by Springer Nature Switzerland AG 2020. All Rights Reserved
R. Zitouni et al. (Eds.): AFRICOMM 2019, LNICST 311, pp. 59–70, 2020.
https://doi.org/10.1007/978-3-030-41593-8_5

Our needs in this study are in fintech's field, another motivation to do an analysis work, [2] business models that are not robust in a lending or financing environment could harm. Indeed, it is a question of realizing a proof of concept which aim of setting up a fintech services platform to do mobile P2P lending adapted to developing countries realities. It will be based on a blockchain technology. The objective is to experiment work based on the assumption that a combination based on Blockchain, Fintech, mobile money, P2P lending and developing countries well-analyzed can promote financial inclusion and lead to an innovative solution. This being the general objective, to be more precise the work aims to define a protocol and a business model that we will gauge by a SWOT analysis.

Given the desired aspect which is the reusability of our work in fintech and blockchain in general, a flexible approach will be adopted consisting in abstracting the needs and solutions before concretizing them with a P2P lending protocol and business model.

2 Approach and Structuring

In this part we describe the adopted approach which explains the structuring.

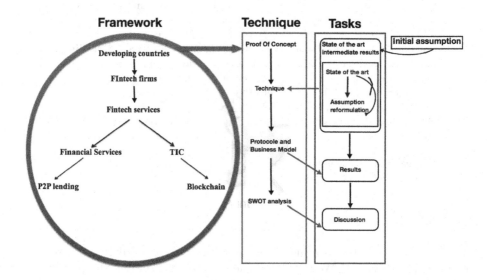

Fig. 1. Approach and structuring.

2.1 The Framework

To better workout our study, the framework is defined. As stated in Fig. 1, our target area is developing countries, we are interested in P2P lending services and the core technology of our study will be the blockchain. So there is talk of offering fintech services adapted to the context of the developing countries and to use the blockchain as underlying technology of this. Hence, the targeted space, services and core technology are defined and it is important for the constituent elements of our technique.

2.2 Technique

The framework is circumscribed, we will describe the study's technique, it integrates into the Proof Of Concept (POC) more particularly to the technical feasibility. The objective is to realize a protocol and a business model adapted to the defined framework, we submit them recursively to a SWOT analysis in order to evaluate it, we stop the analysis once we obtain a satisfactory protocol.

This process will be taken into account in the different tasks that will be performed in this work.

2.3 The Tasks

Each step of the technique is either source or consequence of a task. Indeed, to achieve the technical feasibility part we will make a state of the art, we refer to this last to obtain the protocol. For every verification of our initial hypothesis part, we formulate again the hypothesis. Thus, we will progressively verify our hypothesis by attenuating it as and when we find results. The protocol and intermediate results will be our results. To discuss these last, we will do a SWOT analysis.

This section "approach and structuring", was therefore to give an idea on the philosophy behind the various points that will be addressed in this document.

3 State of the Art

Reviewing the literature to explore the concepts, assets and challenges is important to achieving the objectives.

3.1 Concepts and Definitions

The different concepts, taken individually and/or combined, have aspects that can influence the decisions and the orientations of our study. That's why it is important to browse some scientific papers treating them.

The relationship between these terms and concepts is that mobile money innovations are increasing rapidly in developing countries, where they could extend financial services to billions of unbanked populations [11]. [12] proposes blockchain as underlying technology for entrepreneurial models aiming financial inclusion by adopting the practices of unbanked people. Indeed, properties of integrity, resilience and transparency of blockchain technology cause it to arouse

Table 1. Definitions of concepts

Concepts	Définitions
Fintech	Fintech is the use of financial technology that describes an emerging sector of financial services in the 21st century. [3]
Mobile Money	It is the use of cell phone technology to make financial transactions [4]
P2P lending	These types of fintechs allow individuals and businesses to lend and borrow among themselves [2]
Blockchain	Blockchain technology is a protocol for the secure transfer of money, property and information without the use of a third-party intermediary, such as banks or other financial institutions [5]
Consensus	It allow secure updating of a distributed shared state [6]. A consensus algorithm defines a set of rules to reach agreement on transactions and their order [7]
Smart Contracts	There are code form implemented on the Blockchain. They are based on predetermined factors and are autonomous and auto-executables [8]
SWOT	It is a method used to analyze and position an organization's resources and environment in four areas: strengths, weaknesses, opportunities and threats [9]
Loan motivation	It is the object that wants to acquire (or the service that wants to pay) the borrower. It is specified in the loan application
Financial inclusion	It is about access to financial services from sound and viable institutions at reasonable prices [10]

so much interest [13,14]. Given the promises and risks of such disruptive technology, many financial sector firms are investing in blockchain solutions [1].

To support this need to study our concepts combined, a proof of need is provided below.

3.2   Proof of the Need of Mobile P2P Lending Based on Blockchain in Developing Countries

In this part we will prove the need to use each of the concepts before attacking the need to elaborate the protocol. Remember that our geographical framework is developing countries.

Proof of the Need of Fintech Specifically P2P Lending Service: P2P lending platforms offer innovative solutions for developing countries that have difficulty obtaining traditional channel financing [13]. Henceforth, we can say that the P2P lending could promote the financial inclusion of these countries. Besides, by prescribing five sensitivities to undertake in the field of fintech based on the blockchain and reaching the unbanked population, [12] proposed the P2P network as a solution.

Proof of Need to Access Services via Mobile: In Sub-Saharan Africa, in 2019, mobile penetration has reached 76%, while less than 30% of people have a bank account [11]. In parallel, the use of mobile accounts is more common in these areas [15] (20.% versus a global rate of 4.4%) according to (World Bank, 2018). In addition, in developing markets, more than one billion people have a mobile phone, which can serve as a basis for the development of mobile financial services including payments, transfers, insurance, savings and credit [16]. So the target population is predisposed to mobile services.

Proof of the Need of Blockchain and of Protocol Development: Blockchain has attracted a lot of attentions, investments and developments within FinTech because it addresses two of the most risky aspects of Internet business: transactions and trust [17]. Let's start with the fintech expectations to show that we need to use blockchain as underlying technology.

Fintech faces increasingly demanding customers in terms of speed, ease of use, cost [3], security [12,18] and confidentiality [18] and a law to protect customers transparency and traceability [19]. These needs must be taken into account. In addition, security against theft [12] promotes the transition from cash to digital. Customer management is a challenge for fintech [2]. Note that, when we mention the law in this part we are referring to the case of WAEMU [19]. One of the technological innovations of financial services is the blockchain, which permits it to improve previous applications and deploy new applications that were previously uneconomic or impractical [3]. Indeed, in the field of banking and financial services, blockchain technology can simplify business processes and creating secure and reliable records of agreements and transactions [14]. However, for each of its expectations of fintech, its satisfaction may differ according to the type, consensus mechanism and business model chosen. So we can say that the blockchain could be the underlying technology of this service, however it would be necessary to define the adapted protocol to the needs.

4   Results

First, we define a business concept to achieve expected results. Then we present the latter which are a protocol and a business model allowing to make a P2P lending based on the blockchain in developing countries and accessible via mobile.

4.1   The Business Concept

A part of our hypothesis is verified. In addition, regarding the follow-up of the loan motivation to verify its compliance, this could be an added value to a P2P loan platform. Indeed, for its descriptive statistics for the dependent variables in the estimations [20] mentions Loan-taking motivation in the determinants of financial inclusion in Africa Review of Development Finance. Since this is a determining factor, the transparency of the Loan-taking motivation can encourage participatory financing or an investor to finance a loan.

Initial Hypothesis: A combination based on Blockchain, Fintech, mobile services and developing countries which is properly analysed can promote financial inclusion and lead to an innovative solution.

What is Done: We are starting from the target area (developing countries) to demonstrate the need to combine concepts and to develop a protocol and have announced an innovative approach: follow-up of the loan motivation to verify its compliance. Hence, we can give now the definition of our business concept. The business concept is a business idea that includes basic information such as the service or product, the target demographic group and an unique sales proposal that gives a company an advantage over its competitors [21].

Business Concept: We proof the need to offer to developing countries a blockchain-based mobile P2P lending service. We identify an innovative way to enhance its value. Our proposal is able to verify compliance between the motivation stated as the purpose of financing in general (of a loan in particular) and the use of the amount granted.

Hypothesis Reformulation: In the developing countries context, knowing that it is interesting to set up a P2P lending service based on blockchain technology provided that its protocol is well defined. An analysis work would allow us to adopt a business model and choose the characteristics of the suitable blockchain in accordance with our expectations.

4.2   Protocol and Business Model

We make choices that form the defined protocol. It is about of considering the varieties of each factor and choosing the most suitable for our business concept.

The Blockchain's Type for the P2P Lending: There are three types of blockchain named public, private and federated. The choosen type is private blockchain. Its low transaction costs are adapted to the low incomes characteristic of the target area. Private blockchain is adapted to laws such as those of WAEMU. Indeed, users are identified in the blockchain network with more control [8,13,22]. It has good throughput and maintenance and has a low latency [13], which is very important because of the increasingly demanding users. However, it reintroduces a single point of failure, which can compromise the underlying data [8] and provides low system confidence compared to other types of blockchains.

Choosing a type reduces the range of consensus mechanism choices because not all consensus mechanisms can be used in a private blockchain.

The Blockchain's Consensus Mechanism for the P2P Lending: According to the Table 1 (A comparison of popular blockchain consensus mechanisms), consensus mechanisms compatible with the blockchain private type are: Proof-of-Stake (PoS), Proof-of-elapsed-Time (PoeT) and variations of PBFT [6]. Now, security threat is more serious in Proof-based Consensus algorithm such as PoS and PoeT compared to Vote-based consensus algorithm such as variation of PBFT [23]. In PBFT transactions are confirmed immediately and have a high throughput. The scalability in terms of number of customers is high. It is not a source of energy waste. It should be noted that the target area has energy problems. In addition, with these mechanisms the nodes are identified which is in phase with the requirements of the law. The tolerance towards opponents is certainly 33% of the voting power compared to others as the proof of work which is 25% of the computing power, but this is to be taken into account. The scalability in terms of number of nodes is low. Hence, we choose variations of PBFT.

Borrowers-Investors Matching and the Loans Interest Rate: There are various model to the meeting of borrowers and investors. In a diffused model the platform collects funds from various investors for various loans taking into account guidelines. This is a financial risk management strategy. In addition, the time required to obtain the borrowed amount is shorter. The other model is the direct model where the investor decides how much to lend to the borrower [24]. Given the low incomes characteristic of developing countries, it is very likely that loans requested will be motivated by immediate needs, hence the importance of the short time between the request and the granting of the loan. That's why we choose the diffused model. For greater flexibility, interest rates must be able to vary from one loan to another. For loan interest, in view of the fact that the online P2P credit market is not yet very developed in some developing countries, we have chosen a model that takes this into account. Indeed, the model chosen is such that investors set their maximum interest and borrowers their minimum interest and the platform will match the interest taking into account other elements such as financial risk. The other models are: [24] reverse auction and automatic matching.

Our model is based on customer (borrowers and investor) instructions.

Linear Regression as a Credit Scoring Models: On the one hand, [25] proposes neural network credit scoring model and compared it with the Logistic Regression to evaluate borrowers' creditworthiness. On the other hand [26] classifies some scoring models. By merging the results of [25] and [26], the percentages of correctly classifying a bad customer is recorded in the Table 2 below.

Table 2. Models and their percentages to correctly rank a bad borrower

Models	% ranking a bad borrower	Reference
Linear regression model	87.5	[26]
Poisson model	81.8	[26]
Negative binomial II model	80.6	[26]
Two step procedure	79.8	[26]
Discriminant analysis	78.0	[26]
Neural Network	74.38	[25]
Logistic Regression	61.03	[25]
Probit model	54.1	[26]

To minimize the risks, we chose the linear regression model because. It is the one with the highest percentage. Identifying a bad payer is very important because P2P lending attracts high-risk customers.

Smart Contracts Against the Misuse of Objectives: The absence of an intermediary is one of the greatest advantages of the blockchain, the role played by these trusted third parties should not be overlooked, hence the interest given to consensus. Smart contracts are attractive in many scenarios, particularly those that require money transfers to comply with certain agreed rules [27]. Through smart contracts, various actors can collaborate by pre-defining their logic. Indeed, smart contracts are "if then" type programs, they are executed automatically if their conditions are verified. Thus, to monitor the amount lent to ensure compliance between expenses and the financing motivation, a smart contract could be used to target the accounts to which the amounts will be transferred. In this case, instead of giving the amount directly to the borrower, it will be directly to the accounts of the service provider or the acquisition of which is designated as the reason for the financing. Before answering the how of such an action, let us first specify its interest.

The Interest: Using a smart contract to verify compliance between the stated motives and the use of the amount would be useful for financing requiring proof of expenditure or verification of the acquisition of the good or service designated as the purpose of the financing. Indeed, to generalize the statements of [8], smart contracts provide an elegant way to link accounting, reporting and monitoring of the amount financed. This proven need, let's pass to the analysis and design.

Analysis and Design: Such work requires access to the service supplier's account but also a way to verify the veracity of certain documents. To set up a smart contract to manage this, a few design templates may be requested (Table 3).

Table 3. Useful smart contracts design pattern

Useful design pattern	Solution	In the study context
Oracles	Oracles are contracts which are the interface between contracts and the outside, it can be queried from other contracts. In practice, contract queries an oracle instead of querying an external service; and when the external service needs to update its data, it sends a suitable transaction to the oracle [27]	Ideally all actors would be accessible via the platform offering the service. However, this is not always the case. To use external supporting documents, this contract may be called
Time constraint	Implement time constraints to specify when an action is allowed [27, 28]	If the expenses in accordance with the reason are diverse and their compliance is achieved only if some or all of these expenses are proven. A constrained time will be used. [28] It should also be noted that this one has vulnerabilities described by (Atzei et al. 2017)
ChecksEffects-Interaction Pattern [29]	It allows to follow a recommended functional code order, in which calls to external contracts are always the last step, to reduce the attack surface of a contract manipulated by its own external contracts [29]	To manage vulnerabilities related to contract calls in contracts
Math	Contracts using this model encode the logic that protects the execution of certain critical operations [27]	For example, to avoid subtracting a value from a balance when there are not enough funds in an account [27]. This constraint is useful for tracking an amount
Emergency Stop (Circuit Breaker)	Incorporate an emergency stop function into the contract can be triggered by an authenticated party to disable sensitive functions [29]	To bypass the immutability of the blockchain [29]

Thus we know the patterns that will be used in the solution against the misuse of objectives. These results allow us to verify our reformulated hypothesis. However, in order to assess the relevance of our results, we will discuss them and take the opportunity to identify some ways to improve our results.

5 Discussion

Our results are obtained by comparing the various characteristics and making choices. Now we will gauge the combination of these various characteristics through a SWOT analysis.

Strength of Our Combined Choices: Cost per transaction and latency are low; throughput and maintenance are good [13]. Users are identified within the blockchain network with more control [8,13,22]. The platform matches borrowers and investors according to criteria such as scoring, interest rates. The willingness of stakeholders on the reasons for the loan is taken into account. For the low trust in the system that is relative to the private type: the use of smart contracts will strengthen trust in the system.

Weakness of Our Combined Choices: Scalability in term of number of nodes is low (maximum tested is 20). Malicious tolerance is 33% of voting power. Other weaknesses include: the use of oracle to validate data provenance and run smart contracts.

Opportunity of Our Combined Choices : it offer better compliance with laws such as those of the WAEMU in terms of identity management and better privacy [22]. Transactions confirmation are immediate and have high throughput and high scalability in term of number of clients. Borrowers get money in a short period of time [24]. The probability that each borrower will receive their request for funds is high [24] and diversification of investment is good. The interests of the borrower and the investor converge as a result of the matching of interest rates. The platform promotes financial inclusion and monitors the use of the loan amount.

Threat of Our Combined Choices : there is the threat of data immutability where the pool of participants is small. Private blockchain reintroduces a single point of failure that can compromise the underlying data [8]. The use of oracles can lead to conflicts of interest over data sources.

Our results lead to a Proof of Concept boosting blockchain-based P2P lending in developing countries.

6 Conclusion

The contribution of this study focus on a service, P2P lending, which is an indicator of financial inclusion and on the blockchain. Our starting assumption was: "A combination based on Blockchain, Fintech, mobile money and developing countries properly analysed can promote financial inclusion and lead to an innovative solution".

We verified the hypothesis and consequently, we made a proof of concept materialized by a protocol and a business model for the implementation of a P2P lending based on blockchain technology and adapted to developing countries and accessible via mobile. An approach was defined and used to achieve the results. A business concept with an emphasis on managing the misuse of resources is defined. An analysis and design based on the smart contract of this aspect has been done.

Once the feasibility has been proven, future studies may contribute to each element of choice, taking into account our SWOT analysis.

References

1. Tapscott, A., Tapscott, D.: How blockchain is changing finance. Harvard Bus. Rev. **1**(9), 2–5 (2017)
2. Lee, I., Shin, Y.J.: Fintech: ecosystem, business models, investment decisions, and challenges. Bus. Horiz. **61**(1), 35–46 (2018). https://doi.org/10.1016/j.bushor. 2017.09.003
3. Gomber, P., Kauffman, R.J., Parker, C., Weber, B.W.: On the fintech revolution: interpreting the forces of innovation, disruption, and transformation in financial services. J. Manag. Inf. Syst. **35**(1), 220–265 (2018). https://doi.org/10.1080/ 07421222.2018.1440766
4. Jack, W., Suri, T.: Mobile Money: The Economics of M-PESA (2011). https://doi. org/10.3386/w16721
5. Swan, M.: Blockchain for business: next-generation enterprise artificial intelligence systems. In: Blockchain Technology: Platforms, Tools and Use Cases, pp. 121–162 (2018). https://doi.org/10.1016/bs.adcom.2018.03.013
6. Baliga, A.: Understanding blockchain consensus models, April 2017. https://www. persistent.com/wp-content/uploads/2017/04/WP-Understanding-Blockchain-Co nsensus-Models.pdf
7. Muzammal, M., Qu, Q., Nasrulin, B.: Renovating blockchain with distributed databases: an open source system. Future Gen. Comput. Syst. **90**, 105–117 (2019). https://doi.org/10.1016/j.future.2018.07.042
8. Duchenne, J.: Blockchain and Smart Contracts. Transforming Climate Finance and Green Investment with Blockchains, pp. 303–317 (2018). https://doi.org/10.1016/ b978-0-12-814447-3.00022-7
9. Phadermrod, B., Crowder, R.M., Wills, G.B.: Importance-performance analysis based SWOT analysis. Int. J. Inf. Manag. (2016). https://doi.org/10.1016/j. ijinfomgt.2016.03.009
10. Patwardhan, A.: Financial inclusion in the digital age. Handb. Blockchain Digit. Finance Incl. **1**, 57–89 (2018). https://doi.org/10.1016/b978-0-12-810441- 5.00004-x
11. Lashitew, A.A., van Tulder, R., Liasse, Y.: Mobile phones for financial inclusion: what explains the diffusion of mobile money innovations? Res. Policy (2019). https://doi.org/10.1016/j.respol.2018.12.010

12. Larios-Hernández, G.J.: Blockchain entrepreneurship opportunity in the practices of the unbanked. Bus. Horiz. **60**(6), 865–874 (2017). https://doi.org/10.1016/j.bushor.2017.07.012

13. Viriyasitavat, W., Hoonsopon, D.: Blockchain characteristics and consensus in modern business processes. J. Industr. Inf. Integr. (2018). https://doi.org/10.1016/j.jii.2018.07.004

14. Treleaven, P., Brown, R.G., Yang, D.: Blockchain technology in finance. Computer **50**(9) (2017). https://doi.org/10.1109/MC.2017.3571047

15. World Bank Group. The Little Data Book on Financial Inclusion (2018). https://www.unsgsa.org/files/3815/2511/8893/LDB_Financial_Inclusion_2018.pdf

16. Mobile Money for the Unbanked Programme (2014). Le point sur le secteur: Les services financiers mobiles destinés aux personnes non bancarisées en 2014

17. Kursh, S.R., Gold, N.A.: Adding fintech and blockchain to your curriculum. Bus. Educ. Innov. J. http://www.beijournal.com/images/V8N2_final.pdf#page=6

18. Gai, K., Qiu, M., Sun, X.: A survey on FinTech. J. Netw. Comput. Appl. https://doi.org/10.1016/j.jnca.2017.10.011

19. Meagher, P.: Cadre réglementaire pour les services financiers numériques en Côte d'Ivoire Etude diagnostique, Juillet 2017

20. Zins, A., Weill, L.: The determinants of financial inclusion in Africa. Rev. Dev. Finance **6**(1), 46–57 (2016). https://doi.org/10.1016/j.rdf.2016.05.00

21. Business concept. BusinessDictionary.com, 21 May 2019. http://www.businessdictionary.com/definition/business-concept.html

22. Atlam, H.F., Wills, G.B.: Technical aspects of blockchain and IoT. Adv. Comput. (2018). https://doi.org/10.1016/bs.adcom.2018.10.006

23. Nguyen, G.-T., Kim, K.: A survey about consensus algorithms used in blockchain. J. Inf. Process. Syst. **14**(1), 101–128 (2018). 1976–913X (Print).https://doi.org/10.3745/JIPS.01.0024

24. Omarini, A.: Peer-to-peer lending: business model analysis and the platform dilemma. Int. J. Finance Econ. Trade (IJFET) (2018). (Submitted 1st August 2018, Accepted 24th Sept)

25. Byanjankar, A., Heikkila, M., Mezei, J.: Predicting credit risk in peer-to-peer lending: a neural network approach. In: 2015 IEEE Symposium Series on Computational Intelligence (2015). https://doi.org/10.1109/ssci.2015.109

26. Abdou, H.A., Pointon, J.: Credit scoring, statistical techniques and evaluation criteria: a review of the literature. Intell. Syst. Acc. Finance Manag. **18**(2–3), 59–88 (2011). https://doi.org/10.1002/isaf.325

27. Bartoletti, M., Pompianu, L.: An empirical analysis of smart contracts: platforms, applications, and design patterns. In: Brenner, M., et al. (eds.) FC 2017. LNCS, vol. 10323, pp. 494–509. Springer, Cham (2017). https://doi.org/10.1007/978-3-319-70278-0_31

28. Atzei, N., Bartoletti, M., Cimoli, T.: A survey of attacks on ethereum smart contracts (SoK). In: Maffei, M., Ryan, M. (eds.) POST 2017. LNCS, vol. 10204, pp. 164–186. Springer, Heidelberg (2017). https://doi.org/10.1007/978-3-662-54455-6_8

29. Wohrer, M., Zdun, U.: Smart contracts: security patterns in the ethereum ecosystem and solidity. In: 2018 International Workshop on Blockchain Oriented Software Engineering (IWBOSE) (2018). https://doi.org/10.1109/iwbose.2018.8327565

Smart Cities

A LoRaWAN Coverage Testbed and a Multi-optional Communication Architecture for Smart City Feasibility in Developing Countries

Pape Abdoulaye Barro[1,2]([✉]) [iD], Marco Zennaro[2] [iD], and Jules Degila[1] [iD]

[1] Institute of Mathematics and Physical Sciences (IMSP),
Porto-Novo 3730-301, Benin
pape.barro@imsp-uac.org, pape.abdoulaye.barro@gmail.com
[2] T/ICT4D Laboratory of the Abdus Salam International Centre for Theoretical
Physics (ICTP), 34151 Trieste, Italy

Abstract. Connectivity is key for IoT and smart cities. Unfortunately, a stable Internet connection is scarce in developing countries. LoRaWAN standalone base station solutions can be used to fill the gaps. But since these difficulties may not affect everyone, then, affordable wireless communication, such as Wi-Fi, with direct access to Internet from the collection node, may be useful for data transmission. This article, first, discusses a coverage study based on LoRaWAN autonomous base stations and, then, extends the architectural model proposed in [3] to take into account the Wi-Fi protocol, thus diversifying the implementation choices. A gateway (Wi-IoT) capable of providing Wi-Fi access, on the one hand, and collecting, processing and monitoring data as a mini-server, on the other hand, will be proposed as proof of concept. From the node to the gateway, data will be compressed and sent securely. A user who connects to Wi-IoT will, then, be able to access his data.

Keywords: Sustainability · Smart and future city feasibility ·
IoT/ICT for development · Edge/Fog computing · Wireless and
community network · LoRaWAN · Wi-Fi

1 Introduction

In recent years, LoRaWAN has become the most important sensor network protocol in both research and industrial worlds. This advantage comes from its wide coverage (ranging from 1 to 10 km in urban areas and more than 15 km in rural areas), its low energy consumption and the fact that it is open source, uses the industrial, scientific and medical (ISM) radio bands and also allows a

Supported by organization CEA-SMA, UAC/IMSP, Dangbo, Benin. In collaboration with ICT4D Lab (Marconi-lab), ICTP, Trieste, Italy.

© ICST Institute for Computer Sciences, Social Informatics and Telecommunications Engineering 2020
Published by Springer Nature Switzerland AG 2020. All Rights Reserved
R. Zitouni et al. (Eds.): AFRICOMM 2019, LNICST 311, pp. 73–83, 2020.
https://doi.org/10.1007/978-3-030-41593-8_6

low-cost deployment. LoRaWAN is a communication and architecture protocol that uses LoRa modulation which is a physical layer technology. In LoRaWAN, the data rate is between 0.3 to 5.5 kbps with two high-speed channels at 11 kbps and 50 kbps in FSK modulation and supports secure two-way communication, mobility and location; Spreading factors (SF) ranging from SF7 to SF12 are used to specifically define the data transfer rate with respect to the range. Depending on the environmental conditions between the node and the base station, the network will determine the proper spreading factor to work with. Using an adaptive data rate (ADR), the network is able to manage the data rate and output power of each node individually, in order to optimize battery life, signal range, and overall network capacity. Thanks to their CSS (Chirp Spread Spectrum) modulation and the different phase shifted frequencies used for chirps, the LoRaWAN network is insensitive to interference, multi-path propagation and fading phenomena. Chirps are used to encode the (Tx) side data, while the reverse chirps are used on the (Rx) side to decode the signal.

A first study [2] was conducted on stand-alone LoRaWAN base stations that can operate even when Internet is intermittent or non-existent and, that can communicate with one another [3], form a city size extensive network. In this paper, we will first discuss a coverage study based on LoRaWAN and, then, propose a testbed for this purpose. Noted that [2] and [3] are steps of [1] that aims to study the feasibility of the smart city in developing countries, especially in Africa.

Although Internet can generally be inaccessible or intermittent, acceptable connectivity [3] (with a round-trip time less than 100 ms (see Fig. 1)) can be present at some places. Therefore, it is fair to consider proposing an architectural model offering several options of communication on demand and which will remain flexible for future evolutions. Wi-Fi protocol (which is part of the broad family of radio technologies implementing IEEE 802.11x) is, then, added to the proposed model in [3] to meet the defined objectives. Indeed, it belongs to the Wi-Fi Alliance organization [7] and operates in the frequency band 2.4 GHz (for 802.11b, 802.11g or 802.11n) or 5 GHz for the 802.11a. We also see continuous improvement of its technologies (see Table 1).

Sending bare data over Internet is useless. Ensuring end-to-end integrity is essential. Moreover, in IoT, the data size must not be too large in order to minimize the volume of flux that it can absorb, and remain as close as possible to the real-time. It then becomes, necessary to set up a compression method.

The rest of this paper is as follows: Sect. 2 deals with the coverage study on LoRaWAN Autonomous Base Stations and presents a testbed for this purpose. Section 3 proposes an extension of the architectural model to take into account the Wi-Fi protocol and remains flexible to future developments. Section 4 illustrates the proof of concept and gives test results. The conclusion and some perspectives completes this document.

2   Coverage Study

In LoRaWAN, the gateways can measure, upon reception of the packet, the received signal strength indicator (RSSI) and the signal-to-noise ratio (SNR).

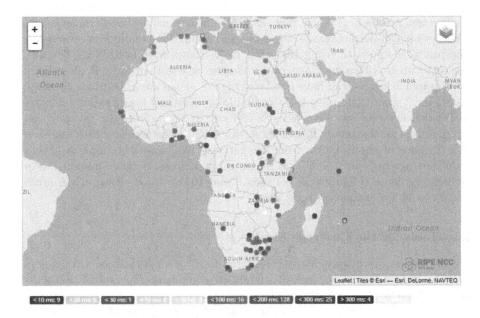

Fig. 1. Internet latency in Africa

The calculation of the radio receiver sensitivity (S), which is the minimum of the detectable signal that can be decoded, helps evaluate the signal quality by monitoring the RSSI, provided that the RSSI is not less than the sensitivity and its limit value, practically not less than -120 dBm, for good coverage. The sensitivity of the receiver (S) in dBm is expressed as a function of the bandwidth (BW) in Hz, the receiver noise factor (NF) in dB and the signal-to-noise ratio (SNR) in dB (see Eq. (1)).

$$S = -174 + 10 \log_{10}(BW) + NF + SNR \tag{1}$$

Table 1. IEEE 802.11 amendments

Standard	Year approved	Max data	Frequency band	Channel width	RF chains width
a	1999	54 Mb/s	5 GHz	20 MHz	1 × 1 SISO
b	1999	11 Mb/s	2.4 GHz	20 MHz	1 × 1 SISO
g	2003	54 Mb/s	2.4 GHz	20 MHz	1 × 1 SISO
n	2009	600 Mb/s	2.4/5 GHz	20/40 MHz	Up to 4 × 4*
ac	2012	3.2 Gb/s	5 GHz	20 to 160 MHz	Up to 8 × 8*, MU
ad	2014	6.76 Gb/s	60 GHz	2160 MHz	1 × 1 SISO
af	2014	426 Mb/s	54 to 790 MHz	6–8 MHz	up to 4 × 4*
ah	2016	@	Below 1 GHz	1–2 MHz	1 × 1 SISO

*: MIMO
@: from 150 kb/s to 347 Mb/s

The test results in [4] show that, as LoRa chooses narrowband transmission, it covers 1 km in-detp coverage situations and about 5 km in outdoor situations. The practical approach using the RSSI in [5] shows that LoRaWAN gateway can cover up to 10 km with a packet loss ratio of less than 30%. It also shows that up to 4–6 km, we can have good coverage in urban areas. Outdoor coverage results in [6] show that, when trees and buildings obstruct line of sight, a 54.33% packet delivery rate was observed at a distance of 2.6 km from the gateway and for an almost unobstructed line of sight, an 84.5% packet delivery rate was seen at a distance of about 4.4 km from the gateway. We can, then, hope to have a good coverage between 1 and 3 km in dense urban areas, between 3 and 6 km in moderately dense urban areas, between 6 and 10 km in low-dense urban areas and up to 15 km or more in rural areas.

2.1   Tools for the Coverage Study

In this Section, we introduce the considered tools in an African context, where there is, most of the time, lack of simulation equipment. The simulation aims at assessing the signal quality, under the constraints imposed by the network and the landscape, for a better presentation and interpretation of the results. To achieve that, the tool must:

- Be able to reveal the current state and the profile of the given area (trees, buildings, watercourses, available materials, etc.) to better take into account the phenomena related to the disturbance of the signal;
- Be able to adjust signal parameters (bandwidth, frequency, spreading factor used, modulation, etc.);
- Propose a good representation of the signal quality in a map with specific collection positions;
- After the simulation, propose a portable recording file, which can be used as needed, without having to repeat the simulation;
- When simulating communications between the base stations, give the acceptable distances and heights to allow good 'line of sight'.

Some tools were covered in [8], but none of them have met our expectations. Finding an open-access tool that can meet our requirements has been a challenge. Radio Mobile [9] can approach the solution but remains limited when it comes to the area conditions. RF Bot [10] is also a good tool for 'Line-of-sight' simulation, but as it is based on SPLAT [11], it requires one goes to generate its scripts. Based on the Pietro Manzoni's scripts [12], we suggest the following testbed that can meet our needs.

2.2   Testbed

The testbed was conducted around the campus of the "Institute of Mathematics and Physical Sciences (IMSP)" and consisted of measuring the received Signal Strength from a node sending data. The purpose of this test is to assess the

Fig. 2. Required types of equipment for the coverage study

coverage despite some obstacles. To expect a strong signal, the RSSI must be closer to zero (0) and the minimum acceptable must be -120 dBm.

To achieve that, we used an eight (8) channel gateway [13] placed at the Institute's computing center and a Pytrack [14], as a mobile node, whose role is to send GPS coordinates, to be able to measure signal strength (RSSI) at a given position. We also used a single channel gateway [15] (see Fig. 2) for the same purposes. The results on the map (see Fig. 3(a)) indicate, when in green that the signal is strong (RSSI higher than -90 dBm), when in yellow that the signal is quite good (RSSI between -90 and -110 dBm) and when in red that the signal is weak (RSSI below -110 dBm).

SPLAT has also been used to simulate the "line of sight" between two sites.

Considering a base station located at the "Ecole normale supérieure" (ENS) of the city of Porto-Novo as a slave, the one located at IMSP as the master, we manage to simulate a line of sight at a distance of 13,25 km (see Fig. 3(b)). The slave can be raised at about 30 m from the ground, while the master height is about 15 m from the ground.

3   Architectures

This vision of the smart city that wants to connect anything to the Internet is undeniably a waste of resources. This type of approach will not be accessible to people who cannot afford it, or even that, the infrastructure will not be stable in

(a)

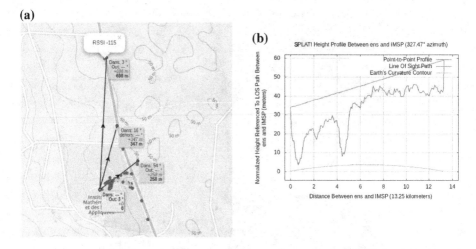

Fig. 3. (a) LoRaWAN network coverage study around the IMSP campus. (b) The line of sight simulation between Slave (ens) and Master (IMSP). (Color figure online)

case of intermittency [3]. However, for people who have access to good connectivity, they can, then, connect their end nodes to Internet using a Wi-Fi interface. The collected data can then be routed to a public Cloud. A local gateway will, then, be able to collect, process and monitor them. We will, therefore, orient our research in this direction and, thus, complete the model proposed in [3] to include this case and, consequently, to diversify the communication modes.

As an illustration, let us consider the scenarios described in [3], with Yao and Benin government. Yao is a businessman and owner of a taxi company and wants to be able to know at any time the position of his taxis. He can easily have access to Internet and capable of building his infrastructure on the latter. Similarly, the Beninese government can also connect its measuring stations to Internet and thus manage the collected data.

The requirements remain the same, and consist of choosing affordable and accessible equipment, implementing a system that uses fewer resources (5 V DC and at least 2.5 A sufficient), with a scalable storage system. The infrastructure must be based on open source and use the free ISM band (industrial, scientific and medical radio bands). The proposed architecture must then meet these requirements and at the same time be flexible for future additions.

We modified the general architecture proposed in [3] by adding the Wi-Fi option as follows (see Fig. 4):

- In "Local Access", we have, at the bottom, the "Measurement Layer", then, the "Messaging Layer" and, between them, the "PublisherInterf" interface.
- In "Remote Access", we first have the "Wi-IoT Services" block, then, the "Application Layer" and, between them, the "MlAppInterf" interface on the one hand and the "MonitorServ" interface on the other.

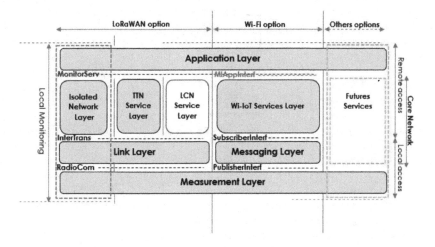

Fig. 4. General architecture

– Between "Local Access" and "Remote Access" we have the "SubscriberInterf" interface. The model is later left flexible to future additions.

When considering an architecture with several communication options, the interoperability problem is present. Also, with a city-sized infrastructure, the centralization of data is considered. The interoperability problem can be handled at the "backup layer" level (central database to which all other communication options converge their data). As a result, remote access to the proposed applications will be required and, each communication option should present data from its "middleware layer" (see Fig. 5).

4   Proof of Concept

In this Section we will discuss the Wi-Fi option implementation methodology. LoRaWAN options descriptions are available in [3].

A choice of equipment (see Fig. 6) must be made first before thinking about programming. So, we chose, on the node side, a Pycom expansion board 3.0 [16] on which we put LoPy 4 [17] and as a sensor, we used a DHT11 [18]. The gateway (Wi-IoT) is developed on a Raspberry pi 3 [19].

In development, the node (embedded system) collects the data, encrypts it, compresses it and publishes it on a broker via Wi-Fi.

– Encryption is based on 128-bit Advanced Encryption Standard (AES),
– The compression is done in 2 steps:
  • First, since the data is transformed into a bitstream, we used a grouping of 4 bits and for each group, a representation character is associated with it. The number of bits must be a multiple of 4, otherwise, the string is filled with zeros at the beginning.

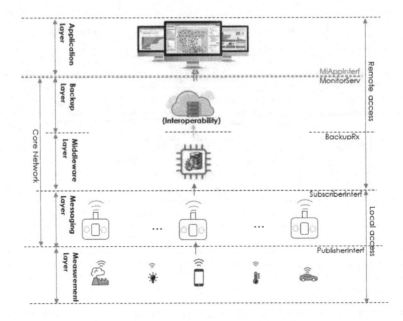

Fig. 5. Infrastructure in each layer

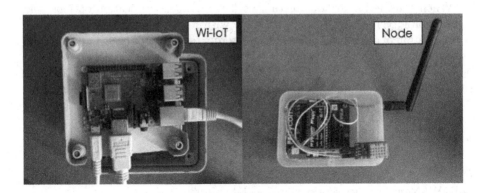

Fig. 6. Required types of equipment to implement the Wi-Fi option

- In a second step, the successive duplicates are identified and listed to be added later to the compression chain by taking the character followed by the number of successive repetitions (like the logic of RLE (Run Length Encoding)).
- Eclipse mosquitto "iot.eclipse.org" is used as a Broker but we could have chosen "test.mosquitto.org", "www.cloudmqtt.com", "mqtt.swifitch.cz" or others ...

Subsequently, the Wi-IoT gateway (which subscribes to the topics of their choice in connected mode) collects data, decompresses, decrypts and stores in

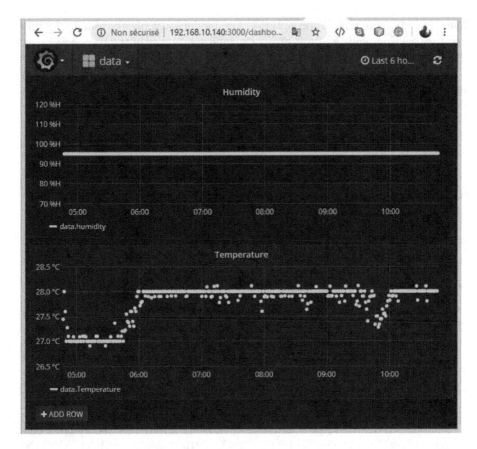

Fig. 7. Display of measurement of temperature and humidity collected

InfluxDB (open-source time-series database). A backup, in the central database for interoperability, and other processing are, then, possible. Grafana (open platform for analysis and monitoring) is, then, accessible on (IP: 3000) by any client connecting to the Wi-IoT gateway (see Fig. 7). The applicability of machine learning is also possible with respect to self-correction, prediction, or decision-making.

5 Conclusion

In developing countries, access to Internet is often a severe problem. Accessibility would be relative, since some of them may claim to have access to acceptable connectivity and will, therefore, prefer to go in that direction. The rest will be satisfied with a good coverage of the LoRaWAN network based on autonomous base stations.

This step consists of completing [2] and [3], which are part of the project described in [1], and extending the architecture by adding the Wi-Fi protocol to diversify radio communication options. The model must always remain flexible to future developments while ensuring the interoperability of the protocols taken into account.

In the future, it will be interesting to propose a complete web application integrating all the constraints for a better LoRa network coverage study. In terms of diversity, it will be interesting to consider the addition of another radio protocol, such as Zigbee [20]. It would also be interesting to discuss the performance of the proposed architecture, given the complexity of the time required to deliver the data.

References

1. Barro, P.A., Degila, J., Zennaro, M., Wamba, S.F.: Towards smart and sustainable future cities based on internet of things for developing countries: what approach for Africa?. EAI Endorsed Trans. Internet Things **4**(13) (2018). https://doi.org/10.4108/eai.11-9-2018.155481
2. Barro, P.A., Zennaro, M., Pietrosemoli, E.: TLTN - the local things network: on the design of a LoRaWAN gateway with autonomous servers for disconnected communities. In: Wireless Days (WD) (2019). https://doi.org/10.1109/WD.2019.8734239
3. Barro, P.A., Zennaro, M., Degila, J., Pietrosemoli, E.: A smart cities LoRaWAN network based on autonomous base stations (BS) for some countries with limited internet access. Future Internet **11**, 93 (2019). https://doi.org/10.3390/fi11040093
4. Bao, L., et al.: Coverage analysis on NB-IoT and LoRa in power wireless private network. Procedia Comput. Sci. J. **131**, 1032–1038 (2018). https://doi.org/10.1016/j.procs.2018.04.252
5. Seye, M.R., Gueye, B., Diallo, M.: An evaluation of LoRa coverage in Dakar Peninsula. In: 8th IEEE Annual Information Technology, Electronics and Mobile Communication Conference (IEMCON) (2017). https://doi.org/10.1109/IEMCON.2017.8117211
6. Yousuf, A.M., Rochester, E.M., Ghaderi, M.: A low-cost LoRaWAN testbed for IoT: implementation and measurements. In: IEEE 4th World Forum on Internet of Things (WF-IoT) (2018). https://doi.org/10.1109/WF-IoT.2018.8355180
7. Wi-Fi Alliance. https://www.wi-fi.org/. Accessed 15 July 2019
8. Fujdiak, R., Mlynek, P., Misurec, J., Strajt, M.: Simulated coverage estimation of single gateway LoRaWAN network. In: IEEE 25th International Conference on Systems, Signals and Image Processing (IWSSIP) (2018). https://doi.org/10.1109/IWSSIP.2018.8439232
9. Radio Mobile. https://www.ve2dbe.com/rmonline_s.asp/. Accessed 15 July 2019
10. Zennaro, M., Rainone, M., Pietrosemoli, E.: Radio link planning made easy with a telegram bot. In: Gaggi, O., Manzoni, P., Palazzi, C., Bujari, A., Marquez-Barja, J.M. (eds.) GOODTECHS 2016. LNICST, vol. 195, pp. 295–304. Springer, Cham (2017). https://doi.org/10.1007/978-3-319-61949-1_31
11. SPLAT. https://www.qsl.net/kd2bd/splat.html. Accessed 15 July 2019
12. Manzoni P.: https://github.com/pmanzoni/pycom_mapper. Accessed 15 July 2019
13. iC880A. https://www.wireless-solutions.de/products/long-range-radio/ic880a.html. Accessed 15 July 2019
14. Pytrack. https://docs.pycom.io/datasheets/boards/pytrack/. Accessed 15 July 2019

15. LoRa expansion board. https://pinout.xyz/pinout/uputronics_lora_expansion_board. Accessed 15 July 2019
16. Pycom expansion board. https://docs.pycom.io/datasheets/boards/expansion3/. Accessed 15 July 2019
17. LoPy. https://docs.pycom.io/datasheets/development/lopy/. Accessed 15 July 2019
18. dht11. https://components101.com/dht11-temperature-sensor. Accessed 15 July 2019
19. Raspberry Pi 3 Model B+. https://www.raspberrypi.org/products/raspberry-pi-3-model-b-plus/. Accessed 15 July 2019
20. Zigbee Alliance. https://www.zigbee.org/. Accessed 15 July 2019

Effective Management of Delays at Road Intersections Using Smart Traffic Light System

Olasupo Ajayi[1,2]([✉]) [iD], Antoine Bagula[1] [iD], Omowunmi Isafiade[1], and Ayodele Noutouglo[2]

[1] Department of Computer Science, University of the Western Cape, Cape Town, South Africa
3944991@myuwc.ac.za, {abagula,oisafiade}@uwc.ac.za
[2] Department of Computer Sciences, University of Lagos, Lagos, Nigeria
olaajayi@unilag.edu.ng
http://www.uwc.ac.za

Abstract. Rapid industrialization coupled with increased human population in urban regions has led to a rise in vehicle usage. The demand for space (road) by motorists for transportation has risen. Unfortunately, infrastructural development has not been at par with vehicular growth thus resulting in congestion along major roads. Traffic lights have been used for years to manage traffic flow. While they serve a good purpose, their underlining principle of operation is to a significant degree inefficient as traffic congestion still prevails and remains a major concern till date. This study seeks to tackle this challenge by proffering a Smart Traffic Management System (STMS) based on image detection. The system incorporates cameras which dynamically capture road situation as images, run them through an image processing algorithm to obtain traffic density then automatically adjust the service times at intersections. To measure the effectiveness of the approach, mathematical models were formulated, analytical comparison as well as experimental simulations were done. Results show that SMTS out-performed the Round-Robin algorithm used by traditional traffic lights, by reducing service interruptions, cutting delay times by at least 50%, while remaining equally fair to all roads at the intersection. This system and its constituent components fall under the Edge computing paradigm as real time data capture, analysis and decisions are made by an embedded computer.

Keywords: Edge computing · Image processing · Scheduling · Smart traffic · Traffic management

1 Introduction

Traffic congestion according to the Merriam Webster dictionary refers to a congestion of vehicles in a particular area thereby hindering the expected flow.

© ICST Institute for Computer Sciences, Social Informatics and Telecommunications Engineering 2020
Published by Springer Nature Switzerland AG 2020. All Rights Reserved
R. Zitouni et al. (Eds.): AFRICOMM 2019, LNICST 311, pp. 84–103, 2020.
https://doi.org/10.1007/978-3-030-41593-8_7

The transportation system in urban cities can be highly unpredictable as free highways can in a matter of minutes be inexplicable gridlocked. This can negatively affects many processes that leverage on transportation for productivity. By extension, road congestion can hinder economic growth by making people arrive late at work and delaying supply of raw materials to factories. In extreme cases it can be a hazardous to health, as drivers and commuters alike experience heightened stress levels daily. As an example, the problem of intra-urban traffic congestion in Lagos, the one-time capital of Nigeria have been examined by Bashiru, et al. [2]. In their work, they showed that 57% of commuters and motorists spend between 30 to 60 min stationary on traffic congested roads. It is therefore a note-worthy subject of interest as the present traffic situation in Lagos and similar cities around the world poses a major challenge to their economies. Reports have shown that most traffic gridlock emanate from road intersections [14]. Numerous traffic management techniques have been deployed over the years, some of which include construction of flyovers and bypass roads, creation of ring roads as well as employing traffic wardens. In recent times, the use of human traffic wardens to manually control vehicular movement at road intersections have been upgraded to traffic lights with their popular "Red, Amber, Green" lights.

While these methods have proven effective to reasonable extents; with human wardens, there is always the risk of being knocked down by reckless drivers and general inefficiencies that comes with employing humans to do repeated activities. Traffic lights have thus been deployed to augment or replace human wardens at road intersections. Traffic lights, though well capable of catering for the human deficiencies, are not without shortcomings. Prominent among which is the lack of human intuition. They simply follow a pre-programmed Round-Robin scheduling technique [24], in which movement access is granted to vehicles on a given lane for a specified time interval before switching to the next lane. The use of traffic lights alone has also proven ineffective, as they are either completely disregarded by impatient drivers or not smart enough to dynamically adjust their timing in response to traffic density on the various lanes they are controlling. The latter is especially common, as many a time, traffic lights repeatedly "pass" lanes with little or no waiting vehicles to the detriment of lanes with long queues. This is one of the major reasons why many drivers get impatient and choose to ignore the lights, ultimately resulting in gridlocks at intersections. Significant improvements are therefore necessary in order to optimize the potentials of the traffic lights. This study proposes a system that combines intelligence (as in the case of the traffic wardens) and the mechanical advantage of a machine to improve the efficiency of the traffic light system. The specific contribution of this paper consists of the design, implementation and performance evaluation of an Intelligent Traffic Management System that:

- uses a lightweight hardware based on Raspberry pi to manage vehicular traffic
- utilizes image processing using the Single-Shot Multibox Detector (SSD) to detect and count the number of vehicles on the road.

- intelligently manages traffic by modelling a T-junction as an M/M/1 queue and utilizes an intelligent algorithm to schedule the departure of vehicles at the junction.

The proposed system falls under the broad umbrella of edge computing, as it involves infusing cameras and processing units into traffic light systems.

The rest of this paper is organized as follows: Related research on traffic management are reviewed in Sect. 2. Section 3, presents the cyber-physical traffic management framework (cyTAC). In Sect. 4, the smart traffic management system (a subset of cyTAC) and its corresponding models are shown. Section 5 details the phases of STMS. System implementation and performance evaluations are discussed in Sects. 6 and 7 respectively. The paper is concluded with future works highlighted in Sect. 8.

2   Related Research

The authors in [14] identified "+" and "Y" junctions as roots of traffic congestion. Their work attempted to pinpoint the exact causes by simulating road traffic situations in software. A hybrid of Structured Systems Analysis and Design Methodology (SSADM) with Fuzzy-Logic based design methodology was used to perform the traffic analysis. Finally they presented a system that could be used to tackle traffic congestion at junctions. The results of the study done in [21] show that poor driving habits, poor road network, inadequate road capacity, and lack of parking facilities constitute the greatest causes of traffic congestion in developing countries. Their work highlighted remedies for improving traffic conditions, which included: good road network, encouragement of mass transport system, proper traffic planning & management and regular education of road users.

Similarly, after a thorough analysis of causes and effects of traffic congestion along certain roads, the following suggestions were also made by [16]: doubling (dual lane) of roads, mounting traffic control devices at junctions, providing designated parking lot along the roads, and removal of shops or markets along the sides of the major roads. Their work investigated only a few roads in Oyo State, Nigeria but many of the observed issues do not apply to roads in other cities.

Bramberger et al. [4] stated that the integration of advanced CMOS image sensors with high-performance processors into embedded systems can be useful. In their work, they implemented a smart camera system for traffic surveillance. The image processing approach used was based on long-term intensity changes of background pixels in videos. Though they recorded positive results, their work assumed consistent ambient light conditions; also stored videos would quickly fill up storage while the transmission over a network for processing would both consume bandwidth and suffer from significant latency, hence limiting real time application.

The authors in [5] proposed an intelligent traffic control system using Radio Frequency Identification RFID. In their work they highlighted the major disadvantages of the timing circuit currently in use by traffic lights. It was noted that existing systems do not take the current volume of traffic on roads at intersections into consideration. Traffic congestion, according to them translates to lost time, missed opportunities and in general wastage. In an attempt to solve these problems, they proposed an Intelligent Traffic Control System (ITCS) using Radio Frequency Identification.

In [11] a system which used RFID to tackle traffic congestion around toll gates was presented. The system was effective as it saved time and reduce the need for manpower in its operation. Their system however required vehicles to be pre-registered into the system and an RFID tag stuck at a visible area on the vehicle. A limitation not considered is the traffic backlogs that would build up if an unregistered vehicles approaches the toll or when drivers do not have sufficient funds in their account.

Similar to the work done in [5], Gadekar et al. [7] also worked on implementing an Intelligent Traffic Control for Congestion, Ambulance clearance, and stolen vehicle detection using RFID. In their model, every vehicle was to have a RFID enabled device that stored the Vehicle Identification Number (VIN), owner details and priority. Vehicles were then divided into 4 categories. The first had the highest priority and experienced little or no delays. The second included school buses which often need to reach their destination on time hence also required fast service. The third category included the car, motorcycle and scooter. The last category catered for heavy vehicles.

Bommes et al. [3] in their work discussed various camera types ideal for different applications in traffic management. Webcam were best suited for quick overview of traffic status. Surveillance cameras were most suited for monitoring road traffic conditions, traffic counts and possibly identifying causes of congestion. While very high resolutions cameras should be used when detailed vehicular identification such as number plates are needed.

There are many related research on vehicle detection. In [10] and [23] for instance, the authors used a computer vision based traffic counting systems. Cameras were used to capture traffic images and passed through image processing models to obtain vehicle count. The most commonly used approaches for traffic image processing are frame differentiation [1] and Landmarking as used in [9].

Image processing library such as OpenCV [15], Single Shot Multibox Detector (SSD) [12], You Only Look Once (YOLO) [17] have also been used. However, according to [25], most of these algorithms use either segmentation or scale based models for object detection. In segmentation based models, pixel-wise predictions are used to determine if a pixel belongs to an object or not. While in scale-based models, a strong classifier is built and used to determine if an image patch belongs to an object. Repeating the process with different resolutions makes objects of different sizes and aspect ratios detectable. In this paper, SSD is used as it has been shown to have a fast prediction time and works well with low resolution images.

Edge Computing is defined in [20], as a computing paradigm in which computing and storage devices are placed at the edge of networks, close to the data sources (sensors) for the purpose of reducing latency and improved utilization of bandwidth. Edge computing is particularly suited for this work because quick decisions are needed in real time. Sending hundreds of captured images over a network to a remote location for processing and then waiting for response before making decisions would be grossly inefficient [22].

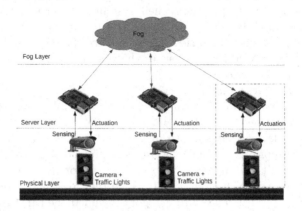

Fig. 1. Cyber-physical traffic management framework (Color figure online)

3   The Cyber-Physical Traffic Management Framework

This paper proposes a cyber-physical traffic management framework called cyTAC. The goal of cyTAC is to introduce human-like decision making process into traffic lights for the purpose of improving the efficiency of traffic management. The proposed framework is shown in Fig. 1 as a layered structure, with layers described as follows:

- **Physical Layer:** This is the lowest layer of the framework and closest to the users. It consists of the traffic lights and cameras. It is responsible for accepting input i.e. sensing the environment and performing specified actions (actuation). Input received are forwarded to the server layer, while output from the server layer are displayed/implemented here.
- **Server Layer:** This layer is responsible for data gathering. It comprises of light-weight computers which accept, analyze and process data received from the physical layer. Output of computational processes are sent back to the physical layer for actuation. Data at this layer are also sent to the Fog layer for storage or further analysis.

– **Fog Layer:** This is the top-most layer of cyTAC and it handles data storage and advanced computation (such as trend analysis and surveillance). It is also responsible for coordinating multiple servers across wide geographical locations.

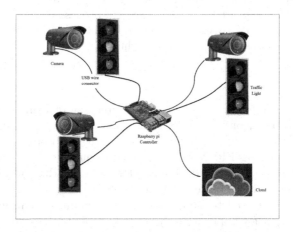

Fig. 2. Smart traffic management system (Color figure online)

In this paper, only a sub-set of the cyTAC framework is presented. This sub-set, enclosed in a dotted block in Fig. 1 is shown in Fig. 2 and referred to as the Smart Traffic Management System (STMS). The rest of this paper would focus on the STMS.

4   Smart Traffic Management System

The Smart Traffic Management System model shown in Fig. 1 is made up of the following parts:

1. **Cameras:** These serve as input source to the system. Though high definition cameras might be desirable, a balance must be struck between crystal clear images and image size. Due to the limited storage capacity of the edge device and because surveillance and/or vehicle identification are not the priority of this work, cameras with capture quality set to 1.3MP were used. Images taken with this resolution were sufficient for the image processor yet minimal in size.
2. **Traffic Light:** The features of the classic traffic lights are retained and used to communicate with the vehicle drivers. It was important to retain the universally understood, red, amber and green lights. The only change made was to the control circuitry, which was changed from basic time switched to a more intelligent image processed switching.

3. **Controller:** This serves as the brain of the system, and where the image processing and switching decisions are done. It is made up of three parts, which are:
   (a) **Input:** Images are received from cameras connected via USB or similar interface
   (b) **Processor:** A Micro-controller such as the Raspberry Pi [19] is to be used. Images captured by the camera are processed here.
   (c) **Output:** Switching decisions obtained from the processed images are sent as output to the connected traffic lights.

4.1   Image Processing

SSD is an object detection algorithm well suited for real-time image identification. It is an extension of the Faster Region Convoluted Neural Networks (FR-CNN) [18] that eliminates the need for the region proposal network. This enables it to be as fast as FRCNN yet utilize lower quality images. A comparison of SSD and some state-of-the-art object detection algorithms has been done in [12] with SSD shown to be better than most. SSD is designed in such away that its primary function is to detect objects present in an image. This unique feature makes it well suited for application in this paper, as the objective is to detect vehicles within an image. SSD works by sliding detection windows of various sizes across an image, it then determines if the windows contains objects of interests or not. The result of this process is a prediction map. As with most computational intelligence algorithms, SSD also has to be trained to identify objects. This training process involves comparing the obtained prediction map against a ground truth (in this case various pictures of vehicles). SSD then compares each presumed object with the ground truth. Matching segments (Intersect over Union (IoU)) are recorded. The higher the IoU, the more likely the presumed object is a target image (in this case a vehicle).

For this work, we are only interested in vehicles, hence our ground truth was made up of pictures of different kinds of vehicles.

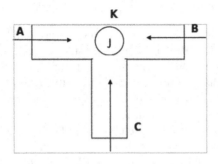

Fig. 3. Sample 'T' road intersection

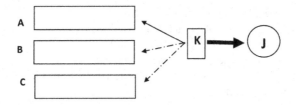

Fig. 4. Road intersection model

4.2   Switching Decision System

The following assumptions are made in establishing the feasibility and reliability of this system:

1. Only T-junctions are considered i.e. three roads connected at an intersection.
2. Each road is single carriage i.e. vehicles move only in one direction on each road.
3. Vehicles have Poisson arrival rates.
4. There are no other factors contributing to traffic congestion (such as bad road or broken down vehicles) except the coordination of the traffic flow.
5. Delays emanating from pedestrian crossings are minute hence not considered.
6. Road switching times are also not considered, that is the time it takes the STMS to switch access between the various roads at the junction.
7. Vehicle depart at a rate of one vehicle per second.

The switching decision system is modelled as follows:

Assume a T-junction, with three connected roads A, B and C, an intersection J and a traffic control light K. This is as shown in Fig. 3. The following are properties relating to the junction:

1. Vehicle Arrival: Vehicles arrive at each road randomly. This can be model using the Poisson model and described in 1

$$VehicleArrival : P_n = \frac{\lambda t^n}{n!} * exp^{\lambda t} \tag{1}$$

Where λ is the arrival rate, t = time interval and n = number of vehicles, Pn is the probability of n vehicles arriving at a given time.
J is the common resource all vehicles need to use. However, allowing all vehicles into J would result in traffic congestion, hence a controller K is required. The situation presented in Fig. 3, is thus analogous to a multi-queue single processor system, or M/M/1. It can thus be remodelled as shown in Fig. 4.
2. Vehicle Scheduling and Departure: Traditionally, the traffic controller K operates using a time-based circuit using a Round-Robin algorithm. It gives each road (A, B or C) access to the junction J for a pre-set time interval t. On expiration of t, it pre-empts the current road and gives the next road access to the Junction, This process is repeated continuously and modelled as follows:

Let λ_a = arrival time of vehicles on road A
Let λ_b = arrival time of vehicles on road B
Let λ_c = arrival time of vehicles on road C
Let μ be departure rate = 1 vehicle/second
Let delay (d) be the time a vehicle has to wait **at the front** of a road for a GREEN signal.

After a time interval t has elapsed, the number of vehicles waiting on each road A, B and C would respectively be:
$\alpha = \lambda_a t$, $\beta = \lambda_b t$, $\gamma = \lambda_c t$ from little's theorem 2

$$N = \lambda * t \tag{2}$$

$\alpha = \beta = \gamma$ *iff* all the arrival rates are equal, in which case the traditional turn based fixed time interval Round-Robin would be fair to all roads and the number of vehicles that leave each road would simply be the time frame allocated per round.

3. Vehicle Delay Time: Let μ_a, μ_b, μ_c be the departure time for each road. The number of vehicles that leave each road per round would thus be:

$$\alpha' = \mu_a t, \beta' = \mu_b t, \gamma' = \mu_c t \tag{3}$$

Traditional traffic lights using Round-Robin assumes that all μ are equal therefore the delay experienced by a vehicle waiting at the front of a road for a GREEN signal when round-robin is used can be given by:

$$d = 2 * \mu * t \tag{4}$$

Let n = number of rounds (i.e. from A to C and back). If at a time t = 0, road A is given access to J; then: At time $0 + t$, A is pre-empted and access is given to road B. At time $0 + t + t = 2t$, B is pre-empted and access given to road C. At time $0 + t + t + t = 3t$, C is pre-empted and access is returned to road A.

From this, road A would next have access to J at time (n*3t) and wait for a period of n*2t. Similarly, road B would next have access at time $(n + 1)*3t$ and wait for a period of $(n + 1)*2t$. Finally, road C would next have access to J at time $(n + 2)*3t$ and wait a duration of $(n + 2)*2t$.

If arrival times were equal across all three roads, then the system would be completely fair to all roads and there would be equal number of vehicles on each road. However this is not always the case, as in reality arrival processes are usually random. Unfortunately, the Round Robin system used in traditional traffic lights does not compensate for this but rather stick to a constant service rate. This invariable results in an unbalanced system and situations were certain roads with short or no queue are being serviced to the detriment of others having long(er) queues. Thus vehicles at the front of a road would have to wait at least $2\mu t$ even if the other roads are empty.

In solving this, STMS takes vehicular density into consideration and in essence converts the Round-Robin to a Priority-Queue. Using this, roads judged to have longer queues are given immediate access to the junction. Using this approach alone would lead to starvation for roads with shorter queues. To avoid this, STMS keeps track of the number of times each road is passed, and progressively increases the priority of the longest waiting road. In essence STMS can be described as a Priority-Queue + Suffrage. The STMS can thus be modelled as follows:

1. Vehicle Arrival: This is similar to the traditional Round-Robin and modelled with 1
2. Vehicle Scheduling and Departure: Similar to the traditional Round-Robin, after a time interval t has elapsed, the number of vehicles waiting on each road A, B and C can also be obtained using 2
3. Vehicle Delay Time: The number of vehicles leaving each road per round is obtained using 3

STMS however improves on the short-coming of Round-Robin by dynamically adjusting the wait time. The delay experienced by a vehicle waiting at the front of a road A, B or C for a GREEN light when STMS is used is be given by:

$$delaytime(d) = \begin{cases} 0, & \text{if the other roads have no queue} \\ \mu t, & \text{if any other roads has longer queue} \\ 2\mu t, & \text{if the other roads have longer queues} \end{cases} \quad (5)$$

Where μ and t are respectively the vehicle departure rate and time elapsed.
From 5, if a vehicle arrives at an intersection:

1. At the best case it would immediately be given the GREEN signal, if there are no waiting vehicles on the two other roads.
2. On the average it would wait μt for the road with the longer vehicle queue.
3. At the worst case it would wait $2\mu t$, as is the case with the traditional Round-Robin based system.

This implies that STMS is better than Round-Robin in 2 of the 3 scenarios and at par in the worst case scenario.

5   Phases of STMS

Smart Traffic Management System (STMS)'s process flow is shown in Fig. 5.

5.1   The Phases of STMS

The system goes through different phases before decisions are made and communicated to the vehicles. These phases are described as follows:

1. Image Capturing: This is the point of entry into the system. For every round of decision, images are first captured. The cameras mounted at strategic locations take shots of the roads and send the images to the controller for processing.

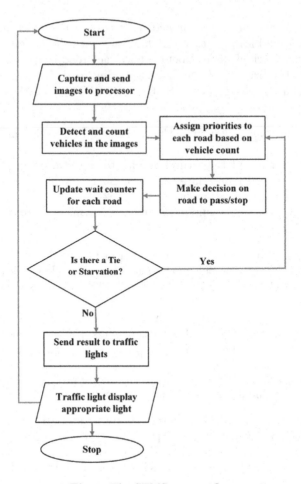

Fig. 5. The STMS process flow

2. Image Detection and Processing: The images are received from the cameras and vehicle detection is done on each of them using the SSD algorithm. The image detection process identifies and counts the vehicles in the image and prioritizes them accordingly. This means that for every image received, there is a priority attached based on the number of vehicles counted.
3. Result Processing: On completion of the detection and prioritization process, a Green signal is sent to the road with the highest priority, while Red signals are sent to the other roads. A time interval is also set for which the signal is to be displayed. After each decision process, a wait counter is updated for each road not passed (Red signal shown). This update, gradually increases the priority of such roads. This is used to prevent starvation or pro-longed denial of service to such roads as well as to break ties (situation where two roads have the same number of vehicles waiting).

4. Optionally, the results obtained alongside images and other useful statistical data could be sent to the Cloud to conserve storage on the Edge device and possibly for further processing.

6   System Implementation

A software prototype was developed using Java and implemented on a system running Windows 10, with 6 GB of RAM and a Core i5 processor. The SSD object detection library used was obtained from Github [6].

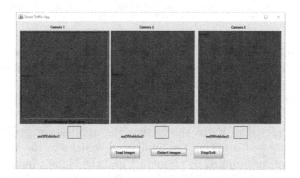

Fig. 6. Interface smart traffic management system

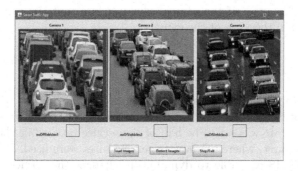

Fig. 7. Smart traffic management system with images loaded

To test the functionality, numerous pictures were captured at different times and at various T-junctions. These pictures were cropped to equal dimensions and saved in a directory on the system. The interface of the program is shown in Fig. 6.

At the start of the simulation, the program randomly selects 3 pictures from the image pool. This is synonymous to the controller receiving pictures from the

Fig. 8. Smart traffic management system with vehicle detection (Color figure online)

attached cameras as shown in Fig. 7. The images are then passed through the SSD object detection algorithm, which detects and counts the number of vehicles present in the 3 images. The obtained results are compared, and the image with the highest number of vehicles gets the GREEN signal. This is as illustrated in Fig. 8.

The image depicted in Fig. 8 shows that the application performed well in terms of identifying and counting the number of vehicles in the supplied images using SSD. The image supplied by Camera 1 had the highest number of vehicles (13) and as such was sent the GREEN signal. It must however be noted that the SSD object detection algorithm was not 100% accurate. For instance in Fig. 8, the image supplied by camera 2 had 11 vehicles, however only 9 were detected. This is possibly because the last two vehicles not detected were further up in the image and not in the camera's perfect line of sight. Increasing the height and re-positioning the angle of the camera could ensure that the captured images are aligned within the view of the camera.

7   Performance Evaluation

Experimental simulations were also carried out for the purpose of determining the efficiency of the proposed model. Five different scenarios were simulated. In the first, arrival rate was set to be half of the service rate, while the second was a variant of the first, wherein adaptive service rates were used. Using adaptive service rate, STMS was able to dynamically changes the service rate for each lane based on the number of vehicles queued. In the third, equal values of arrival and service rate were used, while in the fourth simulation, the arrival rate was set to twice the departure rate. Finally for the fifth experiment, random arrival rates were used.

For each simulation 200 traffic were generated and since the model only considered a T-junction, a simulation run consisted of circling through three (3) lanes. Vehicles were then processed (scheduled) using Round-Robin (as in the case of the traditional traffic lights) and STMS as proposed in this paper. A comparison of both approaches was done using throughput, makespan, service interruptions and fairness index as metrics. These metrics are defined as follows:

1. Throughput: The number of vehicles processed per round and defined as Vehicles Serviced/Number of Rounds. A round is defined as a complete circle through the three lanes. A higher throughput value is desirable.
2. Jain's Index: In order to compare the fairness of the STMS model, Jain's Index [8] is used and shown in 6.
3. Makespan: The amount of time needed to process the last vehicle in the system. A lower Makespan value is desirable.
4. Service interruptions: The number of times service to a given lane is interrupted in favour of a different lane. Lower number of service interruptions are desirable.

$$f(x) = \frac{\sum\limits_{i=1}^{n} x_i^2}{n \sum\limits_{i=1}^{n} x_i^2} \tag{6}$$

With Jain's Index, $0 \leq f(x) \leq 1$, the closer the value of f(x) is to 1, the fairer the system. The results of these simulations are now presented.

7.1   Arrival Rate Equals Half Departure Rate

For this experiment, the number of vehicles arriving at each lane per unit time is set to exactly half the number leaving. The following were observed from this experiment:

1. When departure rate (service rate) is greater than arrival rate, there would be no queue.
2. Similar results are obtained when arrival rate is equal to departure rate.
3. Round-Robin is fair to all the lanes, as vehicles on all the lanes experience equal wait time.
4. STMS (without adaptive service rate) behaves exactly like the traditional Round-Robin.

If however, adaptive service rate is enabled, that is the service rate changes dynamically with respect to the length of each lane, then STMS results in a 50% reduction in delay for all lanes compared to the traditional Round-Robin. This is as shown by the first two columns in Fig. 9. Only make span is shown as all other metrics had similar values.

7.2   Arrival Rate Equals Double Departure Rate

When arrival rate was set to exactly double the value of the departure (service rate), results similar to those of equal arrival and departure rates were obtained. This is as depicted by the last two columns in Fig. 9.

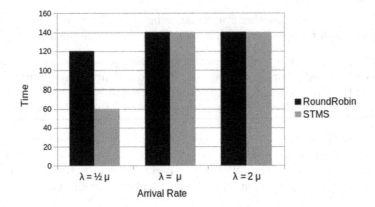

Fig. 9. Variation of Makespan with Arrival rate

7.3   Random Vehicle Arrival

For this experiment, at each run, a number of vehicles were randomly assigned to each lane. This was used to simulate the Poisson arrival of vehicles at an intersection. It is believed that gives a result closer to reality. Other viable models, though not considered in this work are: negative exponential, normal and pearson distribution [13].

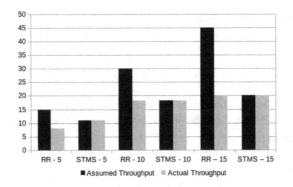

Fig. 10. Throughput comparison

Figure 10 shows a comparison of the throughput values of Round-Robin Scheduling versus STMS based scheduling. In the figure three scenarios are presented; in the first a service rate of 5 vehicles per lane was used, this was increased to 10 and 15 in the second and third scenarios. In the first scenario, the Round-Robin scheduling (RR-5) had an actual throughput of 8 vehicles/round and an assumed throughput of 15 vehicles/round. In the second scenario (RR-10), actual throughput increased to 18 while assumed was 30. In the final scenario with a service rate of 15, RR-15 recorded an actual throughput of 20 versus assumed throughput of 45. Across all three scenarios, Round-Robin resulted in an average of 50.6% lower actual throughput than assumed throughput. This in essence implied that Round-Robin is inefficient with about 50% of its service turns wasted. On the contrary, in all three scenarios, the assumed and actual throughputs of STMS were a perfect match implying zero wasted turn. In this paper, assumed throughput is defined as the number of vehicles assumed to be serviced divided by the number of rounds. In essence, it is approximately the time during which the traffic light is denying service to lanes that have vehicles queued up, in favour of an empty lane.

Round-Robin is known to be a fair algorithm, as it provides all lanes equal access to the intersection for an equal amount of time. To verify the fairness of STMS, the Jain's index was used along side the average throughputs for each of the three service rate scenarios described above. The obtained results are as follows: for the scenario where service rate was set to 5, Round-Robin had an average actual throughput of 8, while STMS has 11. Substituting these values into 6, resulted in a Jain's index value of 0.976. For the two other scenarios, where service rate was set to 10 and 15 respectively; Round-Robin and STMS had equal average throughput values, this resulted in a Jain index value of 1 in both cases. With an index value of approximately 1 in all tested instances, it can be concluded that STMS is as fair to all lanes as Round-Robin is.

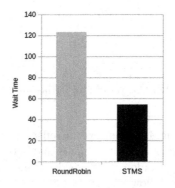

Fig. 11. Comparison of overall Makespan

In Fig. 11, a comparison of the Makespan for both algorithms is shown. Makespan is calculated by multiplying the number of rounds utilized by the number of lanes and service rate (number of vehicles served per run). In this work, service rate is assumed to be one vehicle per second. From Fig. 11, after 200 simulations, the average Makespan for Round-Robin was 123 s, while that of STMS was 54 s. This shows that using STMS on traffic lights, vehicular delay at traffic intersections can be reduced by as much as 56% versus when traditional Round-Robin is used.

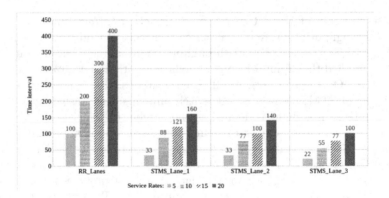

Fig. 12. Per lane delay for random arrival rates

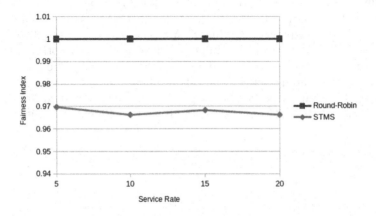

Fig. 13. Comparison of fairness indices

The result shown in Fig. 11 is however a reflection of the overall makespan (delay) of the system. It does not reflect the actual delay on each lane. Owing to the fact that vehicles were randomly assigned to lanes, the obtained result was very sporadic and did not follow any given pattern. To structure the values, a vehicle arrival ratio of 2:3:5 for the three lanes was used and the results of this when compared to the traditional Round-Robin are shown in Fig. 12.

In Fig. 12, the delay on each of the three lanes are compared for both Round-Robin and STMS. Four different service rates were used - 5, 10, 15, 20; and these represented the number of vehicles to serve on each lane. For Round-Robin all three lanes experienced the same amount of delay, and this is represented by the RR_{Lane}. Using STMS, each lane experienced different delays. Ideally, lanes with the shortest queue should experience the maximum delay (due to starvation), but with suffrage limiting feature of STMS, the effect is minimal. The difference between the waiting times for all three lanes is not too pronounced. Particularly, for small service rates (5 for instance), the delays experienced by both lanes 1 and 2 are exactly the same, while lane 3 is not too far off. The fairness indices for both the traditional Round-Robin and STMS, across the four service rates tested are as shown in Fig. 13.

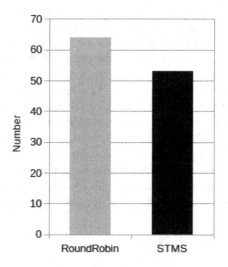

Fig. 14. Service interruptions

Finally, a comparison of the average number of service interruptions of both algorithms was done. The results shown in Fig. 14, shows that after 200 iterations, STMS with an average of 53 interruptions is about 17% better than Round Robin's 64.

8   Conclusion and Future Work

Road traffic congestion is a problem that plagues many societies today. In developing cities, the explosion in number of vehicles and the unmatched infrastructural development results in seemingly unending traffic gridlock on a daily basis. Commuters spend an average of between 30 to 60 min in traffic jams daily. The results of this are wasted man-hours, delays in delivery of raw materials to factories, reduced production powers, among others. These impact negatively on the economy and on human health. The major causes of these traffic gridlocks have been traced to road intersections. Various approaches have been used over the years to tackle this problem, prominent among them is the use of traffic control lights at road intersections. These lights have however proved inefficient as they operate on pre-set time based Round-Robin model and lack human intuition needed to intelligently adjust scheduling and adapt to the traffic situation in real-time. This work proposed a cyber-physical traffic management framework and more specifically a sub-set of this framework called the Smart Traffic Management System (STMS). STMS can run on a light-weight edge device, and utilizes image detection to dynamically alter traffic flow in real time. T-junctions was modelled mathematically and simulations carried out with obtained results showing an average reduction in delay time and service interruptions by as much as 56% and 17% respectively when compared to Round-Robin used in traditional traffic light systems. Overall STMS was at least 50% more efficient in terms of vehicular throughput and delay that Round-Robin yet remained equally as fair. In this work, only software simulations were carried out, however construction of actual physical prototypes would be desirable in future works. An ideal road situation with no vehicle breakdowns or bad roads was assumed. These are interesting factors that plague developing countries and could be considered. Also this paper treated all vehicles with equal priority; in the future, a system that prioritizes special vehicles such as ambulances and emergency services could be considered. Finally, this work focused on a sub-set of the cyber-physical framework, concentrating on detecting and counting vehicles at one intersection; future systems could be designed to consider multiple traffic lights connected to a Fog. With this a lot more information can be captured, analyzed and stored, thus opening up a vista of opportunity for applications in analytics, security and urban city planning.

References

1. Bandarupalli, V.: Evaluation of video based pedestrian and vehicle detection algorithms. Ph.D. thesis, University of Nevada (2010)
2. Bashiru, A., Waziri, O.: Analysis of intra-urban traffic problems in Nigeria: a study of Lagos metropolis. Indonesian J. Geogr. **40**(1), 997–1004 (2008)
3. Bommes, M., Fazekas, A., Volkenhoff, T., Oeser, M.: Video based intelligent transportation systems - state of the art and future developments. Transp. Res. Procedia **14**, 4495–4504 (2016)
4. Bramberger, M., Pflugfelder, R., Maier, A., Rinner, B., Strobl, B., Schwabach, H.: A smart camera for traffic surveillance. In: Proceedings of the 2003 First Workshop on Intelligent Solutions in Embedded Systems, pp. 153–164 (2012)
5. Chattaraj, A., Bansal, S., Chandra, A.: An intelligent traffic control system using RFID. IEEE Potentials **28**(3), 40–43 (2016)
6. Chen, X.: Java SSD object detection (2018). https://github.com/chen0040/java-ssd-object-detection
7. Gadekar, T., Chavare, P., Chipade, K., Togrikar, P.: Implementing intelligent traffic control system for congestion control, ambulance clearance, and stolen vehicle detection. Imperial J. Interdisc. Res. **2**(4) (2016)
8. Jain, R., Durresi, A., Babic, G.: Throughput fairness index: an explanation, pp. 1–13 (1999)
9. Hsieh, J.-W., Yu, S.-H., Chen, Y.-S., Hu, W.-F.: Automatic traffic surveillance system for vehicle tracking and classification. IEEE Trans. Intell. Transp. Syst. **7**(2), 175–187 (2006)
10. Kastinaki, V., Zervakis, M., Kalaitzakis, K.: A survey of video processing techniques for traffic applications. Image Vis. Comput. **21**(4), 359–381 (2003)
11. Khatile, R., Gore, P., Gagre, V., Deshmukh, N.: RFID based traffic control and toll collection. Int. J. Adv. Eng. Res. Dev. **3**(1), 345–360 (2016)

12. Liu, W., et al.: SSD: single shot multibox detector. In: Leibe, B., Matas, J., Sebe, N., Welling, M. (eds.) ECCV 2016. LNCS, vol. 9905, pp. 21–37. Springer, Cham (2016). https://doi.org/10.1007/978-3-319-46448-0_2

13. Mathew, T.: Vehicle arrival models: headway. Transp. Syst. Eng. **39** (2014)

14. Osigwe, C., Oladipo, F., Onibere, A.: Design and simulation of an intelligent traffic control system. Int. J. Adv. Eng. Technol. **1**(5), 47 (2011)

15. Pulli, K., Baksheev, A., Kornyakov, K., Eruhimov, V.: Real-time computer vision with OpenCV. Commun. ACM **55**(6), 61–69 (2012)

16. Raheem, S., Olawoore, W., Olagunju, D., Adeokun, E.: The cause, effect and possible solution to traffic congestion on Nigeria road (a case study of Basorun-Akobo road, Oyo state). Int. J. Eng. Sci. Invention **4**(9), 10–14 (2012)

17. Redmon, J., Divvala, S., Girshick, R., Farhadi, A.: You only look once: unified, real-time object detection. In: Proceedings of the 2016 IEEE Conference on Computer Vision and Pattern Recognition, pp. 779–788 (2016)

18. Ren, S., He, K., Girshick, R., Sun, J.: Faster R-CNN: towards real-time object detection with region proposal networks. In: Advances in Neural Information Processing Systems, pp. 91–99 (2015)

19. Richardson, M., Wallace, S.: Getting Started with Raspberry Pi. O'Reilly Media Inc., Newton (2012)

20. Satyanarayanan, M.: The emergence of edge computing. Computer **50**(1), 30–39 (2017)

21. Ukpata, J., Etika, A.: Traffic congestion in major cities of Nigeria. Int. J. Eng. Technol. **2**(8), 1433–1438 (2012)

22. Varghese, B., Wang, N., Barbhuiya, S., Kilpatrick, D., Nikolopoulos, S.: Challenges and opportunities in edge computing. In: Proceedings of the 2016 IEEE International Conference on Smart Cloud, pp. 20–26 (2016)

23. Velastin, N., Orwell, J.: A review of computer vision techniques for the analysis of urban traffic. IEEE Trans. Intell. Transp. Syst. **12**(3), 920–939 (2011)

24. Yadav, R., Mishra, A., Prakash, N., Sharma, H.: An improved round robin scheduling algorithm for CPU scheduling. Int. J. Comput. Sci. Eng. **2**(4), 1064–1066 (2010)

25. Yadav, V.: Towards a real-time vehicle detection: SSD multibox approach

Binary Search Based PSO for Master Node Enumeration and Placement in a Smart Water Metering Network

Clement N. Nyirenda[1]($\boxtimes$) and Samson G. Nyirongo[2]

[1] ISAT Laboratory, University of the Western Cape,
Robert Sobukwe Road, Bellville, Cape Town 7535, South Africa
cnyirenda@uwc.ac.za
[2] Department of Electrical and Computer Engineering, University of Namibia,
Ongwediva, Namibia

Abstract. A Binary Search based Particle Swarm Optimization (BS-PSO) algorithm is proposed for the enumeration and placement of Master Nodes (MNs) in a Smart Water Metering Network (SWMN). The merit of this proposal is that it can simultaneously optimize the number of MNs as well as their locations in the SWMN. The Binary Search (BS) Mechanism searches a pre-specified range of integers for the optimal number of MNs. This algorithm iteratively invokes the PSO algorithm which generates particles based on the chosen number of MNs. The PSO uses these particles to determine MN coordinates in the fitness function evaluation process within the underlying SWMN simulation. The packet delivery ratio (PDR) is designated as the fitness value for the particle. Results for 10 BS-PSO optimization runs show that the median optimal number of MNs is 15 and that the mean PDR of 96% can be realized. As part of future work, more optimization runs will be conducted to enhance the generalization of the results. The extension of this concept to other optimization algorithms such as Differential Evolution will also be considered.

Keywords: Smart Water · Particle Swarm Optimization · Binary Search

1 Introduction

The rapid developments in ICT have triggered widespread interest in smart water networks (SWNs) [1–3]. From the operation perspective, the major driving force behind the adoption of SWNs is the desire by water utilities to cut down Non-revenue water (NRW). NRW refers to the water that has been produced and is lost before it reaches the customer. It has been reported that more than 60% of clean water is lost due to Non-revenue Water (NRW) [4]. Apart from helping utilities to cut down on NRW, smart water networks (SWNs) also enable them to achieve their quality, productivity, and efficiency targets while,

© ICST Institute for Computer Sciences, Social Informatics and Telecommunications Engineering 2020
Published by Springer Nature Switzerland AG 2020. All Rights Reserved
R. Zitouni et al. (Eds.): AFRICOMM 2019, LNICST 311, pp. 104–118, 2020.
https://doi.org/10.1007/978-3-030-41593-8_8

on the other hand, improving customer service. By implementing SWNs, it is estimated that up to $12.5 billion could be saved annually [5]. According to [1], SWN incorporated the following solution areas: residential metering, water quality monitoring, leak detection, and energy management. This work focuses on SWN based residential metering, which is generally referred to as Smart Water Metering Network (SWMN) [6,7].

1.1 Master Node Location Optimization in Smart Water Metering Networks

Smart Water Metering Networks enable water utilities to collect water consumption data from homes remotely. This cuts out the use of a human meter reader thereby preventing manual data entry errors [8]. Furthermore, meter readings can be collected as frequently as possible thereby enabling customers to keep track of their water usage on a regular basis. This gives customers the ability to optimize their use of water leading to a reduction in water bills. Furthermore, SWMNs also help with early leakage detection, provision of more accurate water rates, and easy detection of water theft.

In SWMNs, the communication infrastructure is extremely important [9]; each smart meter must be equiped with capabilities to reliably and securely transmit meter readings to a central location at the utility. The SWMN adopts hierarchical topology [6]. A limited number of Master Nodes (MNs), which act as the sinks for a group of smart meters within their vicinity, are used to collect metering data from those meters. Smart meters that are far from the MNs use intermediate Smart Meters to relay their data to MNs. MNs relay the aggregated metering data to the Control Center, where the data is processed and analyzed. If the smart meters are few and very close to each other, one MN would be sufficient. This is, however, not the case in practical situations as areas covered by the smart meters are big. In these environments, data transmission from smart meters that are far from the MN may be very poor. Therefore, it may be necessary to implement several MNs in order to solve reachability problems. A high packet delivery ratio (PDR) can be achieved easily by using more MNs and placing them evenly in the network [6]. This will, however, come at a big cost.

In [10], Particle Swarm Optimization (PSO) [12], a population based stochastic optimization technique, has been used to determine the optimal locations of MNs in Smart Water Metering Network (SWMN). The SWMN was simulated in the TinyOS Simulator (TOSSIM) [14], with the Collection Tree Protocol (CTP) [15], as routing protocol. The number of MNs is set *a priori*. In the PSO algorithm, the particle's dimensions is twice the number of MNs in order to cater for the x and y coordinates of each MN. The parameters in the final *global best* particle can easily be extracted and scaled to denote the optimal locations of the MNs. At each PSO function evaluation instant, the underlying TOSSIM script, depicting the SWMNs along with the configured MNs, is triggered and the ensuing Packet Delivery Ratios (PDRs) are recorded. This technique yields good results, but it has a shortcoming in the sense that the determination of the optimal number of MNs is not incorporated in the optimization framework.

1.2 Contribution and Paper Organisation

The work proposed in this paper aims at solving the aforementioned problem by considering the MN placement problem as a two-fold optimization problem. In addition to finding optimal locations for the MNs, the number of MNs must also be optimized dynamically in the same optimization routine. To achieve this, the Binary Search based Particle Swarm Optimization (BS-PSO) algorithm is proposed. The optimisation of the number of MNs as well as the determination of their optimal location in the SWMN are conducted in one optimization routine. The Binary Search is implemented as high level algorithm that fixes the number of MNs, which denotes the search parameter, at every instant and invokes PSO algorithm, which functions as a low level algorithm. An arbitrary number of MNs is used depict the initial upper limit of the search range. At the start of the optimisation run, the PSO algorithm is invoked several times and the ensuing Packet Delivery Ratios (PDRs) are recorded. Then the initial upper limit is doubled and the PSO algorithm is invoked again. T-test is invoked to determine if there is a significant difference between the new upper limit and old one. If there is no significant difference, the old upper limit is construed to the upper limit of the BS approach. Otherwise, the new upper limit is doubled again and the statistical comparison is conducted again until there is no significant difference between the two potential upper limits; the lower one is always chosen. Once the upper limit is fixed, the BS algorithm is employed in order to determine the optimal number of MNs as well as their locations.

The rest of the paper is organized as follows. The SWMN topology is given in Sect. 2. An overview of Particle Swarm Optimization (PSO) is given in Sect. 3. The implementation of the BS-PSO algorithm for MN enumeration and location optimization is presented in Sect. 4. Section 5 presents the experimental setup, the results and discussion, and lastly, conclusions in Sect. 6.

2   Smart Water Metering Network Topology

The Smart Metering concept refers to the use of Smart Meters (SMs) in the collection of water usage data from clients' households. SMs, which are located at the customer's premises, measure water consumption and communicate their readings at regular intervals to the utility [11]. The utility uses this information for monitoring and billing purposes. Unlike conventional metering systems, there is no need for manual meter readers. Allowing each SM to be transmitting its data to the central location is, however, not a cost effective and scalable solution. As a result, the general trend is to deploy hierarchical network topologies in Smart Water Metering Networks [13]. Figure 1 shows a typical topology that is deployed in networks of this type.

The network consists of the following generic system components: Wireless Sensor Nodes (WSNs), Master Nodes (MNs), and the Control and Monitoring Center (CMC). In this work, Smart Meters (SMs) are deployed as a special case of WSNs. In addition to the traditional metering functions, the SMs in SWMNs are equiped with communication and routing functionalities. They are capable of

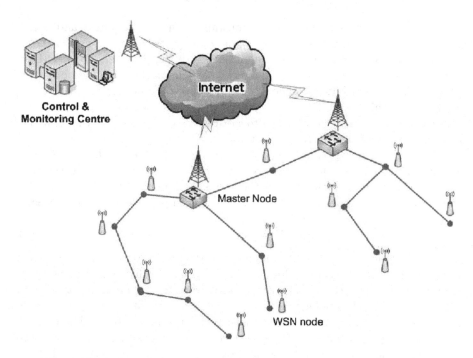

Fig. 1. Typical network topology in Smart Water Metering Networks [13].

transmitting their own metering data, as well as the metering data from neighboring SMs, to the Master Nodes at frequently. The MNs, which are equipped with more memory resources, processing and communication capabilities than the SMs, send the aggregated metering data to the CMC through a higher capacity communication link. MNs are generally fewer in number compared to SMs [11].

3   The Particle Swarm Optimization Algorithm

The Particle Swarm Optimization (PSO) algorithm was introduced by Kennedy and Eberhart in 1995. It draws inspiration from the social behavior of animals living in swarms, such as flocks of birds [12]. PSO is initialized with a population of particles that are generated randomly. Each particle denotes a candidate solution to a problem and is characterized by three main parameters in the search space: its current position, current velocity and the best position ever found by the particle during the search process. The particles fly in the search space in order to find the optimal solution. The trajectory of a particle is influenced by the particle's own experience as well as it's neighboring particles. For a population of N particles, the velocity of the i-th particle is updated at every iteration by using

$$v_i(t) = \omega * v_i(t-1) + c_1 r_1 (p_i^b - x_i(t)) + c_2 r_2 (g^b - x_i(t)), \qquad (1)$$

where $i = 1, 2, \ldots, N$; c_1 and c_2 are constants denoting cognitive and social parameters respectively. The values of c_1 and c_2 are chosen in the range $[0.5, 2.5]$. They are applied to accommodate the influence of the particle's previous best position p_i^b and the best position g^b among all particles in the neighborhood of the i-th particle respectively. Parameters r_1 and r_2 are random numbers uniformly distributed within $[0, 1]$. Parameter ω, known as the inertia weight, helps to dampen the velocities of the particles to assist in the convergence to the optimum point at the end of the optimization iteration.

A further arbitrary parameter $V_m = (v_{m1}, v_{m2} \ldots v_{mD}) \in S$, where D denotes the dimensions of the search space S, was defined to be limit of the velocity. Whenever, a vector element exceeds the corresponding element of V_m, that element is reset to its upper limit. The position of each particle is updated at each iteration by using

$$x_i(t + 1) = x_i(t) + v_i(t + 1). \tag{2}$$

A basic algorithm for PSO technique is illustrated in Algorithm 1. The algorithm begins setting the values for N, c_1, c_2, ω, and G, which denotes the maximum number of iterations. Then it randomly generates an initial population of N particles and initial velocities for each particle. The fitness function values for all N particles are evaluated based on their current positions. The current positions of each particle are set as the personal best positions for the respective particles, and overall best position found so far is set as best solution for the swarm. Then the algorithm goes into the iterative process, which keeps on going on until G iterations are completed or until the stopping criterion is met. At each generation, the particle positions in the search space are updated using Eqs. 1 and 2; fitness function values of all particles are updated based on their new positions. If necessary, personal best and global best values are updated accordingly.

4   The Proposed BS-PSO Algorithm for MN Enumeration and Placement

The proposed Binary Search based PSO algorithm for Master Node (MN) enumeration and optimal placement is based on the approach proposed in [10]. A review of the MN placement optimization problem, conceptualized in [10], is, therefore, revisited in the next subsection before the components of the BS-PSO approach are presented in the subsequent subsection.

4.1   The MN Placement Optimization Problem

A Smart Water Metering Network is assumed to contain n_{sm} smart meters in a rectangular area defined by $L \times M$, where L and M are in meters. Let n_{sm} denote the number of MNs in the area. The location of each MN will be determined by the x and y coordinates. Therefore, the number of variable parameters that have to be encoded in the particle, in order to realize optimal performance, will

Algorithm 1. Particle Swarm Optimization (PSO)

1: Initialize the values for N, c_1, c_2, ω, and G, which denotes the maximum number
   of iterations
2: Randomly generate N particles
3: $F(g^b) \leftarrow 0$
4: **for** $i \leftarrow 1, N$ **do**
5:    Evaluate the fitness function value, $F(x_i)$, for each particle i
6:    $p_i^b \leftarrow x_i$
7:    $F(p_i^b) \leftarrow F(x_i)$
8:    **if** $F(x_i) > F(g^b)$ **then**
9:       $g^b \leftarrow x_i$
10:       $F(g^b) \leftarrow F(x_i)$
11:    **end if**
12: **end for**
13: **while** $t \leq G$ **do**
14:    Update v_i and x_i by using Equations 1 and 2
15:    **for** $i \leftarrow 1, N$ **do**
16:       Evaluate the fitness function value, $F(x_i)$, for each particle i
17:       **if** $F(x_i) > F(p_i^b)$ **then**
18:          $p_i^b) \leftarrow x_i$
19:          $F(p_i^b) \leftarrow F(x_i)$
20:       **end if**
21:       **if** $F(x_i) > F(g^b)$ **then**
22:          $g^b \leftarrow x_i$
23:          $F(g^b) \leftarrow F(x_i)$
24:       **end if**
25:    **end for**
26:    Stop the algorithm if a sufficiently good fitness function value is realized
27: **end while**

$2 * n_{mn}$. For instance, if 5 MNs are used, the number of parameters in the particle will be 10. The goal of the optimization process is to that the best particle must achieve the highest packet delivery ratio (PDR), where PDR is defined by

$$PDR = P_r/P_s, \qquad (3)$$

where P_r is the number of packets received at the MNs, excluding duplicate packets, while P_s denotes the number of packets sent by smart meters. For poorly located DAPs, the PDR will be very low due to reachability issues. The $2 * n_{mn}$ MN coordinate information can be encoded in a particle by using

$$\mathbf{p} = (p_0, p_1 \ldots p_{D-1}), \qquad (4)$$

where p_0 and p_1 are the coordinates of the first MN; p_2 and p_3 are the coordinates of the second MN; p_D and p_{D-1} are the coordinates of the final MN; $D = 2 * n_{mn}$. Each element p_i is defined within $[0, 1]$. To obtain the actual coordinates, the even indexed elements, denoting the x-coordinate, are multiplied by L while odd-indexed elements, denoting the y-coordinate, are multiplied by M.

4.2   BS-PSO Algorithm for MN Enumeration and Placement

In [10], many separate optimization procedures and statistical comparisons were done in order to determine the optimal number of MNs. The proposed approach aims at optimizing the number of MNs along with their placement in the SWMNs in an automated fashion as opposed to [10], where the number of MNs has to be fixed *a priori*. The architecture of the BS-PSO system, as shown in Fig. 2, is composed of three levels. Level 1 depicts the BS algorithm; Level 2 and Level 3 depict the PSO algorithm and the SWMN simulation respectively.

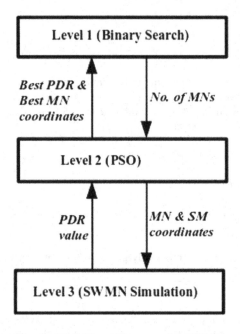

Fig. 2. BS-PSO architecture for SWMNs

The BS algorithm (Level 1) searches a pre-specified range of integers for the optimal number of MNs. At every chosen number of MNs m, it invokes the PSO algorithm (Level 2) k times. The PSO algorithm generates the particle of size $2 * m$. Every function evaluation in the PSO algorithm invokes the SWMN simulation at Level 3, using the MN coordinates extracted from the particle along with the fixed coordinates of the smart meters. The SWMN is implemented in Python in the Tiny Operating System Simulator (TOSSIM) [14], as presented in [10]. The function evaluation routine invokes the Python script several times and computes the average Packet Delivery Ratio (PDR), which denotes the fitness of the particle. Each PSO run generates the *global best* particle, which depicts the optimal locations of the MNs, along with its associated Packet Delivery Ratio (PDR) (see Eq. 3). Invoking the PSO algorithm k times for m MNs generates k particles along with their k associated PDRs. These PDR values are passed from Level 3 to Level 2 by using text files. The Packet Delivery Ratios (PDR) can be presented by using

$$\mathbf{PDR}(m) = (PDR_0(m), PDR_1(m) \ldots PDR_{k-1}(m)), \tag{5}$$

where $PDR_i(m)$ denotes the PDR of the i-th run of the PSO algorithm, when the number of MNs is set to m; $i = 0, 1, \ldots k - 1$.

In the BS algorithm, there is a need to fix the lower bound s_{lb} and the upper bound s_{ub} of the search range. The lower bound s_{lb} is easily set to 1 since this is the lowest possible number of MNs allowed. The upper bound of the range s_{ub} can, however, not be fixed easily. Setting s_{ub} to the same value as the number of the smart meters, n_{sm}, would be a good idea but it will lead to higher computational costs. This is because it might take long time before the search process reaches the optimal value. In this proposal, s_{ub} is, therefore, set to a random integer value, which is uniformly drawn from the range $[1, n_{sm}]$. If s_{ub} is set to a value that is closer to n_{sm}, the behavior will be more or less similar to when $s_{ub} = n_{sm}$. The probability for such an occurrence is, however, lower than when s_{ub} is outrightly set to n_{sm}. On the other hand, if s_{ub} is set to a value that is lower than the desired optimal value, the search will suboptimally converge to s_{ub}. To cater for this latter condition, the Binary Search Upper Bound Initiliazation routine in Algorithm 2 is used. This algorithm scans the upper side of the initial s_{ub} by iteratively comparing $\mathbf{PDR}(\hat{s}_{ub})$ with $\mathbf{PDR}(s_{ub})$, where $\hat{s}_{ub}$ is the potential upper bound. When the condition, $\mathbf{PDR}(\hat{s}_{ub}) \sim \mathbf{PDR}(s_{ub})$, is realized, it implies that increasing the upper bound beyond s_{ub} will not yield any meaningful performance improvement. Therefore, s_{ub} is deemed to be the upper bound. It's associated particle, $\mathbf{p}(s_{ub})$, and $\mathbf{PDR}(s_{ub})$ are also saved for latter use in Algorithm 3.

Algorithm 2. Binary Search Upper Bound Initiliazation

1: **Input:** s_{lb} and n_{sm}
2: **Output:** $s_{ub}, \mathbf{p}(s_{ub}), \mathbf{PDR}(s_{ub})$
3: $s_{ub} \leftarrow \mathcal{U}(s_{lb}, n_{sm})$
4: Set potential upper bound, $\hat{s}_{ub} = 2 * s_{ub}$
5: **if** $\hat{s}_{ub} > n_{sm}$ **then**
6:      $\hat{s}_{ub} \leftarrow n_{sm}$
7: **end if**
8: **while** (1) **do**
9:      Invoke PSO in Algorithm 1, k times with $N = s_{ub}$ to generate $\mathbf{PDR}(s_{ub})$
10:      Invoke PSO in Algorithm 1, k times with $N = \hat{s}_{ub}$ to generate $\mathbf{PDR}(\hat{s}_{ub})$
11:      **if** $\mathbf{PDR}(\hat{s}_{ub}) \sim \mathbf{PDR}(s_{ub})$ **then**
12:          **break**
13:      **else**
14:          $s_{ub} \leftarrow \hat{s}_{ub}$
15:      **end if**
16: **end while**

The BS-PSO algorithm, presented in Algorithm 3 uses s_{lb} as the input. It calls Algorithm 2 in order to determine s_{ub}, $\mathbf{p}(s_{ub})$, and $\mathbf{PDR}(s_{ub})$. It then calls the PSO in Algorithm 1, k times with $N = s_{lb}$ to generate $\mathbf{PDR}(s_{lb})$. Since only one MN is used in the latter case, the PDR realized is normally expected to be the worst. Once the performance at these two extremes of the search range is fixed, the iterative search and PSO optimization process starts. At the start of every iteration, the midpoint s_{mid} of the search range is computed and the PSO algorithm is called several times to generate $\mathbf{PDR}(s_{mid})$. If $\mathbf{PDR}(s_{mid}) \sim \mathbf{PDR}(s_{ub})$, s_{ub} is updated to s_{mid}; $\mathbf{p}(s_{ub})$ and $\mathbf{PDR}(s_{ub})$ are updated to $\mathbf{p}(s_{mid})$ and $\mathbf{PDR}(s_{mid})$ respectively. Once that is done, if the termination condition, $\mathbf{PDR}(s_{mid}) \sim \mathbf{PDR}(s_{lb})$, is reached, the algorithm terminates. Otherwise, if $!(\mathbf{PDR}(s_{mid}) \sim \mathbf{PDR}(s_{ub}), s_{ub})$, s_{lb} is updated to s_{mid}; $\mathbf{p}(s_{lb})$ and $\mathbf{PDR}(s_{lb})$ are updated to $\mathbf{p}(s_{mid})$ and $\mathbf{PDR}(s_{mid})$ respectively, and the iterative search process continues.

Algorithm 3. BS PSO Algorithm

1: **Input:** $s_{lb}, s_{ub}, \mathbf{p}(s_{ub}), \mathbf{PDR}(s_{ub})$
2: **Output:** $s_{lb}, \mathbf{p}(s_{lb}), \mathbf{PDR}(s_{lb})$
3: Determine s_{ub} by invoking Algorithm 2
4: Invoke PSO in Algorithm 1, k times with $N = s_{lb}$ to generate $\mathbf{PDR}(s_{lb})$
5: **while** (1) **do**
6:     $s_{mid} \leftarrow \text{int}(s_{lb} + s_{ub})/2$
7:     Invoke PSO in Algorithm 1, k times with $N = s_{mid}$ to generate $\mathbf{PDR}(s_{mid})$
8:     **if** $\mathbf{PDR}(s_{mid}) \sim \mathbf{PDR}(s_{ub})$ **then**
9:         $s_{ub} \leftarrow s_{mid}$
10:        $\mathbf{p}(s_{ub}) \leftarrow \mathbf{p}(s_{mid})$
11:        $\mathbf{PDR}(s_{ub}) \leftarrow \mathbf{PDR}(s_{mid})$
12:        **if** $\mathbf{PDR}(s_{mid}) \sim \mathbf{PDR}(s_{lb})$ **then**
13:            **break**
14:        **end if**
15:    **else**
16:        $s_{lb} \leftarrow s_{mid}$
17:        $\mathbf{p}(s_{lb}) \leftarrow \mathbf{p}(s_{mid})$
18:        $\mathbf{PDR}(s_{lb}) \leftarrow \mathbf{PDR}(s_{mid})$
19:    **end if**
20: **end while**

---

5   Experiment Setup and Results

5.1   The SWMN Topology and Simulation Parameters

Just like in [6,7,10], the SWMN topology, depicting the Tsumeb East area in Northern Namibia, is used. The area, which is a 400.5 m × 400 m square, has 140 houses, which implies that there are 140 smart meters. Parameters L and

M are, therefore, both set to 400.5 m and 400 m respectively, while n_s is set to 140. The SWMN is set up in TOSSIM using Zuniga's Link Layer Model [16], which is used to generate the Python simulation scripts. Figure 3 illustrates the SWMN; the blue circles denote 140 SMs.

Most PSO parameters, in Eqs. 1, 2 and Algorithm 1, are adopted from [17] and set as follows: $N = 20$, $c_1 = 2.0$, $c_2 = 2.0$, $\omega = 0.9$, and $G = 50$. The particles are initilized between 0 and 1, as described in Sect. 3. These particle parameters are converted to MN coordinates by multiplying them by 400 m. The parameters used in the TOSSIM Simulation are shown in Table 1.

Table 1. Tossim Simulation Parameters [10]

Parameter	Value
Transmission range	70 m
Number of nodes	140
Number of invocations per particle evaluation	3
Simulation time	10 s per simulation

The Binary Search PSO code is written in C language. A personal computer with an Intel Core i7-2670QMCPU@2.20 GHz*8 processor with 4 GB RAM, running on Ubuntu 18.01, is used. Ten BS-PSO optimization routines are conducted in the current implementation due to computing constraints. Each routine incorporated Algorithms 1, 2, and 3 as described in the previous sections.

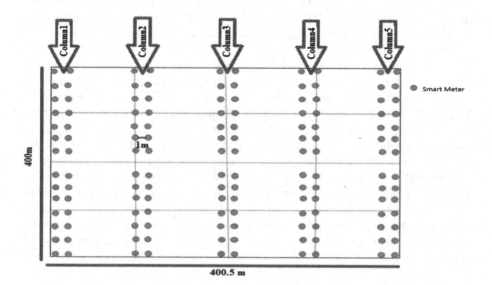

Fig. 3. Smart meters in the Tsumeb SWMN [6]

5.2 Results and Discussion

Ten optimization routines were implemented. For each of the routines, parameter k in Algorithms 2 and 3 is set to 10. Therefore, each optimization routine generates $\mathbf{PDR} = (PDR_0, PDR_1(m) \ldots PDR_9)$ for the realized number of MNs. Table 2 shows the statistical results for the 10 optimization routines.

Table 2. Optimization results from 10 BS-PSO Optimization Routines

Routine no.	Mean PDR (%)	Min. PDR (%)	Max. PDR (%)	No. MNs
1	94.24	96.87	95.95	17
2	94.83	96.19	95.55	15
3	94.19	96.62	95.65	15
4	95.27	97.23	96.06	15
5	94.61	96.26	95.39	12
6	95.55	97.82	96.60	15
7	95.49	97.50	96.51	15
8	92.82	97.89	95.91	15
9	95.60	96.60	96.15	15
10	93.73	97.69	96.03	15

From Table 2, the average PDR is around 96%. The most consistent number of MNs over the 10 routines is 15. Only the first and the fifth routines achieve different results, i.e. 17 and 12 respectively. This is due to the stochastic nature of the Binary Search and the PSO algorithms. From these results it can, therefore, be concluded that the optimal number of MNs for this network is 15, when the BS-PSO algorithm is employed.

To illustrate the spread of the locations of the enumerated MNs in the SWMN, plots of MNs have made on the SWMN based on the realized coordinates from the optimisation process. For brevity of space, only three plots from the best runs for routines 1, 5 and 8 are presented. Figure 4 shows the locations of the 17 MNs realized in the best run in first routine, while Figs. 5 and 6 show the locations of the 12 MNs and 15 MNs realized in the best runs in the fifth and the eighth routines respectively. In some places, the MNs are appear to be cluttered in one place. The crowding of SWMNs in one place, in as much as it is coming from the optimization process, is not a good development. This is because the MNs are actually overlapping, which lead to more interference when packets are being relayed to the MNs. Therefore, there is a need to incorporate an algorithm that will reduce crowding of the MNs in the optimization process in order to maintain a good spread of the MNs in the SWMN topology.

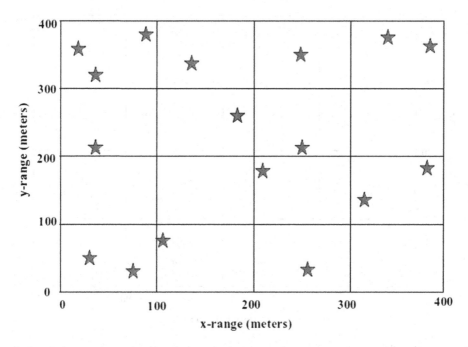

Fig. 4. MN Placement for Run 1, with 17 MNs realized from the optimization process

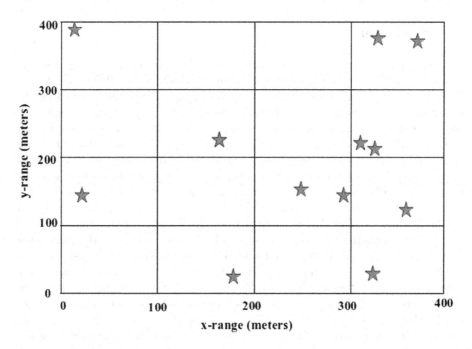

Fig. 5. MN Placement for Run 5, with 12 MNs realized from the optimization process

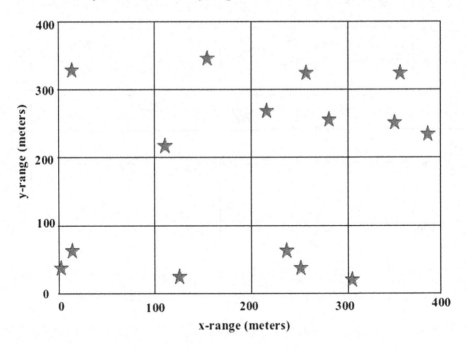

Fig. 6. MN Placement for Run 8, with 15 MNs realized from the optimization process

6 Conclusion

A Binary Search based Particle Swarm Optimization (BS-PSO) algorithm is proposed for the enumeration and placement of Master Nodes (MNs) in a Smart Water Metering Network (SWMN). This proposal was motivated by the desire to simultaneously optimize the number of MNs and their locations in a single run. The system architecture has three levels. Level 1 consists of the Binary Search (BS) algorithm while the PSO algorithm and the SWMN simulation are at Levels 2 and 3 respectively. The Binary Search (BS) Mechanism fixes the upper bound of the search range and then starts searching that range for the optimal number of MNs. The BS algorithm iteratively invokes the PSO algorithm (Level 2) for every potential number of MNs. The PSO algorithm generates particles based on the number of MNs that it receives from the BS algorithm. These particles are used to determine MN coordinates, which it passes to the SWMN simulation (Level 3) in order to determine the Packet Delivery Ratio, which is designated as the fitness function value in this proposal. The Binary Search process uses t-test compare two potential numbers of MNs. Results for 10 BS-PSO optimization routines show that the median optimal number of MNs is 15 and that the mean PDR of 96% can be realized.

The advantage of the proposed BS-PSO algorithm is that the determination of the optimal number of MNs is done automatically in a single run unlike in [10]. The computational requirements are massive to achieve a single optimization.

This is the reason why the number of optimization runs was limited to 10. As part of future work, high performance computing techniques will be employed in order to increase the number of optimization routines and runs to enhance the generalization of the results. Furthermore, future work will also involve the extension of this concept to other optimization algorithms such as Differential Evolution. Dynamic algorithms to cater for the even spreading of MNs in the SWMN will also be developed and analyzed.

References

1. Cahn, A.: An overview of smart water networks. J. Am. Water Works Assoc. **106**(7), 68–74 (2014)
2. Beach, T., Howell, S., Terlet, J., Zhao, W., Rezgui, Y.: Achieving smart water network management through semantically driven cognitive systems. In: Camarinha-Matos, L.M., Afsarmanesh, H., Rezgui, Y. (eds.) PRO-VE 2018. IAICT, vol. 534, pp. 478–485. Springer, Cham (2018). https://doi.org/10.1007/978-3-319-99127-6_41
3. de Azevedo, M.T., Martins, A.B., Kofuji, S.T.: Digital transformation in the utilities industry: industry 4.0 and the smart network water. In: Technological Developments in Industry 4.0 for Business Applications, pp. 304–330. IGI Global (2019)
4. Malcolm, F., Gary, W., Zainuddin, G.: The Manager's Non-revenue water Handbook - A Guide to Understanding Water Losses. USAID, USA (2008)
5. Sensus Research: WATER 20/20: Bringing smart water network into focus. Sensus, North American Headquarters (2012)
6. Shitumbapo, L.N., Nyirenda, C.N.: Simulation of a smart water metering network in Tsumeb East, Namibia. In: International Conference on Emerging Trends in Networks and Computer Communications (ETNCC), pp. 44–49 (2015)
7. Nyirenda, C.N., Nyandowe, I., Shitumbapo, L.: A comparison of the collection tree protocol (CTP) and AODV routing protocols for a Smart Water Metering Network in Tsumeb, Namibia. In: IST-Africa Week Conference, pp. 1–8 (2016)
8. McNabb, J.: Vulnerabilities of wireless water meter networks. J. New Engl. Water Works Assoc. **126**(1), 31–37 (2012)
9. Albentia, S.: Proposal for Smart Metering Networks Solution, ALB-W012-000en, UK (2012)
10. Nyirenda, C.N., Makwara, P., Shitumbapo, L.: Particle swarm optimization based placement of data acquisition points in a smart water metering network. In: Bi, Y., Kapoor, S., Bhatia, R. (eds.) IntelliSys 2016. LNNS, vol. 16, pp. 905–916. Springer, Cham (2018). https://doi.org/10.1007/978-3-319-56991-8_66
11. Mudumbe, J.M., Adnan, M., Abu-Mahfouz, M.: Smart Water Meter System for user-centric consumption measurement. In: 13th International Conference on industrial Informatics (INDIN 2015) (2015)
12. Kennedy, J.: Particle swarm optimization. In: Sammut, C., Webb, G.I. (eds.) Encyclopedia of Machine Learning, pp. 760–766. Springer, Boston (2011). https://doi.org/10.1007/978-0-387-30164-8_630
13. Spinsante, S., Pizzichini, M., Mencarelli, M., Squartini, S., Gambi, E.: Evaluation of the wireless M-Bus standard for future smart water grids. In: 9th International Wireless Communications and Mobile Computing Conference (IWCMC), pp. 382–1387 (2013)

14. Levis, P., Lee, N., Welsh, M., Culler, D.: TOSSIM: accurate and scalable simulation of entire TinyOS applications. In: Proceedings of the 1st International Conference on Embedded Networked Sensor Systems, pp. 126–137 (2003)
15. Fonseca, R., Gnawali, O., Jamieson, K., Kim, S., Levis, P., Woo, A.: The collection tree protocol (CTP). TinyOS TEP **123**(2) (2006)
16. Zuniga, M.: Building a network topology for Tossim. USC Technical Report (2011)
17. Takahama, T.: PSO code. http://www.ints.info.hiroshima-cu.ac.jp/~takahama/download/PSO.html. Accessed 19 July 2019

Internet of Things

State of Internet Measurement in Africa - A Survey

Musab Isah[1], Amreesh Phokeer[1(✉)], Josiah Chavula[2], Ahmed Elmokashfi[3], and Alemnew Sheferaw Asrese[4]

[1] African Network Information Centre (AFRINIC), Ebene, Mauritius
nmusabu@gmail.com, amreesh@AFRINIC.net
[2] University of Cape Town, Cape Town, South Africa
jchavula@cs.uct.ac.za
[3] Simula Metropolitan CDE, Oslo, Norway
ahmed@simula.no
[4] Aalto University, Espoo, Finland
alemnew.asrese@aalto.fi

Abstract. This paper presents the results of a survey aimed at understanding the status of Internet measurement platforms usage, deployment and capabilities in Africa. It presents findings related to prevalence of measurement in the region, the reasons why the different business categories investigated conduct Internet measurement as well as the metrics of interest to these entities. The survey also looked at the popular measurement platforms that the respondents use in their measurement activities as well as the platforms that are hosted by businesses and users in the African region. The survey also recorded responses related to data handling and privacy considerations. A total of 123 responses were received from 34 countries. The survey revealed that Internet measurements are not widely conducted in the region largely due to the inadequacy of deployed measurement platforms, the lack of awareness in the subject, and the lack of relevant skills to carry out the measurement tasks. We outlined some recommendations to remedy these issues.

Keywords: Measurement · Network monitoring · Platforms · Mobile · Metrics · Fixed-line · Measurement-tools

1 Introduction

Internet measurement platforms are infrastructures that are dedicated to periodically running Internet performance and topology measurements. The platforms are broadly categorised as either passive (network traffic monitoring) or active (network probing). Over the years, several such platforms and tools [1–10] have been deployed at strategic locations in access, backbone, behind residential Internet gateways, as well as on user devices. These platforms provide network telemetry, for e.g. to monitor the quality of fixed-line or mobile access networks.

© ICST Institute for Computer Sciences, Social Informatics and Telecommunications Engineering 2020
Published by Springer Nature Switzerland AG 2020. All Rights Reserved
R. Zitouni et al. (Eds.): AFRICOMM 2019, LNICST 311, pp. 121–139, 2020.
https://doi.org/10.1007/978-3-030-41593-8_9

The platforms implement a range of measurement techniques to infer network performance, including through client-side probing and passive monitoring, as well as through remote probing architectures. Remote probing of fixed-line access networks, for instance, is done by injecting packets and using responses received from residential gateways to infer broadband link characteristics [11].

A number of these platforms provide software-based solutions and include Netalyzr [6], SpeedChecker[1], Ookla SpeedTest[2], Glasnost [9], and Shaper-Probe [10], all of which provide a software interface for end users to measure broadband performance. The Netalyzr tool, communicates with a collection of servers to measure key network performance and diagnostic parameters from the perspective of the broadband user.

The hardware-based platforms, on the other hand, use dedicated devices – often termed probes – to run both user-defined measurements or pre-defined measurements with minimal end-user participation. Internet users tend to voluntarily host these probes for the benefit of being able to monitor, among other things, whether their network providers indeed adhere to the advertised service offerings. Internet Service Providers (ISPs), on the other hand, tend to use the data from such platforms to identify and address problems in its eyeball network, as well as to evaluate the Quality of Service (QoS) experienced from their customers' perspective. Popular among these hardware-based platforms are RIPE Atlas [1] and PerfSONAR [3]. RIPE Atlas is a distributed measurement infrastructure deployed by the RIPE NCC and consists of small hardware probes and larger server-like anchors. The hardware probes run active measurements to determine network connectivity and global reachability, whereas the anchors serve as dedicated servers that can act as sources and sinks for the network measurement traffic. Similarly, PerfSONAR is a network monitoring framework focused on measuring end-to-end performance for paths crossing multi-domain networks.

Other systems have been developed mostly for local wireless and mobile networks. Some of the popular mobile platforms include Netradar [5], Portolan [8], MySpeedtest [12], and more recent platforms include Nornet [13], MONROE [7] and LiveLab [14]. Netradar, for instance, is a crowd-based mobile measurement platform that measures link capacity of cellular networks from smartphones and tablets.

While many of these measurement platforms and tools produce the expected results and have gained substantial deployments in many parts of the globe, their availability in Africa and other parts of the developing world still lags. For example, M-Lab has only seven live servers in Africa. Given the limited number of measurement vantage points and limited network resources in Africa, data regarding the Africa's Internet operations remains limited. Generating this high fidelity data could be achieved with the deployment of these measurement probes and conducting short and long term measurement campaigns. These activities will give the Internet community a good understanding of the peculiarities of

---

[1] https://www.speedchecker.com/speed-test-tools/.

[2] www.speedtest.net.

Africa's Internet, which is a key towards building technologies and solutions that will spread the use of Internet in the region by making it cheaper, easily accessible to all, and fast enough.

This paper seeks to establish the awareness and extent to which the various measurement tools and platforms are being adopted and used by various players in Africa's Internet ecosystem. Hence an online survey was instituted and responses collected from different categories of users in the region. The authors found a lack of interest in carrying out measurement by Africa's Internet community as well as a lack of awareness and skills necessary to run a successful measurement campaign. A number of suggestions to remedy the issues discovered were outlined in the conclusion section including the need for Internet bodies and groups to intensify awareness campaigns and increase the number of Internet skills acquisition workshops on Internet measurement as well as the need for the Internet community to host more probes and keep the devices running at all times.

2   Related Work

Recently, there has been a growing interest in measuring different aspects of Internet connectivity and performance in Africa. Gilmore et al. [15] conducted one of the first studies to characterise African Internet connectivity. Using traceroutes, they mapped Internet connectivity from South Africa to all IP blocks that are allocated by AFRINIC[3]. Later, Chavula et al. [16] used active network measurements to quantify the level of local peering and inter-continental traffic exchange among Africa's Research and Education Networks. The study showed that, as of 2013, up to 75% of Africa's inter-university traffic followed circuitous inter-continental routes, and that such traffic was characterised by latencies that were more than double those of traffic exchanged within the continent. More recently, measurement studies by Fanou et al. [17,18] offered a wider view of the AS level topology interconnecting African ISPs using data collected in 2014 from RIPE Atlas probes located in African countries. They highlighted an extreme lack of peering between African ISPs, which results in circuitous routing and consequently very high delays. Gupta et al. [19] collected traceroutes between South Africa, Kenya, and Tunisia to investigate the interconnectivity between African ISPs. The study underscored the poor connectivity between African ISPs and that most of them were more likely to be present at European IXPs than regional IXPs. This resulted in circuitous routing paths and consequently higher round trip delays. Livadariu et al. [20] leveraged RIPE RIS and Routeviews data to examine IPv6 adoption in Africa.

Another wave of studies focused on performance. Chetty et al. [21] studied the performance of mobile and fixed broadband connectivity in South Africa and underscored the importance of peering decisions. Zaki et al. [22] measured

---

[3] AFRINIC is the Regional Internet Registry for Africa and the Indian Ocean.

webpage loading performance for users in Ghana and found that DNS resolution delay is the largest contributor. Recently, Formoso *et al.* [23] used measurements collected by SpeedChecker to quantify inter-country latency in Africa while Fanou *et al.* [24] employed RIPE Atlas to dissect the web ecosystem in Africa revealing that most of the content accessed by users in Africa is still served from outside the continent. With regards to application-level measurements, Phokeer *et al.* [25] ran a quality of experience (QoE) measurement study on local news website in Africa and found that most of Africa's local content is actually hosted in remote locations.

In terms of studying measurement infrastructure and tools, Bajpai *et al.* [26] and Goel *et al.* [27] have provided notable surveys. Bajpai *et al.* [26] detailed a taxonomy of measurement platforms on the basis of deployment use cases, and analysed the coverage and scale of measurement tools. Goel *et al.* [27] focused on mobile measurement tools and examined approaches to end-to-end mobile network performance measurement. They compared the available tools, highlighting their weaknesses and limitations in meeting the needs of developers, researchers, network operators, and regulators.

While the previous surveys [26, 27] largely focused on the technology, our study sheds new light by focusing on the users' understanding and awareness of the measurement infrastructure, as well as highlighting measurement infrastructure that is potentially deployed within corporate networks and largely hidden from the research community. In addition, while it is clear that the previous measurements in Africa have largely drawn upon existing platforms like RIPE Atlas, SpeedChecker and Routeviews or small scale local setups, Africa-grown platforms are notably absent. Furthermore, there is a clear gap when it comes to measuring the performance of mobile broadband both in terms of studies and measurements infrastructures. This is unfortunate, given that most Internet access in Africa is mobile.

As the efforts to understand Africa's Internet intensifies, there is a need to find out more information about the platforms that enable the assessment of the Internet in the region and how these tools are utilised. Hence, the survey was conducted with a number of objectives in mind. Firstly, to improve the current understanding of Internet performance measurement in Africa. Secondly, to establish the state of Internet measurement platforms availability, capabilities, and challenges in the continent. And finally, to establish a good understanding of the needs of the African Internet community in terms of Internet measurement.

3   Survey Description

The online survey was run for the period of eight weeks between 2019-02-28 and 2019-04-14. It was made up of 31 questions and a total of 234 responses were received from 34 African countries.

3.1   Survey Sections

The survey opening section was made up of questions related to the respondents' country and their business/network category. This was followed by the "General section" – the first of five major sections – where we collected data about whether a business runs any measurement campaign or not and the related detail if campaign is currently running/was run in the past. The next four sections included "Metrics section", where we established the relevant metrics important to the different businesses; "Data Handling section", which established the type of data collected, the duration of the data collection, methods used to process, store, and report the data, etc.

The "Measurement Infrastructure" section asked questions about Internet measurement tools hosted/used by the networks and the respondents' level of satisfaction with the available tools. The last section is termed "Conclusion", where open-ended questions were asked including any remarks the respondents have as related to Internet measurement in the African region.

3.2   Collected Data and Cleanup

The countries where these responses came from included South Africa with 20 respondents as the first, Nigeria came second with 16, Sudan third with 8, Ethiopia and Uganda fourth with 7, while Kenya, Morocco, and Ghana came fifth with 4 responses each. These 9 countries constitute almost half the population of Africa and together with the responses from the other 24 countries, the composition gives us some confidence that our data has a continent-wide spread. The list of countries also shows that there are responses from all the 6 sub-regions of the continent[4].

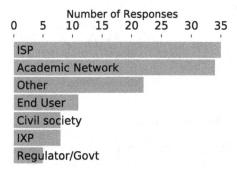

Fig. 1. Business categories that responded

---

[4] AFRINIC divides its Africa service region into 6 sub-regions, namely, Northern, Western, Central, Eastern, Southern and the Indian Ocean, https://AFRINIC.net/service-region.

The respondents also represented different business categories as shown in Fig. 1. ISPs group, which forms the bulk of the responses also comprised of Telecom Operators and Wireless Network providers. There were also responses from Academic Networks (included in this group were Academic Institutions network and National Research and Education Networks) with the second largest number of responses. Responses were also received from Internet eXchange Points (IXP), Civil Society, Regulator/Government Agency, End-user (Home/Mobile Broadband), and the 'Other' category, which comprised of Enterprise Network, Community Network, ccTLD/DNS Operator, Data Centre, and Cable Operator.

For the purpose of cleaning, all incomplete responses from the 234 attempts were removed and 123 entries were left.

4   Status of Internet Measurement

In this section, the paper examines some of the responses received in relation to prevalence of Internet measurements, the purpose of running measurements, and the metrics that are important to the different businesses in the region.

Table 1. Internet measurement by business category

Business category	Total responses	Number running	
		Campaign [%]	Measurement [%]
ISP	35	7 [20]	24 [69]
Academic Network	34	7 [21]	14 [41]
IXP	8	1 [13]	4 [50]
Civil society	8	5 [63]	6 [75]
Regulator/Govt	5	0	2 [40]
End User	11	4 [36]	3 [27]
Other	22	7 [32]	15 [68]

4.1   Prevalence of Measurement

As the first question related to measurement in the survey, we asked "Have you ever run any internet measurement campaign - either as a business owner or a home broadband/mobile device user?" in order to get the percentage of business running measurements in the region. Only 31 (25.20% of the) respondents answered with a YES. This small number was quite a surprise considering that the bulk of the responses, as highlighted in Sect. 3.2, came from networks that serve a lot of users and should, in theory, want to know how their networks perform. Although not intended, the question was understood by our respondents

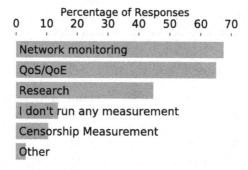

Fig. 2. The main purpose of running measurement

to mean measurement campaigns of some significance likely involving some specialised devices and one that ran for a good number of weeks/months.

This became apparent from two other aspects of the survey as follows. When the 31 respondents with 'YES' in the question above were later asked to provide more detail, we received responses such as "Regular user satisfaction measurement campaign,"I have been the lead collaborator with the Open Observatory of Network Inference (OONI) on Internet censorship research in Nigeria.", "we host perfSONAR measurement nodes which are part of the Academic Network measurement probes for multidomain measurements.", and other similar responses. Secondly, when we later asked a question about performance metrics of interest and followed up with the question, "Do you collect data for the metrics selected in the previous question?" 55.28% of the 123 respondents answered positively – that they have collected some measurement data.

We could understand from the 55.28% figure that while measurement campaigns are not popular with the different business categories, a good number of the networks have conducted some Internet measurement in the past – see Table 1 for more detail.

4.2   Purpose of Running Measurement

Here, we try to understand what is the main purpose that the different businesses are carrying out measurements on their networks for. As highlighted in Fig. 2, about 67% of respondents said that they run measurement for network monitoring, 65% for QoS/QoE, about 45% for research, and a small percentage going for censorship and other reasons. Network monitoring and QoS being the most prevalent reason why measurements are carried out is in line with the dominant source of the survey responses, the ISPs.

Looking at the data, of the 83 respondents that selected network monitoring from the options, 29 of them are ISPs followed by Academic Networks with 21. It is also quite impressive that research comes third among the reasons why businesses conduct measurement on their network. The research option indicates that apart from the business side of measurement, there is some level of interest in Internet measurement research in the African region.

4.3 Metrics of Relevance

While understanding the general purpose of running measurement gives us some clue about 'why measurement' in general, we also asked a question about metrics of interest to have a better understanding of the performance parameters that are of relevance to the different business categories. It turned out that bandwidth/throughput is the most popular metric in general, chosen by 111 of the total respondents. This is followed by latency chosen by 99 respondents, route reachability, 78, and network utilisation came fifth with 75, among others. With ISPs – especially – and Academic Networks leading the survey responses, it is understandable that bandwidth and latency are the prevalent answers.

The different responses by category are shown in Fig. 3 and we could see that for some networks such as that of Civil Society, 'performance of certain applications' is more important than the second overall popular metric, latency. We could also see for 'Other' networks (such as enterprise, cable operator, community network, etc.) network utilisation is of more importance than latency. It is also instructive that most of the respondents are sure of the metrics that are vital to their businesses as there were only two selections for the option 'Not sure!'.

We have also learned from the survey that data aggregation during measurement is mostly done at the country level, followed by autonomous system (AS) level, and then the point of presence level. AS level, as could be expected, is the popular level for ISPs.

5   Measurement Tools and Infrastructure

5.1   Popular Measurement Platforms

Systems: We asked the respondents about the measurement tools they use to collect data and their answers included the use of popular platforms such as RIPE Atlas and Speedchecker, the use of tools developed in-house, the use of interviews, etc. The survey question outlined six platforms, which included the two mentioned above, as well as M-Lab/NDT, CAIDA Ark[5], PerfSONAR, and Bismark Nodes[6], as well as an option to choose personal computer (PC) where measurement platforms were not involved. We also provided an option, 'Other,' where respondents could type the name of a measurement tool(s) they used on their network.

We counted more than 30 different measurement systems mentioned in the 'Other' section. The measurement systems were mostly PC software/web-based including, Uptime Robot, Netflow, View response PRTG, MRTG, Cacti,

---

[5] http://www.caida.org/projects/ark/.

[6] http://projectbismark.net/.

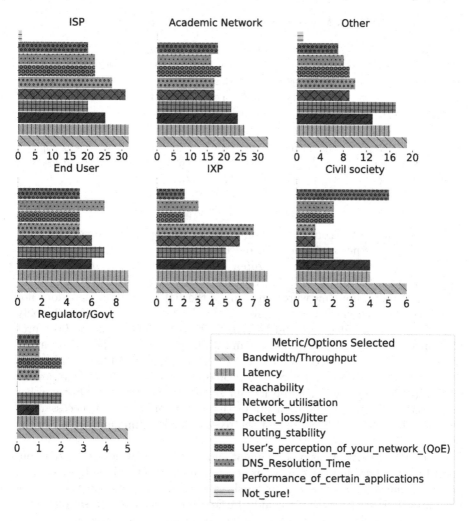

Fig. 3. Metrics of interest

WANkiller, etc. This explains why the option PC was the most popular choice from the list as shown in Table 2. The different platforms/systems chosen as the responses indicate the diverse nature of the tools deployed for Internet measurement in the region.

RIPE Atlas, selected by 29% of respondents, is the most frequently used platform in the region. This is likely because RIPE probes are the most-widely deployed of hardware measurement platforms in Africa with 231 active probes and anchors, as of 10 May 2019, distributed in 126 Autonomous Systems (ASes) (39 of which have both IPv4 and IPv6 connectivity). This represents quite a little coverage of 7.3% of the 1,728 ASNs issued by AFRINIC. What is surprising, however, is that the other measurement platforms were not as patronised

Table 2. Measurement platforms usage by percentage

Business category	Academic Network	ISP	Other	End user	Civil society	IXP	Regulator/ Govt agency	Total responses [%]
PC	25.49	23.53	27.45	11.76	3.92	3.92	3.92	51 [41.50%]
RIPE Atlas	28.57	30.95	14.29	11.90	4.76	9.52	0	42 [34.10%]
Speed checker	26.92	26.92	15.38	15.38	7.69	3.85	3.85	26 [21.10%]
Perf SONAR	70	20	0	10	0	0	0	10 [8.1%]
CAIDA Ark	37.5	25	0	12.5	0	25	0	8 [6.5%]
M-Lab/ NDT	33.33	0	33.33	0	33.33	0	0	3 [2.40%]
Bismark	0	0	0	0	0	0	0	0

by networks across the continent despite the fact they allow for some vital measurement projects not available with RIPE.

For instance, bandwidth/throughput is the most popular metric as discussed in Sect. 4.3 and PerfSONAR is a software-based tool that allows for TCP/UDP throughput measurement, unlike the RIPE platform that does not have such a measurement feature, nevertheless, PerfSONAR was chosen by only 10 respondents. Speedchecker and M-Lab/NDT are two platforms that also provide throughput measurement feature and while the former is the second most-voted platform, M-Lab had only 3 votes. Speedchecker's ease of use could be the reason for its popularity as the software could be installed on hand-held devices or be directly integrated into websites for seamless measurement. On the other hand, the size and the requirements of the server infrastructure necessary to deploy M-Lab/NDT is likely one of the reasons for its minimum spread in the region.

What made RIPE Atlas more popular and added to its widespread adoption, apart from the fact that the project has been around for a number of years, could be the organisation's strategic partnerships with many entities in the African region, such as AFRINIC. We could also attribute the poor utilisation of the useful features provided by the other measurement platforms to lack of awareness from the side of the businesses under review.

Mobile Apps: With Africa's Internet mostly accessed through mobile devices, we investigated the use of mobile apps to measure Internet. While businesses could utilise these apps to understand what customers receive, the customers, on the other hand, could use the apps to know if their networks is at the level expected. As could be seen from Fig. 4, mobile measurement apps are not as popular as the measurement platforms discussed, with more than half of our respondents not using any of the apps. This could be understood considering the fact that apps are mostly popular with end users and they form a small number of our respondents. However, the End User category with a total of only

11 respondents had the highest selection of apps per group in comparison to other categories[7].

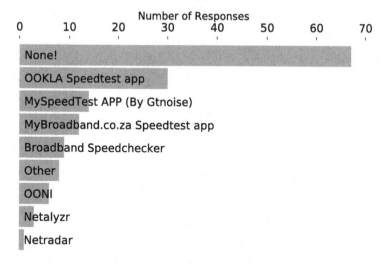

Fig. 4. Measurement apps for mobile devices

5.2   Hosting Measurement Platforms

Having established the popular measurement platforms, we attempted to understand the number of businesses which are currently hosting a measurement probe. 65 of the 123 respondents answered that they host no measurement platform, which indicates some level of disinterest in participation in Internet measurement activity by networks in the African region. The most noticeable of this disinterest is in the case of Regulators/Government Agency group with no probe hosted.

Furthermore, ISPs and Academic Networks accounted for 62% of the total number of the platforms hosted, which means that only a few businesses, outside these 2 categories, are supporting Internet measurement projects. In line with the responses in Sect. 5.1, RIPE Atlas probes are the most popular with 41 devices hosted followed by Ookla Speedtest Server as a distant second with 13. SamKnows, OONI Probe, Bismark Node, and M-Lab pod are the least patronised platforms in the region as detailed in Table 3.

Lastly, we used a Likert scale to get respondents to state their satisfaction level with the current measurement platforms in Africa from 'Highly Satisfied' to 'Highly Disappointed'. As shown in Fig. 5, about 70% are either OK, Satisfied, or highly satisfied with what is available and the other 30% are disappointed with the current measurement platforms.

---

[7] End User: 11 respondents, 18 selections; ISP: 35 respondents, 34 selections; etc.

Table 3. Measurement platforms hosting responses

Business category	RIPE Atlas	Ookla	Perf-SONAR	CAIDA ark monitor	M-Lab pod	Bismark Node	OONI Probe	Sam-Knows
ISP	18	9	1	1	0	0	0	0
Acad. Network	13	1	9	2	2	0	0	0
IXP	6	1	0	2	0	0	0	0
End user	4	0	1	0	0	1	0	0
Civil society	1	0	0	0	0	0	1	0
Regulator/Govt	0	0	0	0	0	0	0	0
Other	6	2	0	0	0	0	0	0
Total	49	13	11	5	2	1	1	0

Fig. 5. Level of satisfaction with the existing measurement platforms

5.3   Data Handling

We mentioned in Sect. 4.3 that data aggregation during measurement as reported by respondents is mostly done at the country level, followed by AS level, and then the point of presence level. We asked further questions regarding the measurement data that the respondents collect. These questions bothered on the duration of collected data necessary for analysis, the tools used for the analysis, and the sort of reporting the respondents produced from the data. As for the duration of collected data, 43 of the respondents chose 'Less than a year' option from the question – which is in line with the preference of short term measurements over long term campaigns discussed in Sect. 4.1 – 38 chose '1–2 years', 13 went for '2–3 years' and 11 chose the 'More than 3 years' options. There are up to 18 respondents who chose the 'Not sure!' option.

Our question related to the tools used for data analysis/visualisation provided three different tools as options, MS Excel, Python tools, and R tools. There is also an option to select whether a respondent was not conducting any analysis as well as the 'Other' option to name the tool that was used if different, or in addition, to the provided options. More than 20 different tools were highlighted by respondents who chose the 'Other' options and their responses included Netflow, Tcpdump, ELK, "Custom dev," "provided by nagios," "utils developed by the University of Reunion", etc. MS Excel was the popular tool used and was voted by 43 respondents, 15 for python and 12 for R. Note that this is a multiple choice question and some respondents chose more than one tool for their answer. Hence, users may be utilising one tool for an aspect of their data analysis and another for a different aspect. Lastly, 52 of the respondents reported not to be carrying out any analysis/visualisation and this figure is closed to the number of respondents who are not running any measurement as reported earlier.

For the question related to reporting the measurement data, respondents included termly reports (daily, weekly, monthly, and yearly), real-time monitoring, research analysis, and reporting a one-off performance analysis on a need-basis, as the different ways that the data measured was reported.

6   Discussion

6.1   Conducting Measurement

Our survey results show that Internet measurement campaigns are not a commonplace in the African region. Measurement campaigns that could run for a considerable amount of time were not very popular with the different business categories, as discussed in Sect. 4.1, despite the benefits that could be derived therefrom. Only 25.20% acknowledged to have run some measurement campaign in the past. Most networks prefer short-term measurement exercises, apparently to understand what was happening at that moment, which could be adequate in some instances. There seemed to be no interest in carrying out a continuous measurement, which could give the businesses a bigger picture of their networks and/or that of their customers.

Furthermore, with only 55.28% of respondents carrying out some measurement, it means that almost half of the members of the networks surveyed are not carrying measurements on their networks. We have also mentioned in the previous section that 52 of the respondents indicated that they do not carry out analysis/visualisation of any measurement data. As will be elaborated in the following subsection, there is a lack of awareness on what Internet measurement entails, what available tools are out there, what benefits it brings to a business, etc.

We could also see some poor handling of issues related to measurement when we look at statistics from an external body, such as RIPE NCC. RIPE Atlas records show that, of the 1026 probes delivered to users across the African region between 13 June 2014 and 10 May 2019, only 231 (22.5%) are currently connected as depicted in Fig. 6. Around 10% of the probes were never connected to the Internet and a whopping 60% of the nodes were abandoned (meaning they have not been connected for a long period of time). While we should take into account many possible reasons for disconnecting the probes – for instance, equipment damage, loss, and users who disconnected the probes because the devices were no more needed – when counting the number of abandoned probes, it is still a large number of devices that are left unconnected to the network for a very long time. While it is important that platform providers distribute more probes and for businesses and individuals to accept and deploy the devices, an important factor in the success of Internet measurement is keeping the devices running all the time for as long as possible. The 7% disconnected nodes on the figure are devices that have been offline for a short period of time.

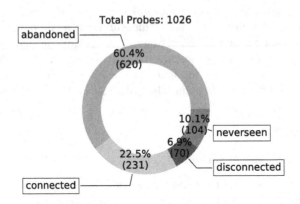

Fig. 6. Status of RIPE Atlas probes in Africa as of 10 May 2019

6.2   Awareness and Skills Development

We asked a question in the survey regarding the lack of use of Internet measurement platforms in order to understand the reasons for the apathy in conducting Internet measurement in the region. As it can be observed from Fig. 7, "Lack of technical know-how" was cited as the number one reason indicating the need for skills development. The second option, "Lack of data processing and visualisation tools," is also an indication that there is a need for awareness and skills development campaigns to introduce some of the users concerned to many open source platforms that they could use for analysis and data visualisation. There are some answers from the 12 respondents who chose the 'Other' option, which included "My laptop is sufficient because I share the same WI-FI connections with my phone", "Not sure", "do not have any", "not aware of their existence", etc. These responses all point to the fact that there is a need for some awareness campaign regarding Internet measurement.

The need for skills is a recurring decimal in other questions that were asked in the survey. To establish the factors hindering Internet measurement in Africa, a question about the factors provided a number of options for respondents to choose from as well as the 'Other' option for respondents who would add factors not captured in our list. Respondents chose different factors as shown in Fig. 8 and the two votes for 'Other' came with the following statements: "Lack of awareness of tools and the importance of the subject" and another response "I don't think enough people care enough to do it." In addition, we could see from the figure that "Lack of well-trained personnel" is the most voted factor with 73

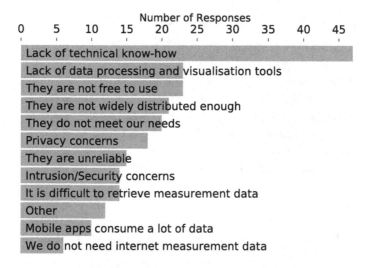

Fig. 7. Reasons respondents were not using the measurement platforms

followed by lack of interest with 57 all pointing to the need for training in order for Internet measurement to pick up pace in Africa.

Similarly, when we asked an open-ended question "What do you think is currently missing in the available measurement platforms/tools in Africa?" we got 47 answers mostly pointing on the need to develop skills. Following are some of the views of the respondents: "... Nous avons des ingénieurs sur place mais il faut de renforcement de capacité sur les outils/plateformes de métrologie de l'internet." which means "We have engineers on site but we need capacity building on the tools/platforms for measuring the Internet." "Some training and accessibility to the tools will help", "more training and know-how sessions across Africa", "Enough service to the rural communities," "Make internet scalable and available for every one," "Enabling law that protect privacy," "knowledge about the tools", etc.

6.3 Privacy and Security

Privacy and security concerns could have an impact on the adoption of Internet measurement in the region. To understand whether privacy and security rules and regulations have impacted on the prevalence of Internet measurement in Africa, we asked the respondents whether there are rules regulating passive Internet measurement in their countries and provided them with three options to choose from, 'YES', 'NO', and 'Not Sure!'. As can be seen from Fig. 9 most of the respondents (52.85%) are not aware if such laws exist in their country. Roughly a third of the respondents (30.08%) answered that such Internet privacy and security laws do not exist in their country. A small fraction of the respondents, 17%, answered positively on the availability of a privacy and security laws in their country. When we grouped the responses by country, we realised that, with the

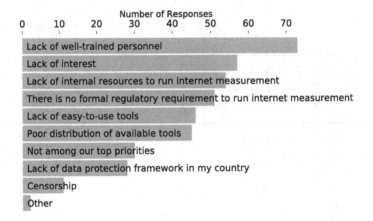

Fig. 8. Factors hindering internet measurement in Africa

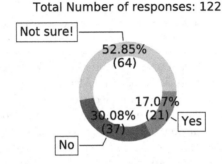

Fig. 9. Presence and level of awareness about privacy Laws

exception of Ghana where the four respondents answered 'YES', responses from same countries were alternating between 'YES', 'NO', and 'Not Sure!'. It is clear that even if such laws exist in countries where some respondents answered in the positive, the majority are not aware of the regulations.

There is no evidence from our data to show that privacy and security laws have any bearing on the prevalence of measurement in the region.

7   Conclusions and Recommendations

There has been a growing interest in measuring the different aspects of Internet connectivity and performance in Africa. This could be seen in the rise in measurement probes deployment across the continent and the number of research literature produced in recent years. The region, however, lags in terms of substantial deployment of probes in comparison with other regions across the world. This issue and the other areas of concerned discussed in the paper – including the poor rate at which Internet measurement is conducted and the lack of awareness and the necessary skills to handle measurement campaigns – need to be addressed in order to generate high fidelity data regarding the continent's Internet operations. We believe the following points could help in this regard.

1. There is a need for Internet bodies and groups in Africa, such as AFRINIC, *NOGs, ISOC, IGF, etc., to actively sensitise the Internet community in the region of the benefits of participating in Internet measurement projects – with some focus given to the wireless networks as the number one source of connectivity in Africa. Local chapters of these bodies and groups should also create awareness about any existing laws regulating the use of traffic data.

2. The Internet bodies and groups should also increase the number of skills acquisition workshops where network administrators and users are taught the skills needed to conduct Internet measurement and data analysis. The local chapters should be encouraged to organise workshops of capacity building in the Internet measurement area. Internet measurement training programs and resources should be made available via online MOOCs or offline for the thousands who may not be able to attend training events.

3. There is a need for businesses, institutions, and individuals in Africa to host more probes/servers to increase the number of measurement vantage points in the region. It is also vital that these devices should be kept running at all time. Platform providers and their ambassadors should increase distribution and follow-up to ensure that probes stay connected to the Internet.

4. There is a need for collaborations between researchers in the academia and between them and the network engineers running the Internet. The researchers could use the practical knowledge of and insights from the engineers in building research questions that reflect reality. The Internet bodies should facilitate these collaborations.

5. While there is no evidence to show that privacy and security laws have any bearing on the prevalence of measurement in Africa, the governments in the region need to be proactive in coming up with laws that govern the usage of user traffic for the purpose of conducting Internet measurement. The governments should create awareness of the new or any existing law in this area and ensure compliance.

6. Our study also reveals that there is no silver bullet in terms of measurement platforms as a one-size-fits-all solution. Most if not all the existing platforms were built in the context of the developed world and did not take into account the particularities of African networks (or the developing world). In many African countries, there is a high prevalence of mobile phones/wireless networks and any new measurement initiative should take into account this reality. As such, incorporating spectrum sensing and QoE metrics could be an interesting improvement to existing solutions.

7. Moreover, the lack of interoperability between platforms and the lack of standardisation in the data models limit the sharing of information between platforms – feature that can be used to correlate different metrics for e.g. congestion and QoE. This could be another area of improvement.

Acknowledgment. Authors would like to thank Roderick Fanou of CAIDA/UC San Diego for his many vital pointers during the course of this study.

References

1. RIPE Atlas: A global internet measurement network. Internet Protocol J. **18**(3) (2015). https://atlas.ripe.net/
2. Dovrolis, C., Gummadi, K., Kuzmanovic, A., Meinrath, S.D.: Measurement lab: overview and an invitation to the research community. ACM SIGCOMM Comput. Commun. Rev. **40**(3), 53–56 (2010)
3. Hanemann, A., et al.: PerfSONAR: a service oriented architecture for multi-domain network monitoring. In: Benatallah, B., Casati, F., Traverso, P. (eds.) ICSOC 2005. LNCS, vol. 3826, pp. 241–254. Springer, Heidelberg (2005). https://doi.org/10.1007/11596141_19
4. Nikravesh, A., Yao, H., Xu, S., Choffnes, D., Mao, Z.M.: Mobilyzer: an open platform for controllable mobile network measurements. In: Proceedings of the 13th Annual International Conference on Mobile Systems, Applications, and Services, pp. 389–404. ACM (2015)
5. Sonntag, S., Manner, J., Schulte, L.: Netradar-measuring the wireless world. In: 2013 11th International Symposium and Workshops on Modeling and Optimization in Mobile, Ad Hoc and Wireless Networks (WiOpt), pp. 29–34. IEEE (2013)
6. Kreibich, C., Weaver, N., Nechaev, B., Paxson, V.: Netalyzr: illuminating the edge network. In: Proceedings of the 10th ACM SIGCOMM Conference on Internet Measurement, pp. 246–259. ACM (2010)
7. Khatouni, A.S.: Speedtest-like measurements in 3G/4G networks: the MONROE experience. In: 2017 29th International Teletraffic Congress (ITC 29), vol. 1, pp. 169–177. IEEE (2017)
8. Faggiani, A., Gregori, E., Lenzini, L., Luconi, V., Vecchio, A.: Smartphone-based crowdsourcing for network monitoring: opportunities, challenges, and a case study. IEEE Commun. Mag. **52**(1), 106–113 (2014)
9. Dischinger, M., Marcon, M., Guha, S., Krishna Gummadi, P., Mahajan, R., Saroiu, S.: Glasnost: enabling end users to detect traffic differentiation. In: NSDI, pp. 405–418 (2010)
10. Kanuparthy, P., Dovrolis, C.: ShaperProbe: end-to-end detection of ISP traffic shaping using active methods. In: Proceedings of the 2011 ACM SIGCOMM Conference on Internet Measurement Conference, pp. 473–482. ACM (2011)
11. Dischinger, M., Haeberlen, A., Gummadi, K.P., Saroiu, S.: Characterizing residential broadband networks. In: Internet Measurement Conference, vol. 7, pp. 43–56 (2007)
12. Muckaden, S.: MySpeedTest: active and passive measurements of cellular data networks. In: Proceedings of ISMA (2013)
13. Gran, E.G., Dreibholz, T., Kvalbein, A.: NorNet core-a multi-homed research testbed. Comput. Netw. **61**, 75–87 (2014)
14. Shepard, C., Rahmati, A., Tossell, C., Zhong, L., Kortum, P.: LiveLab: measuring wireless networks and smartphone users in the field. ACM SIGMETRICS Perform. Eval. **38**, 15–20 (2011)
15. Gilmore, J., Huysamen, N., Krzesinski, A.: Mapping the African internet. In: Proceedings Southern African Telecommunication Networks and Applications Conference (SATNAC), Mauritius (2007)
16. Chavula, J., Feamster, N., Bagula, A., Suleman, H.: Quantifying the effects of circuitous routes on the latency of intra-Africa internet traffic: a study of research and education networks. In: Nungu, A., Pehrson, B., Sansa-Otim, J. (eds.) AFRICOMM 2014. LNICST, vol. 147, pp. 64–73. Springer, Cham (2015). https://doi.org/10.1007/978-3-319-16886-9_7

17. Fanou, R., Francois, P., Aben, E.: On the diversity of interdomain routing in Africa. In: Mirkovic, J., Liu, Y. (eds.) PAM 2015. LNCS, vol. 8995, pp. 41–54. Springer, Cham (2015). https://doi.org/10.1007/978-3-319-15509-8_4

18. Fanou, R., Francois, P., Aben, E., Mwangi, M., Goburdhan, N., Valera, F.: Four years tracking unrevealed topological changes in the African interdomain. Comput. Commun. J. **106**, 117–135 (2017)

19. Gupta, A., Calder, M., Feamster, N., Chetty, M., Calandro, E., Katz-Bassett, E.: Peering at the internet's frontier: a first look at ISP interconnectivity in Africa. In: Faloutsos, M., Kuzmanovic, A. (eds.) PAM 2014. LNCS, vol. 8362, pp. 204–213. Springer, Cham (2014). https://doi.org/10.1007/978-3-319-04918-2_20

20. Livadariu, I., Elmokashfi, A., Dhamdhere, A.: Measuring IPv6 adoption in Africa. In: Odumuyiwa, V., Adegboyega, O., Uwadia, C. (eds.) AFRICOMM 2017. LNICST, vol. 250, pp. 345–351. Springer, Cham (2018). https://doi.org/10.1007/978-3-319-98827-6_32

21. Chetty, M., Sundaresan, S., Muckaden, S., Feamster, N., Callandro, E.: Measuring broadband performance in South Africa. In: Proceedings of the 4th Annual Symposium on Computing for Development (2013)

22. Zaki, Y., Chen, J., Pötsch, T., Ahmad, T., Subramanian, L.: Dissecting web latency in Ghana. In: Proceedings of the 2014 Conference on Internet Measurement Conference, pp. 241–248. ACM (2014). Review **38**(3), 15–20 (2011)

23. Formoso, A., Chavula, J., Phokeer, A., Sathiaseelan, A., Tyson, G.: Deep diving into Africa's inter-country latencies. In: IEEE INFOCOM 2018-IEEE Conference on Computer Communications, pp. 2231–2239. IEEE (2018)

24. Fanou, R., Tyson, G., Fernandes, E.L., Francois, P., Valera, F., Sathiaseelan, A.: Exploring and analysing the African web ecosystem. ACM Trans. Web (TWEB) **12**(4), 22 (2018)

25. Phokeer, A., et al.: On the potential of Google AMP to promote local content in developing regions. In: 2019 11th International Conference on Communication Systems and Networks (COMSNETS), Bengaluru, India, pp. 80–87 (2019)

26. Bajpai, V., Schönwälder, J.: A survey on internet performance measurement platforms and related standardization efforts. IEEE Commun. Surv. Tutor. **17**(3), 1313–1341 (2015)

27. Goel, U., Wittie, M.P., Claffy, K.C., Le, A.: Survey of end-to-end mobile network measurement testbeds, tools, and services. IEEE Commun. Surv. Tutor. **18**(1), 105–123 (2015)

I2PA, U-prove, and Idemix: An Evaluation of Memory Usage and Computing Time Efficiency in an IoT Context

Ibou Sene[1,2]([✉]), Abdoul Aziz Ciss[1], and Oumar Niang[1]

[1] Laboratoire de Traitement de l'Information et des Systèmes Intelligents (LTISI),
Ecole Polytechnique de Thiès, P.O. Box A10, Thiès, Senegal
senei@ept.sn
[2] Ecole Doctorale Développement Durable et Société (ED2DS),
Université de Thiès, P.O. Box 967, Thiès, Senegal
{aaciss,oniang}@ept.sn

Abstract. The Internet of Things (IoT), in spite of its innumerable advantages, brings many challenges namely issues about users' privacy preservation and constraints about lightweight cryptography. Lightweight cryptography is of capital importance since IoT devices are qualified to be resource-constrained. To address these challenges, several Attribute-Based Credentials (ABC) schemes have been designed including I2PA, U-prove, and Idemix. Even though these schemes have very strong cryptographic bases, their performance in resource-constrained devices is a question that deserves special attention. Therefor, this paper aims to conduct a performance evaluation of these schemes on issuance and verification protocols regarding memory usage and computing time. Recorded results show that both I2PA and U-prove present very interesting results regarding memory usage and computing time while Idemix presents very low performance with regard to computing time compared to I2PA and U-prove.

Keywords: ABC · Anonymity · Credential · IoT · Performances · Privacy · Lightweight cryptography

1 Introduction

Out of several emerging technologies and concepts, the Internet of Things is a new paradigm that brings both challenges and opportunities [1]. According to Ashton Kevin, to whom we owe the term "Internet of Things", the IoT has the potential to change the world, as did the Internet, maybe even more [2]. The Internet of Things represents a vision in which the Internet extends into the real world embracing everyday objects [3]. However, as mentioned above, it brings many challenges including issues about users' privacy preservation and constraints about lightweight cryptography [4]. We are among those who

R. Zitouni et al. (Eds.): AFRICOMM 2019, LNICST 311, pp. 140–153, 2020.
https://doi.org/10.1007/978-3-030-41593-8_10

think that the protection of privacy is a fundamental right and its loss would lead to the restriction of freedom [5]. Lightweight cryptography is a strong constraint because IoT devices are qualified to be resource-constrained. Indeed, these devices have three major constraints namely low energy autonomy, very limited storage capacity and very low computing power [4]. From there, were designed several schemes and the most promising include I2PA [4], Idemix [6], and U-prove [7]. These schemes are based on recognized robust cryptosystems. However, the question of their applicability in an IoT context, therefore in resource-constrained devices, is of capital importance. Roughly results recorded in [4] on issuance and verification of credentials made up of 10 attributes show that I2PA and U-prove are more efficient than Idemix regarding computing time efficiency. However, what about memory usage and computing time efficiency on different number of attributes? In this paper, we provide a deeper evaluation by regarding memory usage and computing time while issuing and verifying credentials made up of 1, 5, and 10 attributes respectively.

The rest of this paper is organized as follows. Section 2 is related to background review while related works are presented in Sect. 3. Section 4 describes experimental set-up whereas recorded results and discussions are depicted in Sect. 5. This paper is ended by a conclusion and perspectives in Sect. 6.

2 Background Review

We now recall few notions about Attribute-Based Credentials (ABC), Elliptic Curves Cryptography (ECC), Binary Scalar Multiplication (BSM), and Extended Homogeneous Coordinates (EHC). We refer readers to [4,8–11] for more details about discussed concepts in this section.

2.1 Attribute-Based Credential

Attribute-Based Credentials are mechanisms of authentication that allow to flexibly and selectively authenticate different attributes about an entity without revealing additional information about that entity. As a result, they do not necessarily identify the user, as they only provide authentic assertions about the user [4,8,9]. They are building blocks that aim at protecting users' privacy preservation.

2.2 Elliptic Curve Cryptography

Elliptic Curve Cryptography (ECC) was presented independently by Koblitz [12] and Miller [13] in the 1980s. Their structure of group and performance in computing time they offer make them a new direction in cryptography [4]. They offer good level of security with smaller key size. They are also less Central Processing Unit (CPU) intensive so they are ideal for resource-constrained devices.

2.3 Binary Scalar Multiplication

The fundamental operation of ECC is point scalar computation (also known as scalar multiplication) of the form [4]:

$$Q = k.P = \underbrace{P + P + \ldots + P}_{k \text{ times}}$$

Security in ECC is based on Elliptic Curve Discrete Logarithm Problem (ECDLP) [4,10] that can be summarized as follows. Given an elliptic curve E defined over a finite field $\mathbb{F}_p$. Let $P, Q \in E(\mathbb{F}_p)$, find $k \in \mathbb{F}_q$, if it exists, such that $Q = k.P$ (q denotes the order of P). Scalar multiplication can be performed efficiently when tackling small numbers. However, when numbers hold in many bits (160 for instance), this might take lot of time. Several methods have been designed so far to speed up these operations including the double-and-add algorithm also known as binary algorithm. This algorithm is a very elegant technique to perform multiplication of big numbers. Two versions of this algorithm exist that either scan the scalar in a left to right or right to left direction [14]. Let k be an integer such that $k_{(10)} = (k_n k_{n-1} \ldots k_1 k_0)_{(2)}$, where $k_i \in \{0, 1\}, k_n = 1$ and $n \geq 1$. The left to right version is described in "Algorithm 1".

Algorithm 1. Left to right double-and-add

Input: $P \in E(\mathbb{F}_p), k \in \mathbb{F}_q$
Result: $k.P \in E(\mathbb{F}_p)$
1 R ←P
2 **for** $i \leftarrow n - 1$ **to** 0 **do**
3   R ←2.R
4   **if** $k_i = 1$ **then**
5   R ←R+P
6   **end**
7 **end**
8 **return** R

The "Algorithm 1" is simple, efficient and has an average complexity of $nD + \frac{n}{2}A$ (D and A denote respectively the number of double and add operations). Implementations of I2PA and U-prove are based on this technique seeing its simplicity, its low complexity, and its easy implementation in place of other methods like Non-Adjacent Form (NAF) also known as Signed Binary Representation (SBR) which presents a more interesting complexity ($nD + \frac{n}{3}A$) but requires a supplementary treatment on the representation of the scalar. Let us consider a device with a processor clocked at $1\,\text{GHz}$ and $k = 2^{40}$. Computing $k.P$ with decimal representation of k would require around $19\,\text{min}$ while with binary representation, this would take less than $1\,\text{ms}$. We remind that the number of bits required to represent a positive integer n in radix 2 is at most equal to $ceil(log_2(n)) + 1$, where $ceil(x)$ denotes the rounds of x up to the nearest integer. These results show how relevant it is to use this technique instead of decimal representation.

2.4 Extended Homogeneous Coordinates

According to our experimental parameters (see Sect. 4.3), Josefsson et al. [11] recommended to use extended homogeneous coordinates (EHCs). In the EHCs representation, (x, y) is represented as $(X : Y : Z : T)$ where $x = \frac{X}{Z}$, $y = \frac{Y}{Z}$ and $xy = \frac{T}{Z}$. The neutral point $(0, 1)$ is equivalent to $(0 : Z : Z : 0)$ for any nonzero Z. Coordinates $(X : Y : Z : T)$ and $(\lambda X : \lambda Y : \lambda Z : \lambda T)$ are equivalent for any nonzero λ. EHMs avoid inversion operations and, as a result, improve computing time efficiency. We refer readers to [11] for more details. Details of add and double formulas are presented respectively in "Algorithm 2" and "Algorithm 3".

Algorithm 2. Add formula
Input: $P_1, P_2 \in E(\mathbb{F}_p)$
Result: $P_1 + P_2 \in E(\mathbb{F}_p)$
1 $A \leftarrow (Y_1 - X_1)(Y_2 - X_2)$
2 $B \leftarrow (Y_1 + X_1)(Y_2 + X_2)$
3 $C \leftarrow 2dT_1T_2$
4 $D \leftarrow 2Z_1Z_2$
5 $E \leftarrow B - A$
6 $F \leftarrow D - C$
7 $G \leftarrow D + C$
8 $H \leftarrow B + A$
9 $(X, Y, Z, T) \leftarrow (EF, GH, FG, EH)$
return $(X : Y : Z : T)$

Algorithm 3. Double formula
Input: $P \in E(\mathbb{F}_p)$
Result: $2.P \in E(\mathbb{F}_p)$
1 $A \leftarrow X^2$
2 $B \leftarrow Y^2$
3 $C \leftarrow 2Z^2$
4 $D \leftarrow (X + Y)^2$
5 $H \leftarrow B + A$
6 $E \leftarrow H - D$
7 $G \leftarrow A - B$
8 $F \leftarrow C + G$
9 $(X', Y', Z', T') \leftarrow (EF, GH, FG, EH)$
return $(X' : Y' : Z' : T')$

3 Related Works

The Internet of Things brings both challenges and opportunities [1]. Indeed, in an IoT context, performance, privacy preservation, and lightweight cryptography are key aspects that must be taken into account with special attention. To the best of our knowledge, the best way of protecting users' privacy preservation remains using Attributes-Based Credentials (ABC) also known as Privacy-ABC. Many ABC schemes have been designed so far including I2PA, U-prove, and Idemix. However, few works evaluate the efficiency of these schemes in an IoT context. On a theoretical level, authors of [15,16] have addressed the importance of computational efficiency in resource-constrained devices. Veseli et al. [17] have evaluated the computational efficiency of Idemix and U-prove. Their results shown that U-prove is more efficient than Idemix for the User operation (proving) and in general when a credential has more attributes. They have also stated that Idemix is more efficient in the rest of the cases, especially when advanced presentation features are used. Their simulation uses a computer with a processor of 1.8 GHz Intel Core i7 and both schemes are instantiated using the RSA cryptosystem. Veseli et al. [18] have addressed storage and communication efficiency of Idemix and U-prove. Their results suggest that for storage, Idemix is more efficient than U-prove, since a single credential provides multiple-show unlinkability. They have also pointed out that, in terms of communication efficiency, Idemix is more efficient for issuance, whereas U-prove is more efficient for presentation of credentials. They have developed a number of experiments in Java, which have been executed on a computer with a processor of 1.8 GHz Intel Core i7 and schemes are based on the RSA cryptosystem. Vullers et al. [19] have presented an efficient selective disclosure on smart cards using Idemix (using the MULTOS platform). Their implementation is based on a 1024 bits security level. They asserted that Idemix's selective disclosure can be efficiently implemented on a smart card. Mostowski et al. [20] provided an efficient U-prove implementation for Anonymous Credentials on smart cards (Using the MULTOS platform). Their implementation aims at making the smart card independent of any other resources, either computational or storage. Their performance results strongly support their idea to use a stand-alone U-prove smart card rather than the Microsoft device-protection approach, which seems to overlook the current capabilities of smart cards. SENE et al. [4] have conducted a comparison of I2PA, U-prove, and Idemix on issuance and verification regarding computing time for credentials made up of 10 attributes. They have instantiated U-prove using ECC and their results have shown that U-prove presented more interesting results than Idemix regarding computing time on issuance and verification protocols. I2PA and U-prove present nearby performance even though I2PA's results are more interesting. Although these works have presented interesting results, most of them have focused on the efficiency of a particular implementation of a particular technology, and on a particular platform. Some of them were interested in many schemes or many aspects of privacy preservation but used computer which does not give any idea on low-resource devices efficiency. To the best of our knowledge, this is the first contribution that evaluates efficiency of I2PA, U-prove and Idemix in an IoT context regarding computing time and memory usage. Furthermore, as far as we know, it is also the first one that considers ECC-based U-prove instantiation in low-resource devices.

4   Experimental Setup

This section describes both hardware and software setup. It also describes curve and parameters used to perform this evaluation.

4.1   Hardware Setup

The hardware setup consists of a smartphone and a Raspberry Pi. The Raspberry Pi ("Fig. 1") is used to deploy both issuer and verifier. We describe some of its characteristics below:

- Model Pi 3 B+
- 1 Go of SDRAM LPDDR2
- A 64-bit quad core processor clocked at 1.4 GHz
- Raspbian operating system

- Dual Band 2.4 GHz and 5 GHz IEEE 802.11. b/g/n/AC Wireless LAN
- Enhanced Ethernet performance over USB 2.0 (maximum throughput of 300 Mbps)

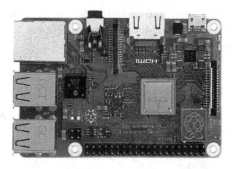

Fig. 1. Hardware environment

The smartphone ("Fig. 2") acts as a user. Some of its characteristics are depicted below:

- Model TECNO SPARK KB7j
- RAM 2 GB
- ROM 16 GB
- CPU 2.0 GH*4
- Battery 3500 mAh
- Memory 16 GB

(a) Initial view   (b) Processing view   (c) Result view

Fig. 2. Android application's screenshots.

4.2   Software Setup

The software environment is made up of three major components that are issuer, verifier, and user ("Fig. 3"). Issuer and verifier are Java Socket while user is an Android application. We are running both the issuer and the verifier on the same device (the Raspberry Pi) while the user is running on a smartphone. The "Fig. 3" is an overview of software components.

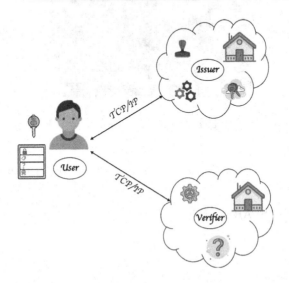

Fig. 3. Software environment

4.3   Parameters

Edwards' curves are known to offer better performances among all Elliptic Curve (EC) families [21]. The $Curve25519$ was introduced as an ECDH (Elliptic Curve Diffie-Hellman) function but it is known today as the underlying elliptic curve designed for use with ECDH key agreement scheme ($X25519$) or with ECDSA (Elliptic Curve Digital Signature Algorithm) signature ($Ed25519$). It was first introduced in its Montgomery form $E : v^2 = u^3 + 486662u^2 + u$ over the prime field defined by $p = 2^{255} - 19$. This curve ensures a 128-bit security level as the fastest known attack on the discrete logarithm problem [22]. Nowadays, it is used in Protocols, Networks, Operating Systems, Software, SSH Software, TLS Libraries, etc. [23]. Below, we describe parameters used in our performance evaluation and they are adapted from [22]. The parameter k defines keys' size for schemes I2PA and U-prove while k' defines Idemix's keys size. The parameter p defines the field $\mathbb{Z}_p$, d defines the elliptic curve $E_d : x^2 + y^2 = 1 + dx^2y^2$. Values x_0 and y_0 define the coordinates of the base point P with order q. The component Z_0 defines the third component in extended homogeneous coordinates of the base point. We refer reader to [10,24] for keys' size justification. Parameters' values are depicted below:

- $k = 160$
- $k' = 1024$
- $p = 2^{255} - 19$
- $d = 37095705934669439343138083508754565189542113879843219016388785533085940283555$
- $x_0 = 15112221349535400772501151409588531511454012693041857206046113283949847762202$
- $y_0 = 46316835694926478169428394003475163141307993866256225615783033603165251855960$
- $Z_0 = 1$
- $q = 2^{252} + 27742317777372353535851937790883648493$

At the core of ABC schemes, we have attributes. An attribute is a characteristic or a qualification of a person [4]. It certifies that an entity has skill, knowledge, qualification, etc. An attribute certified by a third party is known as a claim. Whatever the nature of an attribute, it can be represented in a decimal format. Therefore, attributes' values used in this evaluation are described below:

- $a_0 = 3022871045856445402$
- $a_1 = 2303921356947$
- $a_2 = 63990592803$
- $a_3 = 63188281798077$
- $a_4 = 233454418592768000150715$
- $a_5 = 72478959060716899515$
- $a_6 = 132108418240270107954363$
- $a_7 = 53359477949683103$
- $a_8 = 393090009322226684739352798186683$
- $a_9 = 2930303348526267$

5 Results and Discussion

This section depicts and comments results of our performance evaluation. Unless explicitly stated, time will always be expressed in milliseconds (ms) and memory in Megabyte (MB). It should also be noted that, for memory metrics, all values are rounded to two decimal places. We remind that U-prove and I2PA are instantiated using ECC as mentioned before. The implemented versions of U-prove and Idemix are based on schemes presented by Gergely Alpár [9] while I2PA implementation is based on the scheme presented by SENE et al. [4]. We point out that every simulation is carried out with new random parameters except system's parameters and attributes' values.

5.1 Limitations

We note some limitations that should be taken into account while exploring results presented thereafter.

- Our results are based on the openly available versions of U-prove and Idemix.
- During the issuance phase and at user side, when the issuer takes lots of times to issue credential, recorded minima in terms of memory usage at user side may be biased. The user may remain idle for a while which considerably lowers used resources. This is the case with Idemix since its issuance requires lots of times (See "Fig. 7").
- During the verification phase, in order not to impact memory usage, we first issue a credential and then verify it immediately instead of storing all credentials that should be verified. This may impact the recorded minima at verifier side if the issuance of a credential takes lots of times. The later may remain idle for a while what considerably lowers used resources. This is the case with Idemix that requires a lot of times to issue a credential (See "Fig. 7").

5.2   Memory Usage Evaluation

This section describes results about memory usage. Figures presented below are recorded with VisualVM 1.3.9 [25] using "Tracer-Monitor Probes" plugin. Evaluations involve 100 simulations on issuance and verification of credentials made up of 1, 5, and 10 attributes respectively.

5.2.1   Issuance

In this section, we describe memory evaluation at issuer and user sides. At issuer side (respectively at user side), we evaluate the memory required to issue (respectively to get) a credential.

At Issuer Side: Recorded results from issuance of credentials made up of 1, 5, and 10 attributes respectively are presented in "Fig. 4".

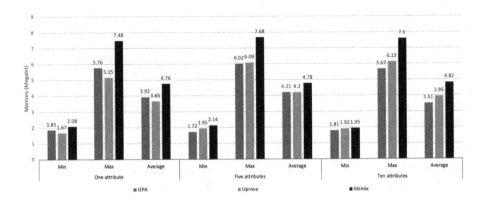

Fig. 4. Issuance memory usage at issuer side

As shown in "Fig. 4", the three schemes present nearby performance regarding memory usage at issuer side while issuing credentials. At first glance, this may seem paradoxical seeing keys' size (160 for I2PA and U-prove, 1024 for

Idemix). However, this can be explained by the usage of extended homogeneous coordinates while instantiating U-prove and I2PA. Nevertheless, in all cases, Idemix requires more resource in average and records highest maxima. U-prove and I2PA, in three cases, have nearby average consumptions; 3.92 against 3.65 (respectively 4.21 against 4.2, and 3.51 against 3.95) for issuance of 1 attribute (respectively 5 and 10 attributes).

At User Side: This section describes memory usage at user side while issuing credentials of 1, 5, and 10 attributes respectively. We shall not evaluate the memory usage in the verification phase since the user only presents her credential; she performs no operation. Due to limitations noted in the mobile application while recording memory usage at user side, we recorded these results with a user implemented using Java socket and running in a Raspberry PI. The "Fig. 5" is an illustration of recorded results.

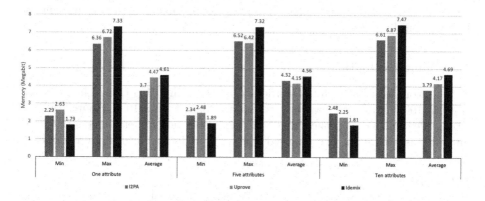

Fig. 5. Issuance memory usage at user side

"Figure 5" shows that, as we have already pointed out in the limitations (Sect. 5.1), Idemix has very low minima (1.79, 1.89, and 1.81) compared to other schemes (2.29, 2.34, and 2.48 for I2PA, 2.63, 2.48, and 2.25 for U-prove). Despite the fact that three schemes present nearby consumptions, Idemix has higher maxima and requires more resources on average.

5.2.2 Verification

If the credentials to verify are generated and stored beforehand, this may greatly affect memory usage and then influences recorded results. We verify a credential after generating it. This frees the memory once the credential is verified. "Figure 6" illustrates recorded results while verifying credentials of 1, 5, and 10 attributes respectively.

"Figure 6" shows that, globally, tendencies recorded here do not differ from those presented in previous sections. We can note that on average, Idemix, requires more memory than I2PA and U-prove. Except for the verification of

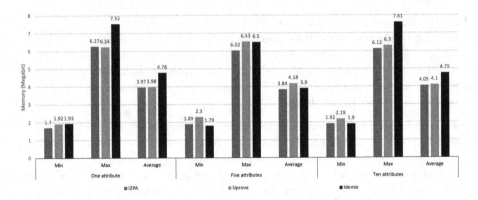

Fig. 6. Verification memory usage at verifier side

credentials made up of 5 attributes, Idemix presents the highest average values. I2PA, in all three cases, has an average value smaller than that present by U-prove and Idemix.

5.3   Time Evaluation

This section describes results recorded regarding computing time. These results concern 100 simulations involving credentials of 1, 5, and 10 attributes respectively. We shall consider the time required at user side to get a credential from an issuer as well as the one required to have a credential verified by a verifier.

5.3.1   Issuance

Results recorded from issuance of credentials made up of 1, 5, and 10 attributes are illustrated in "Fig. 7". We illustrate minima, maxima, as well as average values.

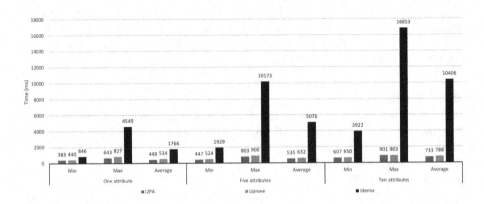

Fig. 7. Time issuance comparison

"Figure 7" shows that I2PA and U-prove have similar performance regarding computing time efficiency. However, I2PA presents more interesting result than U-prove. Idemix, meanwhile, has very low performance compared to I2PA and U-prove. The time it requires for issuance is on average at least 3 times (respectively 8 and 13) more important than that required by I2PA and U-prove for issuance of credential made up of 1 attribute (respectively 5 and 10 attributes). Regarding distribution of time for credential containing 1 attribute (respectively 5 and 10 attributes), 33% (respectively 45% and 50%) of simulations have duration higher or equal to the average for I2PA, 38% (respectively 45% and 49%) for U-prove, and 35% (respectively 39% and 51%) for Idemix. Finally, regarding computing time efficiency, I2PA and U-prove present more interesting result than Idemix. What should be the number of attributes (1, 5, or 10), I2PA and U-prove require less than 1 s for credential issuance, what can be considered as relevant.

5.3.2 Verification

As for the issuance, this section describes recorded results while verifying 100 credentials of 1, 5, and 10 attributes respectively. "Figure 8" illustrates registered results.

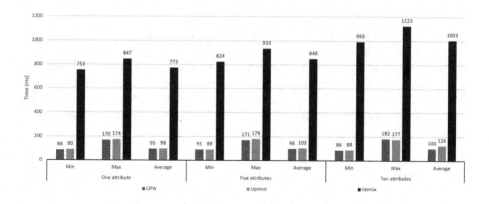

Fig. 8. Time verification comparison

"Figure 8" shows that, as for the issuance, I2PA and U-prove present similar performances on the verification protocol regarding computing time efficiency. However, except the maximum recorded during the issuance of credentials made up of 10 attributes, I2PA requires less computing time compared to U-prove. Idemix, meanwhile, has very low performance compared to I2PA and U-prove. The time it requires for verification is on average at least 7 times (respectively 8 and 8) more important than that required by I2PA and U-prove for verification of credentials made up of 1 attribute (respectively 5 and 10 attributes). Regarding distribution of time for credentials of 1 attribute (respectively 5 and 10 attributes), 22% (respectively 10% and 21%) of simulations have duration higher or equal to the average for I2PA, 13% (respectively 13% and 50%) for U-prove and 39% (respectively 54% and 12%) for Idemix. Finally, regarding computing time efficiency, we can safely assert that I2PA and U-prove present more interesting result than Idemix on verification protocol. They can thus be envisaged in a context of resource-constrained devices.

6   Conclusion and Future Works

In this paper, the performance evaluation of I2PA, U-prove, and Idemix we conducted in low-resource devices, was focused in evaluating computing time and memory usage efficiency. Three types of conclusions can be drawn:

- In terms of memory usage at issuer, user or verifier sides, I2PA, U-prove, and Idemix present nearby consumptions if I2PA and U-prove are instantiated using ECC and ECH representation. However, in average, Idemix requires more memory than I2PA and U-prove.
- In terms of computing time efficiency, Idemix has very low performances compared to I2PA and U-prove. The time it requires for issuance (respectively verification) is at least 3 times (respectively 7 times) more important than that requires by I2PA and U-prove.
- Even though EHC representation speeds up operations over the curve, it increases memory usage.

Finally, for computing time and memory usage efficiency criteria, I2PA and U-prove are two schemes that can be envisaged in an IoT context. However, for an effective choice, other criteria must be taken into account including issuance unlinkability, multi-show unlinkability, selective disclosure, randomization, etc. This evaluation, for reasons of completeness, could be extended by studying randomization and selective disclosure protocols efficiency as well as bandwidth usage.

References

1. Chen, Y.-K.: Challenges and opportunities of internet of things, pp. 383–388, January 2012. https://doi.org/10.1109/ASPDAC.2012.6164978
2. Ashton, K.: That "Internet of Things" Thing (2009). https://tools.ietf.org/html/draft-josefsson-eddsa-ed25519-03. Accessed 28 June 2019
3. Mattern, F., Floerkemeier, C.: From the internet of computers to the internet of things. In: Sachs, K., Petrov, I., Guerrero, P. (eds.) From Active Data Management to Event-Based Systems and More. LNCS, vol. 6462, pp. 242–259. Springer, Heidelberg (2010). https://doi.org/10.1007/978-3-642-17226-7_15
4. Sene, I., Ciss, A.A., Niang, O.: I2PA: an efficient ABC for IoT. Cryptography 3(2), 16 (2019). https://doi.org/10.3390/cryptography3020016
5. Toumia, A., Szoniecky, S.: Prétopologie et protection de la vie privée dans l'Internet des Objets. Open Science-Internet des objets 2(1) (2018)
6. Camenisch, J., Van Herreweghen, E.: Design and implementation of the idemix anonymous credential system. In: Proceedings of the 9th ACM Conference on Computer and Communications Security, pp. 21–30. ACM (2002)

7. Paquin, C., Zaverucha, G.: U-prove cryptographic specification v1. 1. Technical report, Microsoft Corporation (2011)
8. Alpár, G., Jacobs, B.: Credential design in attribute-based identity management (2013)
9. Alpár, G.: Attribute-based identity management: [bridging the cryptographic design of ABCs with the real world]. [Sl: sn] (2015)
10. Ciss, A.A.: Trends in elliptic curves cryptography. IMHOTEP: Afr. J. Pure Appl. Math. **2**(1), 1–12 (2015)
11. Josefsson, S., Liusvaara, I.: Edwards-curve digital signature algorithm (EDDSA). Technical report (2017)
12. Koblitz, N.: Elliptic curve cryptosystems. Math. Comput. **48**(177), 203–209 (1987)
13. Miller, V.S.: Use of elliptic curves in cryptography. In: Williams, H.C. (ed.) CRYPTO 1985. LNCS, vol. 218, pp. 417–426. Springer, Heidelberg (1986). https://doi.org/10.1007/3-540-39799-X_31
14. Rivain, M.: Fast and regular algorithms for scalar multiplication over elliptic curves. IACR Cryptology ePrint Archive, p. 338 (2011)
15. Baldimtsi, F., Lysyanskaya, A.: Anonymous credentials light. In: Proceedings of the 2013 ACM SIGSAC Conference on Computer & Communications Security, pp. 1087–1098. ACM (2013)
16. Camenisch, J., Groß, T.: Efficient attributes for anonymous credentials. ACM Trans. Inf. Syst. Secur. (TISSEC) **15**(1), 4 (2012)
17. Veseli, F., Serna, J.: Evaluation of privacy-ABC technologies - a study on the computational efficiency. In: Habib, S.M.M., Vassileva, J., Mauw, S., Mühlhäuser, M. (eds.) IFIPTM 2016. IAICT, vol. 473, pp. 63–78. Springer, Cham (2016). https://doi.org/10.1007/978-3-319-41354-9_5
18. Veseli, F., Olvera, J.S.: Benchmarking privacy-ABC technologies - an evaluation of storage and communication efficiency, pp. 198–205, June 2015. https://doi.org/10.1109/SERVICES.2015.37
19. Vullers, P., Alpár, G.: Efficient selective disclosure on smart cards using idemix. In: Fischer-Hübner, S., de Leeuw, E., Mitchell, C. (eds.) IDMAN 2013. IAICT, vol. 396, pp. 53–67. Springer, Heidelberg (2013). https://doi.org/10.1007/978-3-642-37282-7_5
20. Mostowski, W., Vullers, P.: Efficient U-prove implementation for anonymous credentials on smart cards. In: Rajarajan, M., Piper, F., Wang, H., Kesidis, G. (eds.) SecureComm 2011. LNICST, vol. 96, pp. 243–260. Springer, Heidelberg (2012). https://doi.org/10.1007/978-3-642-31909-9_14
21. Liu, Z., Seo, H., Xu, Q.: Performance evaluation of twisted Edwards-form elliptic curve cryptography for wireless sensor nodes. Secur. Commun. Netw. **8**(18), 3301–3310 (2015)
22. El Housni, Y.: Edwards curves. Working Paper or Preprint, December 2018. https://hal.archives-ouvertes.fr/hal-01942759
23. IANIX. Things that use Ed25519 (2019). https://ianix.com/pub/ed25519-deployment.html. Accessed 25 Jan 2019
24. Sinha, R., Srivastava, H.K., Gupta, S.: Performance based comparison study of RSA and elliptic curve cryptography. Int. J. Sci. Eng. Res. **4**(5), 720–725 (2013)
25. Sedlacek, J., Hurka, T.: VisualVM, All-in-One Java Troubleshooting Tool (2017). https://visualvm.github.io/. Accessed 05 Mar 2019

A Hybrid Network Model Embracing NB-IoT and D2D Communications: Stochastic Geometry Analysis

Athanase M. Atchome[1]($\boxtimes$), Hafiz Husnain Raza Sherazi[2], Rodrigue Alahassa[3],
Frantz Tossa[1], Thierry O. Edoh[4], Luigi Alfredo Grieco[2],
and Antoine C. Vianou[1]

[1] Ecole Doctorale Des Sciences de l'Ingénieur (ED-SDI)/UAC, Cotonou, Benin
`atchomeathanase@gmail.com,tossafrantz@gmail.com,avianou@yahoo.fr`
[2] Department of Electrical and Information Engineering, Politecnico di Bari,
Bari, Italy
`{sherazi,alfredo.grieco}@poliba.it`
[3] Institut de Mathématiques et de Sciences Physiques(IMSP)/UAC,
Porto-Novo, Benin
`bidossessi.alahassa@gmail.com`
[4] RFW-Universität of Bonn, Technische Universität München, Munich, Germany
`oscar.edoh@gmail.com`

Abstract. A narrow-band system introduced in Release 13 of 3GPP has recently gain momentum to support a range of IoT use-cases. Narrowband-Internet of Things (NB-IoT) comes with low-cost devices characterized by extremely low power consumption, offering a battery life of more than 10 years, and broad radio coverage to target tens of kilometers, but on the cost of low data rate and higher end-to-end latency. NB-IoT can be deployed in three different modes of operation; standalone, in-band, and within the guard-band of existing LTE carrier. In this paper, a hybrid network model embracing both NB-IoT and D2D technologies has been introduced. we first present an analytical framework to derive analytical rate expressions for D2D in NB-IoT networks. Then, the performance gains of network model are investigated through numerical evaluations that demonstrate the superiority of proposed model over the traditional NB-IoT network.

Keywords: NB-IoT networks · Cellular networks · Spectrum sharing · Stochastic geometry

1 Introduction

The 3rd Generation Partnership Project has latterly introduced a number of key features to support a variety of IoT use-cases in its latest release 13 [1]. The main purpose of these features is to improve the existing for mobile Communications [2] and LTE (Long-Term Evolution) [3], respectively, in order to better serve for

R. Zitouni et al. (Eds.): AFRICOMM 2019, LNICST 311, pp. 154–165, 2020.
https://doi.org/10.1007/978-3-030-41593-8_11

rapid deployment as well as for the best use case of the Internet of Things. A third track, NB-IoT [4] as well shares these objectives as well. NB-IoT is a new narrowband IoT system built on the top of existing LTE framework: it possible to reuse the same hardware while sharing the LTE spectrum [5,6]. It can be deployed into three different modes of operation: stand-alone, in-band , and within the guard-band of an existing LTE carrier. In stand-alone deployments, NB-IoT can occupy one GSM channel while for in-band and guard-band deployments, it will use one or more physical resource blocks (PRBs) of LTE (180 kHz). The low-cost devices, high coverage, long device battery life and massive capacity with relaxed latency are some of the major design considerations of NB-IoT [6,7] (see Fig. 1).

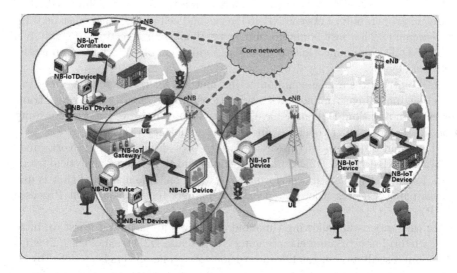

Fig. 1. Hybrid network model embracing NB-IoT and D2D communications coexisting with cellular networks.

For NB-IoT networks deployment , one or more PRBs are reserved, for example In-band mode of operations. The following four access modes can generally be identified in NB-IoT network:

Direct Access to an Evolved NodeB: An NB-IoT device can joint an eNB in hybrid networks without an intermediate device that is ordinary communication. Although this is the easiest direct access method, it can lead eNB congestion due to the large number of NB-IoT devices on the hybrid network.

Gateway Access: NB-IoT devices can benefit from cellular connectivity via NB-IoT gateways. An NB-IoT gateway is a dedicated device with features different from those of conventional NB-IoT objects. NB-IoT gateways transmit data between eNBs and a group of NB-IoT objects but do not generate their own data traffic. This NB-IoT gateway can be used by connecting a set of NB-IoT objects. This NB-IoT gateway can be used to connect a set of NB-IoT objects.

NB-IoT Device Coordinator Access: In some cases, adjacent NB-IoT devices can be grouped together to reduce redundant signaling and avoid congestion. A group-derived NB-IoT device can act as a coordinator to communicate with eNB, acting as a temporary NB-IoT gateway for its group. This access mode minimizes the power consumption of NB-IoT devices and extends the life of devices with battery constraints.

UE Access: NB-IoT devices can obtain connectivity via a cellular UE. Secondly, interoperability between NB-IoT users and cell phone users must be taken into account. This last configuration is particularly interesting to analyse in light of D2D communication technologies, which enable direct communication between devices.

D2D introduces a new communication method for commercial services that are close, including social network applications, public security, local data transfer [8,9]. In addition, D2D may have benefits such as improved energy consumption, increased cellular coverage, and spectral efficiency [10,11].

The main objectives of this article are to provides a hybrid network model embracing NB-IoT and D2D Communications and to develop a analytical framework for the analysis with a performance evaluation. The main tool that is used in this paper study is stochastic geometry, namely the Poisson Point Processes (PPP).

In this paper, the following threefold objectives are achieved. First we introduce a hybrid network model embracing NB-IoT and D2D technologies, in which a random distribution of Euclidean positions of mobile objects is modeled by the Poisson Point Process (PPP) [13,14]. Second, we present an analytical framework and third, we derive analytical rate expressions for D2D communications in NB-IoT networks.

The paper is organized as follows: In Sect. 2, we provide more details on the joint adoption of D2D and NB-IoT technologies. We introduce a hybrid network model embracing NB-IoT and D2D technologies in Sect. 3, in which the random and unpredictable distributions, mainly in Euclidean spaces of mobile users are modeled by PPP. While an analytical framework to derive analytical rate or throughput expressions for D2D in NB-IoT networks is presented in Sect. 4. In the last spring, concluding remarks are mentioned in the Sect. 5.

2   Background and Related Work

2.1   D2D Communication

D2D communication in traditional cellular networks is defined as direct communication between two mobile users with a proximity distance without passing through the eNB. In [15], Doppler *et al.* demonstrated that D2D communications supported, by a cellular infrastructure, can contribute to four types of profits. The communication between nearby devices can allow a very high bit rate, low delays and high energy consumption. Secondly, the jump gain refers to the use of a single link in D2D mode rather than the use of an uplink and downlink resource when exchanging between an device and eNB in cellular mode. Third, the re-use gain implies that radio resources can be used simultaneously by cellular links and D2D links, thus reinforcing the re-use factor even the re-use system. Finally, the matching gain refers to the degree of selection freedom of the UEs communicating with the eNB and UE pairs using a direct link of the same time and the same frequency resources [16,17].

Based on the spectrum usage of D2D users, D2D communications are classified into two groups: in-band D2D communications and out-band D2D communications. In in-band D2D communications, D2D terminals use licensed spectrum. The in-band communications can further be divided into underlay and overlay. Underlay D2D communications occur where cellular and D2D nodes share the same spectrum. On the contrary, overlay D2D communications eliminate intra-cell interference between cellular service and D2D communications by dividing the licensed spectrum into two part through orthogonal channel assignment. Out-band D2D communications use unlicensed spectrum which eliminates the interference between D2D and cellular communication [17,18].

Currently, several research projects have focused on D2D communication, using stochastic geometry. In [19], Xin *et al.* develop a model to analyze the performance of hierarchical data transmissions in the D2D underlying network based on spatio-temporal mathematical tools, the work conducted in [20] proposed a poisson point process model to design an interference-free network. Subhankar *et al.* [21] develop a stochastic geometry namely Poisson point process-based network modelling and performance analysis in heterogeneous wireless network and Basem *et al.* [22] consider an analytical approach to evaluate the outage behavior of the (D2D) communication, which is underlaid with hybrid networks, as an enabling technology for IoT.

2.2 NB-IoT In-Band Cellular Networks

Deployment of NB-IoT can be done in three different modes of operation: guard-band, stand-alone and in-band. In this article, we focus on the mode of operation in the band in existing cellular networks. For NB-IoT in-band operation, one or more PRB LTEs are reserved for NB-IoT. A NB-IoT carrier intended to facilitate the initial synchronization of the UE is called an anchor carrier. For example, in a 10 MHz LTE carrier, the NB-IoT anchor carriers are 4, 9, 14, 30, 35, 40, 45 [23,24].

Figure 2 shows the different options of NB-IoT deployment. The PRB of the bandwidth above the DC subcarrier (PRB# 25) is centered at 97.5 kHz. The DC LTE subcarrier is placed on the 100 kHz frame, the center of the PRB# 25 is located at 2.5 kHz from the nearest 100 kHz grid. The same is for PRB# PRB# 30, PRB# 35, PRB# 40 and PRB# 45 which are also centered at 2.5 kHz from the nearest 100 kHz grid [24, 25]. A PRB that does not have a value greater than 7.5 kHz of the 100 kHz frame can be considered and used as the NB-IoT anchor carrier. In addition, an NB-IoT anchor carrier should not be one of the six LTE carrier middle PRBs [24, 25]. In fact, these six middle PRBs are occupied by the LTE synchronization and diffusion channels, which makes their use difficult by the NB-IoT.

The eNB power is used between the LTE and the NB-IoT with a better possibility to use the increase of the spectral power density. This sharing allows for more efficient use of the spectrum for better performance and continuous capacity growth, as more devices can be added to the system faster and easier.

Currently, several research projects have focused on the deployment of NB-IoT. In [26], Nitin textit et al. uses existing LTE infrastructure by studying the deployment of NB-IoT, the work in [27] develops a monitoring system to monitor the drop rate and volume of a patient's real-time infusion losses. They also discuss future challenges for building a smart hospital using IoTs.

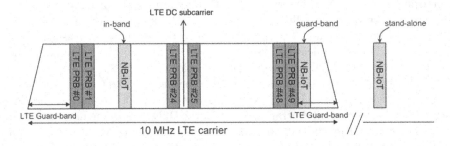

Fig. 2. Examples of NB-IoT deployments [28].

3   System Model

3.1   Network Model

We consider hybrid networks consisting of both NB-IoT, cellular, cellular D2D, and NB-IoT D2D links. Based on [15, 18, 28], we consider a circular cell of radius R with an evolved NodeB (eNBs) equipped with an omni-directional antenna located at the center of each cell that consists N_n orthogonal NB-IoT users, N_{dn} orthogonal NB-IoT D2D links , N_c orthogonal cellular users and N_{dc} orthogonal cellular D2D links uniformly distributed in the cell. The Fig. 3 show the system model and approximate interference analysis. Specifically, a fraction β of the spectrum is allocated to the cellular D2D objects data transmission and the remaining $1 - \beta$ is allocated to the cellular objects data transmission, where $0 \leq \beta \leq 1$. In the same way, a fraction γ of the spectrum is allocated to the NB-IoT D2D objects data transmission and remains $1 - \gamma$ is allocated to NB-IoT objects data transmission, where $0 \leq \gamma \leq 1$. Founded on [29–31], denoting by

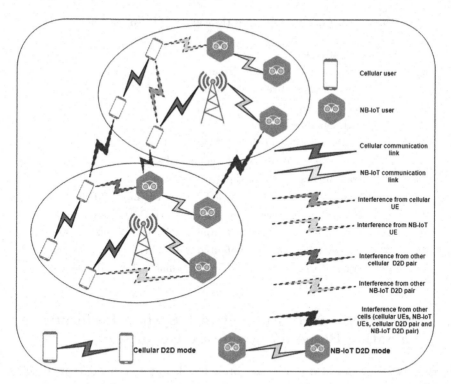

Fig. 3. Network model embracing NB-IoT technologies and D2D communications

$1/\lambda_b$ in the hybrid networks the area of a hexagonal cell, λ_b can be regarded as the average number of (eNB) per unit area. The spatial PPP corresponds to a uniform distribution of NB-IoT users and cellular users in the hybrid network, which is the baseline assumption for many mobile system studies [29]. Denote by $\Phi \in \mathbb{R}^2$ the unmarked PPP $\{X_i\}$ with intensity λ_1. The transmit user equipment (NB-IoT UEs and Cellular UEs) are randomly distributed and modeled by an independently market Poisson Point Process PPP denoted as $\{\tilde{\Phi}_1, \tilde{\Phi}_2\}$ with $\tilde{\Phi}_1 = \{(X_i, \delta_i, L_i, P_i)\}$ and $\tilde{\Phi}_2 = \{(Y_j, \delta_j, L_j, P_j)\}$. where X_i denote the spatial locations of NB-IoT UEs. Each UE has its associated defined parameters that collectively form a marked PPP $\tilde{\Phi}$. L_i is the distance between the ith NB-IoT UE and P_i is the transmit power of the ith NB-IoT UE. The parameter δ_i indicates the inherent type of the ith transmit NB-IoT UE which may be a potential NB-IoT D2D UE with probability $q_1 = \mathbb{P}(\delta_i = 1)$ or a NB-IoT UE with probability $1 - q_1$, where $q_1 \in [0, 1]$. For national simplicity, we denote by L_n the link length between a typical NB-IoT UE and the associated eNB. Similarly, L_{dn} represents the link lengh between a typical NB-IoT D2D UE and NB-IoT D2D receiver UE.

The parameters Y_j, L_j, P_j, δ_j in cellular networks respect the same assumptions as those of NB-IoT networks. The notations and simulation parameters used are summarized in Tables 1 and 2.

Table 1. Set of notations used throughout the proposed model

Parameter	Description
δ_i	Inherent type of the ith NB-IoT UEs
δ_j	Inherent type of the ith cellular UEs
β	Spectrum factor
α	Path-loss exponent
X_i	Spatial locations of the ith NB-IoT UEs
Y_i	Spatial locations of the ith cellular UEs
P_i	Transmitting power of the i-th UEs
P_n	Transmitting power of NB-IoT UEs operating in NB-IoT mode
P_{dc}	Transmitting power of potential NB-IoT D2D in D2D mode
P_{dn}	Transmitting power of potential cellular D2D in D2D mode
$\bar{P}_{dc}$	Transmitting power of potential NB-IoT D2D in cellular mode
$\bar{P}_{dn}$	Transmitting power of potential cellular D2D in NB-IoT mode

4   Framework for Hybrid Network System Performance Evaluation Based on Stochastic Geometric

In this section, analytical results are presented laying the foundation stone for the paper under study of underlay D2D in-band deployed in legacy cellular networks.

Mobile transmitters including mobiles NB-IoT devices and Potential NB-IoT D2D devices in NB-IoT operation mode form a PPP Φ_n with intensity λ_n :

$$\lambda_n = (1 - q_1)\lambda_1 + q_1\lambda_1\mathbb{P}(D_1 \geq \mu_1) \tag{1}$$

Potential NB-IoT D2D devices in D2D operation mode form a Φ_{dn}, Poisson Point Processes with intensity λ_{dn}

$$\lambda_{dn} = q_1\lambda_1\mathbb{P}(D_1 < \mu_1) \tag{2}$$

From (2) and (3) we obtain:

$$\lambda_n + \lambda_{dn} = \lambda_1 \tag{3}$$

We assume $\lambda_1 \geq \lambda_b$, which is reasonable as the uplink transmitter density is usually larger than the (eNB) density. At the same time, for cellular devices and cellular D2D devices in cellular mode form a poisson point processes Φ_c with intensity λ_c :

$$\lambda_c = (1 - q_2)\lambda_2 + q_2\lambda_2\mathbb{P}(D_2 \geq \mu_2) \tag{4}$$

Potential cellular D2D devices in D2D mode form Poisson Point Processes Φ_{dc} with intensity λ_{dc}

$$\lambda_{dc} = q_2\lambda_2\mathbb{P}(D_2 < \mu_2) \tag{5}$$

Table 2. Simulation/numerical parameters

System assumptions	Value
Density of macro cells	$(\pi 500^2)^{-1}\text{m}^{-2}$
Density of UEs	$10 * (\pi 500^2)^{-1}\text{m}^{-2}$
Potential NB-IoT D2D UEs q_1	0.2
mode selection threshold μ_1	200 m
ℸ, Aloha access probability	1
n, spectrum partition factor	0.2
β, spectrum access factor	1
sub-channels number	1
Value of l-th moment	1
$SINR_m$	10 dB
B	1 MHZ
Path Loss exponent α (Urban Area)	2,7–3,5

From (5) and (6), we obtain:

$$\lambda_c + \lambda_{dc} = \lambda_2 \tag{6}$$

In this paper, we use the channel inversion for power control, *i.e.*, $P_i = L_i^{\alpha}$, where $\alpha > 2$ denotes the path loss exponent. Similarly, we use P_n, P_{dn}, P_c, and P_{dc} to denote the transmit powers variables of NB-IoT users, potential NB-IoT D2D users, cellular users and potential cellular users, respectively.

4.1 Spectral Efficiency

Either a typical pair receiver and transmitter scrambled by a type of heterogeneous interference. We focus on frequency narrowband channels. Under these assumptions above, $SNIR$ for the two modes:

$$SINR = \frac{P_i L_i^{-\alpha} G_i}{I + \sigma^2} \tag{7}$$

where P_i is a transmitting power, $L_i^{-\alpha_i}$ is a link length for NB-IoT and G_i is a channel fading, and interference power I. In our model networks we have a multiple interference, interference due to mobile NB-IoT UEs I_n in NB-IoT mode, interference due to other NB-IoT D2D UEs in NB-IoT D2D mode I_{dn}, interference due to cellular UEs I_c and interference due to cellular D2D UEs I_{dc}.

In this paper we focus our study from D2D in NB-IoT deployed in legacy cellular networks. We consider channel inversion, i.e $P_i L_i^{-\alpha_i} = 1$, so we obtain $P_i L_i^{-\alpha_i} G_0 = G_0$. Based on result given by [29–31], the following model can be derived:

$$I = I_n + I_{dn} + I_c + I_{dc} \tag{8}$$

Lemma 1: The received $SNIR_{dn}$ and $SNIR_n$ for NB-IoT D2D mode and NB-IoT mode our model are given by

$$SINR_{dn} = \frac{G_0}{I_{dn}^{D2D^{mode}} + \sigma^2} \tag{9}$$

where

$$I_{dn}^{D2D^{mode}} = \sum_{X_i \in \Phi_{n,i}} P_{n,i} G_i ||X_i||^{-\alpha} +$$

$$\sum_{X_i \in \Phi_{dn,i}\backslash\{o\}} P_{n,i} G_i ||X_i||^{-\alpha} + \sum_{X_j \in \Phi_{c,j}} P_{c,j} G_j ||X_j||^{-\alpha}$$

$$+ \sum_{X_j \in \Phi_{dc,j}} P_{c,j} G_j ||X_j||^{-\alpha}$$

and

$$SINR_n = \frac{G_0}{I_n^{NB-IoT^{mode}} + \sigma^2} \tag{10}$$

where

$$I_n^{NB-IOT^{mode}} = \sum_{X_i \in \Phi_n\backslash\{o\}} P_{n,i} G_i ||X_i||^{-\alpha} +$$

$$\sum_{X_i \in \Phi_{dn}} P_{n,i} G_i ||X_i||^{-\alpha} + \sum_{X_j \in \Phi_c} P_c, G_j ||X_j||^{-\alpha}$$

$$+ \sum_{X_j \in \Phi_{dc}} P_{c,j} G_j ||X_j||^{-\alpha}$$

Corollary 1: Suppose $SNIR = \frac{P_i L_i^{-\alpha_i} G_0}{I + \sigma^2}$, where $P_i L_i^{-\alpha_i} = 1$, $G_0 \sim exp(1)$ denote Rayleigh fading, I denote interference powers and σ^2 denote the noise power.I, G_i are independent and we have:

$$\mathbb{E}[log(1 + SINR)] = \int_0^\infty \frac{e^{-\sigma^2 x}}{1+x} \mathscr{L}_I(x) dx \tag{11}$$

where, $\mathscr{L}_I(s) = \mathbb{E}[e^{-sI}]$ denotes the Laplace transform of I .

Next we define the effective throughput R, which combines modulation and codding schemes in the physical layer and multiple access protocols in the medium access control layer. It could be expressed :

$$R = \mathbb{E}[\tau.log(1 + SNIR)] \tag{12}$$

where *tau* indicates the time or frequency on the one hand or the time and frequency resources on the other hand accessed in hybrid networks by the typical link.

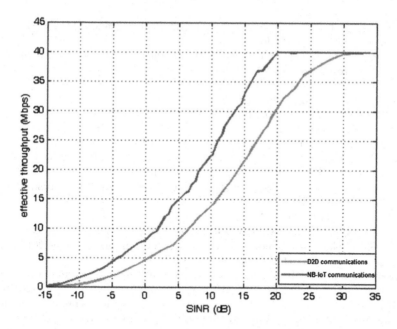

Fig. 4. Effective throughput for NB-IoT and D2D communications in system model

Figure 4 shows the effective throughput of NB-IoT and D2D NB-IoT in a hybrid network model embracing NB-IoT and D2D Communications. The effective throughput of NB-IoT device is much greater than the throughput of D2D NB-IoT device. This effective throughput of D2D NB-IoT in this hybrid network contributes to improve the data transmission, although it is impacted by multiple interference.

5   Conclusion

In this paper, a D2D network overlaid on an uplink cellular network was considered where the locations of the mobile UEs (e.g., NB-IoT and Cellular UEs) as well as the eNBs were modeled as PPP. A novel stochastic geometric approach was exploited for evaluating the D2D network performance in hybrid network presenting an analytical framework and derived analytical rate expressions for D2D scenarios in NB-IoT networks. The numerical results demonstrate the performance gains of D2D communications in comparison with conventional NB-IoT networks.

References

1. Holma, H., Toskala, A., Reunanen, J.: LTE Small Cell Optimization: 3GPP Evolution to Release 13. Wiley, Hoboken (2015)

2. Dahlman, E., Parkvall, S., Sköld, J.: 4G: LTE/LTE-Advanced for Mobile Broadband. Academic Press, Oxford (2011)
3. Stuckmann, P.: The GSM Evolution: Mobile Packet Data Services. John Wiley and Sons, West Sussex (2003)
4. Qualcomm, Incorporated, "Narrowband IoT (NB-IoT)," RP-151621, 3GPP TSG RAN Meeting 69, September 2015. http://www.3gpp.org/ftp/tsg_ran/TSG_RAN/TSGR_69/Docs/RP-151621.zip
5. Ratasuk, R., Vejlgaard, B., Mangalvedhe, N., Ghosh, A.: NB-IoT system for M2M communication. In: IEEE WCNC, Doha, April 2016
6. Nair, K.K., Abu-Mahfouz, A.M., Lefophane, S.: Analysis of the narrow band internet of things (NB-IoT) technology. In: 2019 Conference on Information Communications Technology and Society (ICTAS), 02 May 2019 (2019). https://doi.org/10.1109/ICTAS.2019.8703630
7. Vejlgaard, B., Lauridsen, M., Nguyen, H., Kovacs, I.Z., Mogensen, P., Sorensen, M.: Coverage and capacity analysis of Sigfox, LoRa, GPRS, and NB-IoT. In: 2017 IEEE 85th Vehicular Technology Conference (VTC Spring), 4–7 June 2017 (2017). https://doi.org/10.1109/VTCSpring.2017.8108666
8. Corson, M., Laroia, R., Li, J., Park, V., Richardson, T., Tsirtsis, G.: Toward proximity-aware internetworking. IEEE Wirel. Commun. 17(6), 26–33 (2010)
9. 3GPP TR 22.803 V1.0.0, 3rd generation partnership project; technical specification group SA; feasibility study for proximity services (ProSe)(release 12), Technical Report, August 2012
10. Fodor, G., et al.: Design aspects of network assisted device-to-devicecommunications. IEEE Commun. Mag. 50(3), 170–177 (2012)
11. Lin, X., Andrews, J.G., Ghosh, A., Ratasuk, R.: An overview of 3GPP device-to-device proximity services. IEEE Commun. Mag. 52(4), 40–48 (2014)
12. TR 45.820 v13.1.0, Cellular system support for Ultra low complexity and low throughput internet of things, November 2015. http://www.3gpp.org/ftp/Specs/archive/45_series/45.820/45820-d10.zip
13. Andrews, J.G., BAccelli, F., Ganti, R.: A tractable approach to coverage and rate in cellular networks. IEEE Trans. Wirel. Commun. 12(11), 3122–3134 (2011)
14. Lin, X., Ganti, R.K., Fleming, P.J., Andrews, J.G.: Towards understanding the fundamentals of mobility in cellular networks. IEEE Trans. Wirel. Commun. 12(4), 1686–1698 (2013)
15. Doppler, K., Rime, M., Wijting, C., Ribeiro, C.B., Hugl, K.: Device-to-Device communication as an underlay to LTE-advanced networks. IEEE Commun. Mag. 47(12), 42–49 (2009)
16. Doppler, K., Rinne, M., et al.: Device-to-Device communication as an underlay to LTE-advanced networks. IEEE Commun. Mag. 47(12), 42–49 (2009)
17. Corson, M.S., Li, J., Park, V., et al.: Toward proximity aware internetworking. IEEE Wirel. Commun. 17(6), 26–33 (2010)
18. Wei, L., Hu, R.Q., Qian, Y., Wu, G.: Enable device-to-device communications underlaying cellular networks: challenges and research aspects. IEEE Commun. Mag. 52(6), 90–96 (2014)
19. Xin, J., Zhu, Q., Liang, G., Zhang, T.: Performance analysis of D2D underlying cellular networks based on dynamic priority queuing model. J. Mag. 7, 27479–27489 (2019). https://doi.org/10.1109/ACCESS.2019.2894678
20. Qamar, F., Dimyati, K., Hindia, M.N., Noordin, K.A., Amiri, I.S.: A stochastically geometrical poisson point process approach for the future 5G D2D enabled cooperative cellular network. J. Mag. 7, 60465–60485 (2019)

21. Chakrabarti, S., Das, S.: Poisson point process-based network modelling and performance analysis of multi-hop D2D chain relay formation in heterogeneous wireless network. Int. J. Commun. Netw. Distrib. Syst. **22**(1), 98–122 (2018). https://doi.org/10.1504/IJCNDS.2019.096522

22. ElHalawany, B.M., Ruby, R., Wu, K.: D2D communication for enabling internet-of-things: outage probability analysis. IEEE Trans. Veh. Technol. **68**(3), 2332–2345 (2019). https://doi.org/10.1109/TVT.2019.2891648

23. Wang, Y.P.E., Lin, X., et al.: A primary on 3GPP narrowband internet of things (NB-IoT). arXiv:1606.04171 (2016)

24. Ratasuk, R., Mangalvedhe, N., Ghosh, A.: Overview of LTE enhancements for cellular IoT. In: IEEE PIMRC, Hong Kong, September 2015

25. Wang, Y.P.E., et al.: A Primer on 3GPP narrowband internet of things (NB-IoT) networking and internet architecture (cs.NI); Information Theory (cs.IT). arXiv:1606.04171 [cs.NI]. Accessed 13 June 2016

26. Mangalvedhe, N., Ratasuk, R., Ghosh, A.: NB-IoT deployment study for low power wide area cellular IoT. In: 2016 IEEE 27th Annual International Symposium on Personal, Indoor, and Mobile Radio Communications (PIMRC), 4–8 September 2016 (2016). https://doi.org/10.1109/PIMRC.2016.7794567

27. Zhang, H., Li, J., Wen, B., Xun, Y., Liu, J.: Connecting intelligent things in smart hospitals using NB-IoT. IEEE Internet Things J. **5**(3), 1550–1560 (2018). https://doi.org/10.1109/JIOT.2018.2792423

28. Lin, X., Andrews, J.G., Ghosh, A.: Spectrum sharing for device-to-device communication in cellular networks. IEEE Trans. Wirel. Commun. **13**(12), 6727–6740 (2014)

29. Baccelli, F., Blaszczyszyn, B.: Stochastic geometry and wireless networks - Part I: Theory. Found. Trends Netw. **3**(3–4), 249–449 (2009)

30. Stoyan, D., Kendall, W., Mecke, J.: Stochastic Geometry and its Applications. Wiley, New York (1995)

31. Lin, X., Andrews, J.G.: A general approach to SINR-based performance metrics with application to D2D and carrier aggregation. In: Proceedings of Asilomar Conference on Signals, Systems, and Computers, pp. 1–5, November 2013

Data Management and IT Applications

Laws and Regulations on Big Data Management: The Case of South Africa

Patrick Sello[1], Antoine Bagula[2(✉)], and Olasupo Ajayi[2]

[1] Department of Information Systems, University of the Western Cape,
Cape Town 7535, South Africa
[2] Department of Computer Science, University of the Western Cape,
Cape Town 7535, South Africa
abagula@uwc.ac.za

Abstract. A growing global trend has been witnessed in many developing countries where efforts and resources are been invested in advancement of electronic health information. The expectation is to improve the quality of health care, increase universal health coverage, and reduce both Legal Cases and healthcare costs in a changing world where data collected while providing healthcare produces big data sets which can provide useful insights for the advancement of healthcare services. The challenge is a greater risk for legal regulations to keep up with the accelerated global changes resulting from Big Data, and loss of information privacy created by digital transformation. In some countries, legal, privacy and ethical issues related to use and access to personal health data still causes foreseeable challenges. This article reviews the South African laws and regulations in handling, processing, storing, accessing and big data analytics on digital health data.

Keywords: Big data management · Laws · Regulations · Healthcare

1 Introduction

The digital revolution has changed how modern medicine is practiced as the use of information technology in healthcare delivery has grown rapidly in recent years. With it, volumes of digital health data are generated; which in turn improves the delivery of healthcare services, helps to address easy access to public healthcare, reduces information duplications and challenges faced by health professionals. A digital health record is the digital version of the patient's health record. Digital records are becoming common practice as more digital records are being created [2]. The creation of digital data records can assist in evidence based medical practice [4]. Privacy of information collected during healthcare processes is necessary because of the sensitivity content, stipulation of various legislations and protection of the patient's identity. With growing demand on the need for remote consolidation of digital health data, big data analytics, artificial intelligence and machine learning, the current legislative frameworks are no

R. Zitouni et al. (Eds.): AFRICOMM 2019, LNICST 311, pp. 169–179, 2020.
https://doi.org/10.1007/978-3-030-41593-8_12

longer able to cover and protect patient privacy. Most of the machine resources required for big data analytic, machine learning and artificial intelligence are only available in Cloud computing. However, this requirement for Cloud computing has encounter resistance within the public health sector due to legislative restriction on where and how digital health data can be stored and analysed. The management and access to digital health data requires [5]:

- Protection of information security, confidentiality and patient privacy always.
- Promoting information governance consensus among all stakeholders to use information better.
- Getting the basics right in terms of infrastructure, connectivity, basic ICT literacy, human resources and affordability planning.
- Taking an incremental approach.
- Adhering to the NHIS/SA principles for information management

Applicable security technologies exist and have proved effective in the banking and military sectors but experience is lacking to ascertain whether current technologies are satisfactory for health care. As yet, no model security implementations exist in any clinical computing environment, [6] although awareness of risks and of possible technical solutions is increasing [7]. This article will review the South African laws and regulations in handling, processing, storing, accessing and big data analytics on digital health data. The rest of this paper is arranged as follows, in Sect. 2 regulations for collection of digital health records are discussed, while Sect. 3 discusses regulations for processing of digital health records. In Sect. 4, focuses on storage of digital health records. Sections 5 and 6 focus on data management and access to digital healthcare data respectively. Section 7 discusses big data analytics in healthcare, while Sect. 8 focuses on integration and interoperability. Conclusion and potential future works are discussed in Sect. 9.

2   Digital Health Data Creation and Regulations

The benefits of digital health record include providing accurate, up-to-date, and complete information about patients at the point of care [2]. This:

- Enables quick access to patient records for more coordinated and efficient care
- Allows for sharing electronic information with patients and other clinicians in a secure manner
- Helps providers diagnose patients more effectively, thereby reducing medical errors.
- Improves patient-provider interaction and communication, as well as health care convenience
- Enables safer and possibly more reliable drug prescription.
- Helps promote legible, accurate and complete documentation as well as streamlined coding and billing

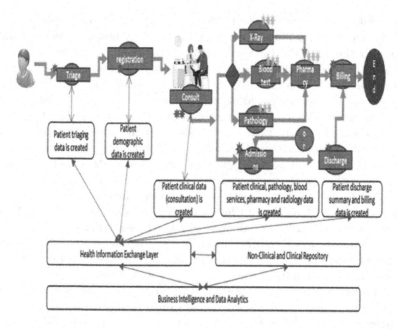

Fig. 1. Patient visit at academic hospital

- Enhances privacy and security of patient data
- Helps providers improve productivity and work-life balance
- Enables providers improve efficiency and meet their business goals
- Reduces costs by decreasing paperwork and duplicated tests.

Digital health data is created at every point of care within the patient journey in a hospital. Figure 1 depicts a high-level process flow of a patient's visit to an academic hospital.

The figure shows that data is created at triage, patient registration, consultation, radiology, pathology, admission and at the pharmacy. Data created in triage mostly comprises of patients' vitals which forms part of the clinical record. This data is collected by the healthcare professional. A Health Information System (HIS), is used by the healthcare professional to create, capture and collect digital health data during consultation with the patient. The system is used for patient administration, billing and collecting clinical data. The National Health Act 61 of 2003 Sect. 2, stipulate that, no health services can be provided to a patient without informed consent of the patient, unless the patient is unable to provide an informed consent. According to the Protection of Personal Information Act, 2013, a consent is defined as "any voluntary, specific and informed expression of will in terms of which permission is given for the processing of personal information" [10]. The Act is clear on the right of the patient being required for the data to be created, captured and collected. Patient demographics data is collected during registration, this data is used to identify the patient, provide next of kin, verify the economic status of the patient or the person responsible for the payment of the services, to be rendered. The registration process to capture, create and collect digital health data is carried-out by hospital clerks or administrators. Section 14 of the National Health Act stipulates that "all information concerning a patient, including information relating to his or her health status, treatment or stay in a health establishment, is confidential" [7]. However, the Act allows for the following exceptions to this general rule: (a) when the user consents to that disclosure in writing; (b) when a court order or any law requires that disclosure; or (c) when the non-disclosure of the information represents a serious threat to public health. The Act is limited on processes for vetting people who are capturing, creating and collecting digital health data. This has led to a wide range of abuse and misuse of digital health data by academic institutions, NGO's, NPO's, government departments and other independent agents. As an example, an international NGO which had a partnership with Gauteng Department of Health (GDoH), was allowed to use its own employees to assist the department in capturing, creating and collecting digital health data of patients with chronic diseases. It was later discovered that, the NGO used most the data for research on behalf of international pharmaceutical companies. The NGO was rendering a legitimate service as agreed with GDoH, however, because of shortfalls within the legislative framework it is a difficult process to provide vetting for people responsible for collecting digital health data. The confusion and vulnerability is further exacerbated by the same National Health Act, which also states that, "a healthcare professional or healthcare worker that has access to the health records of a patient can disclose such personal information to any other healthcare professional as is necessary for any legitimate purpose within the ordinary course and scope of his or her duties where such access or disclosure is in the interests of the patient." This make digital health data privacy difficult to police and monitor adherence regulations [8].

3   Digital Health Data Ingestion (Processing) and Regulations

The European Union's General Data Protection Regulation (GDPR) states that, "higher protection standards for health data and delineates a variety of definitions and conditions that apply to such data," it highlights the required conditions that must be meet for health data to be processed [11]. The conditions include explicit consent of the patient, clear purpose of why the data must be processed and public interest. The ingestion of digital health data starts as soon as the data is collected using the Health Information System (HIS). Health information technology apply information processing tools both hardware and software to the storage, retrieval, sharing, and use of health care information, data, and knowledge for communication and decision making [13]. Health Information Systems thus facilitate the process of storing and retrieval of individual records with the aid of computers interconnected through a computer network. Once the digital health data is captured (as described in the previous section), a patient unique identifier is generated and allocated to the patient. The patient unique identifier becomes the Master Patient Index (MPI) which forms part of Enterprise Master Patient Index (EMPI). An EMPI is a patient database used by Healthcare facilities to maintain current and accurate digital health data across multiple healthcare systems. The allocated patient unique identifier is presented only once across all healthcare systems. South African National Department of Health has recently launched a Health Patient Register System (HPRS), the system is aimed to process digital health data and create single patient identifiers across the country which will allow patient to receive healthcare services across provinces. Once the data has been processed, there are multiple storage platforms which are in use and available for the data to be stored. With respect to storage, the Protection of Personal Information Act 2013, stipulate that, the responsible party must ensure that the conditions set out in Chap. 3 condition 1 of the Act is met "and all the measures that give effect to such conditions, are complied with at the time of the determination of the purpose and means of the processing and during the processing itself." The Act goes further to stipulate that, "the data must be processed lawfully, in a reasonable manner that does not infringe the privacy of the data subject and only be processed if, given the purpose for which it is processed, it is adequate, relevant and not excessive". Section 2 of the National Health Act covers only research related data, there is no clear guidelines or regulated related to how general digital health data must be processed. At the international level, systems for surveillance and monitoring of diseases and epidemics, and initiatives to share knowledge and data for health research and health development are progressing. WHO continues to track the adoption of eHealth and Universal Health Coverage (UHC) goals and measuring the achievement of Sustainable Development Goals (SDGs). Two particular work areas continue to advance eHealth agenda in this respect: the Health Data Collaborative and the implementation of the WHO Framework for Integrated People-Centred Services [15]. In some countries there is still a need to build a strong eHealth foundation including necessary infrastructure, standards, legislation and workforce. Rules and regulation are very limited on how digital health data can be processed and the legality of how digital health data must be processed. Legal, privacy and ethical issues related to use and access to personal health data still causes foreseeable challenges in many countries. However,"WHO is expanding its focus on digital health, the Organisation has been working in this area for years, for example, through the development of the eHealth Strategy Toolkit in 2012, published in collaboration with International Telecommunications Union (ITU)" [3]. Because of these gaps within the legislative framework, academic institutions across the world have found ways of processing digital health data for research purpose which is collected from public healthcare facilities, while absolving themselves of any form of responsibility as stipulated in the Protection of Personal Information Act.

4   Storage of Digital Data

The National Health Act, stipulate that, "Subject to National Archives of South Africa Act, 1996 (Act No. 43 of 1996), and the Promotion of Access to Information Act, 2000 (Act No. 2 of 2000), the person in charge of a health establishment must ensure that a health record containing such information as may be prescribed is created and maintained at that health establishment for every user of health services."

Figure 2 depicts multiple stage where digital health data is stored. The figure provides a high-level view of were the data is generated versus stored. All the data generated during consultation with the patient is a relational database linked to a module within the HIS. Different types of digital health data are created at each stage, the data is later stored in a clinical repository which provides access to data analytic, big data and data visualization. Condition 3 Section 14 of the Protection of Personal Information Act stipulate that, "Subject to subsections (2) and (3), records of personal information must not be retained any longer than is necessary for achieving the purpose for which the information was collected or subsequently processed, unless;

(a) retention of the record is required or authorised by law;
(b) the responsible party reasonably requires the record for lawful purposes related to its functions or activities;
(c) retention of the record is required by a contract between the parties thereto; or
(d) the data subject or a competent person where the data subject is a child has consented to the retention of the record".

This is in support of the National Health Act, which provides guidelines on how long health records can be kept in a healthcare facility. The Health Professional Council of South Africa (PCSA) offers the following guidance on the retention of medical records: (a) Records must be stored for 6 year after becoming dormant. (b) Records of people under 21 must be kept until they reach 21 years. (c) Mental health records must be kept until the death of the patient receiving treatment [17]. These regulations and guidelines were formulated on a paper-based records approach. These records had a limited time span, were prone to damage and required huge warehouse storage. Unlike paper-based records, digital health data can be stored and archived for many years in digital warehouses, data centres, Cloud storage and on-premise storage devices. Digital data can also be stored anywhere in the world if there is adequate connectivity, however, this creates a gap on legislative requirements on how and where the data is stored, and the duration for which such data can be stored. The legislative framework requires digital health data to be stored where the patient is receiving treatment. The Protection of Personal Information Act stipulate that, "no personal information which includes digital health data can be transferred outside the Republic unless, the third party who is the recipient of the information is subject to a law, binding corporate rules or binding agreement which provide an adequate level of protection". This means that, data cannot be shared outside the healthcare facility where the patient is receiving treatment. It also means that any form of international collaboration will not be possible. The major limitation to the framework is that, with the growing demand for more computer resources for big data analytics, machine learning and artificial intelligence, which Cloud

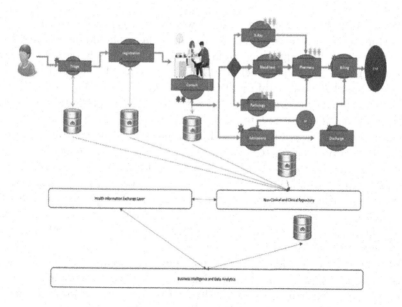

Fig. 2. Digital health data

computer can provide. Unfortunately, these computing power are hosted in first world developed countries, and because of legislative limitations digital health data cannot cross country boarders. This limitation is due to the failure of policy makers to accelerate digital transformation in public healthcare facilities. A gap has been however been created for academic intuitions to extract and collect digital health data. The approach is to provide an electronic health record system which is used by intern doctors to capture data related to patients, the intern doctors are incentivized by being able to use the collected data as portfolio of evidence(s) for their community service.

5   Data Management

Data integrity and quality of the data collected must be of high standard at all time. The data contains information about the medical history of the patient which must be accurate and updated whenever there is an encounter with the patient. The Protection of Personal Information Act provides legal guidelines on steps to ensure that the personal information is complete, accurate, not misleading and updated where necessary. In taking these steps, the responsible party must have regard to the purpose for which personal information is collected or further processed. Data Ownership is a legal and regulatory complex discussion. The health information is owned by the patient as directly prescribed in the Protection of Personal Information Act and Protection of Access to Information Act. The discussion has always been on the person responsible for creating the record, or where the record was created as been the custodians of the record.

"In the case of public health institutions, where records e.g. radiographs are the property of the institution, original records and images should be retained by the institution. Copies must however, be made available to the patient (or referring practitioner) on request for which a reasonable fee may be charged in terms of the Promotion of Access to Information Act (Act No. 2 of 2000)" Data Security is one of the difficult aspects associated with the creation of digital health data. The Nation Health Act stipulate that, "the person in charge of a health establishment in possession of a user's health records must set up control measures to prevent unauthorised access to those records and to the storage facility in which, or system by which, records are kept". The Protection of Person Information Act also puts the responsibility of securing personal records on the person responsible for the collecting the information. It further states that, reasonable technical and organisational measures must be put in place to prevent: (a) loss of, damage to or unauthorised destruction of personal information; and (b) unlawful access to or processing of personal information."

This can be done by identifying all reasonably foreseeable internal and external risks to personal information stored within the facility or organisation. The responsible party must have due regard to generally accepted information security practices and procedures which may apply to it generally or be required in terms of specific industry or professional rules and regulations.

6   Access to Digital Health Data

The Health Act states that, "no health care practitioner shall make information available to any third party without the written authorisation of the patient or a court order or where non-disclosure of the information would represent a serious threat to public health". This Act has an inherent limitation as it allows for health data to be disclose during legal matters, where non-disclosure of the medical information has a threat to public health and/or where it is in the interest of the wellbeing of the patient and there is a health risk to the patient if the information is not disclosed. Measures must therefore be put in place that will provide audit trail of any other person(s) who has access to the information and the purpose linked to that access.

7   Access for Big Data and Analytics

The introduction of Big Data has revolutionized how we manage, analyse and take advantage of data to provide healthcare and management decision making. Healthcare is one of the promising early gains in the use of big data for management decision making and planning. As data is collected within multiple healthcare systems in high volume, high velocity and high variety, it becomes para-important for deploying mechanisms for mining and analysing data. As an example, Discovery Holdings, a company which specialises in health and life insurance, has been using big data technology to promote healthier behaviour. The approach has been studied to produce the required outcomes base on a study conducted by RAND Europe [18]. There are couple of technological platforms such as Hadoop and Spark which can be can be used in the public healthcare for predictive analysis, real-time patient monitoring (with IoT), medical equipment monitoring (with IoT), Electronic Health Records (EHRs), genomics, Tracking of communicable disease in boarder crossing, reduction of re-admissions and building artificial intelligence models for early detection of cancers and other disease, etc. Most governments have not progressed in reshaping national policies to improve the use of big data while adhering to internal regulations on data privacy, confidentiality and security. According to the WHO's Global Observatory for eHealth, only 21 (17%) of the 125 Member States reported having a policy or strategy regulating the use of big data in their health sectors [19]. The responsibility of creating progressive legislation on big data has been left to academic institutions whose interest does not align with government policies on universal health coverage and digital health. However, even basic health data can be misused, potentially leading to discrimination, especially of the vulnerable populace [20].

8   Integration and Interoperability

There can be over 200 parties in a standard public healthcare environment, this creates standardisation challenges in the system and results in most systems and data being fragmented. As depicted in Fig. 1, data is created in multiple points and collected across systems which are incompatible to each other. The business process of generating such data are also not aligned and imputable. The Health Normative Standards provides a set of standards-based profiles which must guide any interoperability function within healthcare. It has been shown in multiple studies that, poor coordination of technology and lack of standards are limiting factors for facilitate collaboration. Standardisation of business processes within healthcare can assist in addressing such challenges. The traditional based regulations are limited when covering integration regulations.

9   Conclusion and Future Work

The continues increase of technology within the healthcare will require coordination across all stakeholders to ensure that benefits to healthcare are truly achieved [20]. Policy makers will have to review and make necessary amendments to realise full benefit of big data and data collaborations in healthcare. The answer lays in the interaction between institutions of higher learning and policy makers within government. There must be a strategy to coheres exiting academia knowledge that can be used to accelerate amendments of policies related to digital data privacy and collaboration analytics. The focus must be on getting the basics right, taking incremental approach, looking for early wins and advocating the benefits to healthcare. As an avenue for future research, the work presented in this paper in the South African context can be adapted to guiding policy in the implementation of cyberhealthcare systems [21–26] in both rural and urban areas of the world and especially in developing countries.

References

1. Barrows, R.C., Clayton, P.D.: Privacy, confidentiality, and electronic medical records. J. Am. Med. Inf. Assoc. **3**(2), 139–148 (1996). https://doi.org/10.1136/jamia.1996.96236282
2. Rouse, M.: "What is electronic health record (EHR)? - Definition from WhatIs.com", SearchHealthIT. https://searchhealthit.techtarget.com/definition/electronic-health-record-EHR. Accessed 30 May 2019
3. "What are the advantages of electronic health records? — HealthIT.gov", Healthit.gov, 2019. https://www.healthit.gov/faq/what-are-advantages-electronic-health-records. Accessed 30 May 2019
4. South African Minister of Health, eHealth Strategy, p. 8 (2012)
5. Shea, S.: Security versus access: trade-offs are only part of the story. JAMIA **1**, 314–5 (1994)
6. Barrows, R., Clayton, P.: Privacy, confidentiality, and electronic medical records. J. Am. Med. Inf. Assoc. **3**(2), 139–148 (1996). https://doi.org/10.1136/jamia.1996.96236282
7. National Health Act 61 of 2003
8. Promotion of Information Act 2 of 2000
9. Agarwal, T.K.: Vendor neutral archive in PACS. Indian J. Radiol. Imag. **22**(4), 242–245 (2012). https://doi.org/10.4103/0971-3026.111468. Accessed 1 June 2019
10. Cognizant 20–20 Insights, "The U.S. Healthcare Implications of Europe's Stricter Data Privacy Regulations (2018)
11. Almunawar, M., Anshari, M.: Health Information Systems (HIS): concept and Technology (2012). Accessed 2 June 2019
12. Protect of Personal Information Act 2013
13. Geneva, 14 to 18 May 2018, Commission on science and technology for development (CSTD) (2018)
14. Purtova, N., Kosta, E., Koops, B.-J.: Laws and regulations for digital health. In: Fricker, S.A., Thümmler, C., Gavras, A. (eds.) Requirements Engineering for Digital Health, pp. 47–74. Springer, Cham (2015). https://doi.org/10.1007/978-3-319-09798-5_3
15. Chaib, F., Garwood, P.: WHO releases first guideline on digital health interventions (2017). https://www.who.int/news-room/detail/17-04-2019-who-releases-first-guideline-on-digital-health-interventions. Accessed 27 May 2019
16. HPCSA, Guidelines on the Keeping of Patient Records, paragraph 9 (2008)
17. Marr, B.: This Health Insurance Company Tracks Customers' Exercise And Eating Habits Using Big Data And IoT(2019). https://www.bernardmarr.com/default.asp?contentID=1884. Accessed 03 Jun 2019
18. World health organization., global diffusion of ehealth. World health organization, geneva (2017)
19. Vayena, E., Dzenowagis, J., Brownstein, J., Sheikh, A.: Policy implications of big data in the health sector. Bull. World Heal. Organ. **96**(1), 66–68 (2017). https://doi.org/10.2471/blt.17.197426
20. Taylor, K.: Digital health the future of healthcare — life sciences and healthcare — Deloitte Southern Africa. https://www2.deloitte.com/za/en/pages/life-sciences-and-healthcare/events/digital-health-the-future-of-healthcare.html. Accessed 26 May 2019

21. Mandava, M., Lubamba, C., Ismail, A., Bagula H., Bagula, A.: Cyber- healthcare for public healthcare in the developing world. In: proceedings of the 2016 IEEE Symposium on Computers and Communication (ISCC), Messina-Italy, 27–30 June 2016, pp. 14–19 (2016)
22. Bagula, M.F., Bagula, H., Mandava, M., Kakoko Lubamba, C., Bagula, A.: Cyber-healthcare kiosks for healthcare support in developing countries. In: Mendy, G., Ouya, S., Dioum, I., Thiaré, O. (eds.) AFRICOMM 2018. LNICST, vol. 275, pp. 185–198. Springer, Cham (2019). https://doi.org/10.1007/978-3-030-16042-5_18
23. Celesti, A., et al.: How to develop IoT cloud e-health systems based on FIWARE: a lesson learnt. J. Sens. Actuator Netw. 8(1), 7 (2019)
24. Bagula, A., Mandava, M., Bagula, H.: A framework for healthcare support in the rural and low income areas of the developing world. J. Netw. Comput. Appl. 120, 17–29 (2018). https://doi.org/10.1016/j.jnca.2018.06.010
25. Bagula, A., Lubamba, C., Mandava, M., Bagula, H., Zennaro, M., Pietrosemoli, E.: Cloud based patient prioritization as service in public health care. In: 2016 ITU Kaleidoscope: ICTs for a Sustainable World (ITU WT), pp. 1–8. IEEE (2016)
26. Lubamba, C., Bagula, A.: Cyber-healthcare cloud computing interoperability using the HL7-CDA standard. In: 2017 IEEE Symposium on Computers and Communications (ISCC), pp. 105–110. IEEE (2017)

Big Data Processing Using Hadoop and Spark: The Case of Meteorology Data

Eslam Hussein[2], Ronewa Sadiki[2], Yahlieel Jafta[2],
Muhammad Mujahid Sungay[2], Olasupo Ajayi[1,2], and Antoine Bagula[1,2(✉)]

[1] ISAT Laboratory, University of the Western Cape, Cape Town 7535, South Africa
abagula@uwc.ac.za
[2] Department of Computer Science, University of the Western Cape, Cape Town
7535, South Africa

Abstract. Meteorology is a branch of science which can be leveraged to gain useful insight into many phenomenon that have significant impacts on our daily lives such as weather precipitation, cyclones, thunderstorms, climate change. It is a highly data-driven field that involves large datasets of images captured from both radar and satellite, thus requiring efficient technologies for storing, processing and data mining to find hidden patterns in these datasets. Different big data tools and ecosystems, most of them integrating Hadoop and Spark, have been designed to address big data issues. However, despite its importance, only few works have been done on the application of these tools and ecosystems for solving meteorology issues. This paper proposes and evaluate the performance of a precipitation data processing system that builds upon the Cloudera ecosystem to analyse large datasets of images as a classification problem. The system can be used as a replacement to machine learning techniques when the classification problem consists of finding zones of high, moderate and low precipitations in satellite images.

Keywords: Hadoop · MapReduce · Spark · Hive · Meteorology · Big data

1 Introduction

Meteorology is a branch of science which studies the earth's atmosphere with its physical occurrences [1]. It helps to gain a better understanding of the meteorological related phenomena, such as weather precipitation forecasting, cyclones, thunderstorms and climate changes. Each of these can have significant impacts on our daily lives [2]. For instance, precipitation is considered to be the primary source of fresh water. It plays an important role in industry and agriculture, but when in excess might lead to flooding or related natural disasters. One recent disaster occurred in Mozambique and its neighbouring countries in April 2019, where almost 750 lives were lost to a cyclone in Southern Africa. Figure 1 shows the outcomes of that disasters [3]. Such consequences explain the importance of

© ICST Institute for Computer Sciences, Social Informatics and Telecommunications Engineering 2020
Published by Springer Nature Switzerland AG 2020. All Rights Reserved
R. Zitouni et al. (Eds.): AFRICOMM 2019, LNICST 311, pp. 180–185, 2020.
https://doi.org/10.1007/978-3-030-41593-8_13

Fig. 1. An image of the disaster that occurred in Mozambique [3].

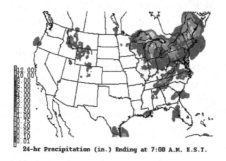

24-hr Precipitation (in.) Ending at 7:00 A.M. E.S.T.

Fig. 2. An image from the National Centers for Environmental Prediction data set

developing an accurate forecasting system to provide early alarms for governments to manage potential disaster(s) [4].

Meteorology is one of the fields that has always been highly data-driven [8], big data analytics can thus find good application in Meteorology [5]. One of the largest databases in the world is data related to climate known as *The World Data Center for Climate* (WDCC), and includes 340 terabytes of earth observations data [6]. A number of research work have utilized different platforms to maintain and analyze these huge data [7]. However, due to its volume and variety, we consider big data platforms to be well suited to taking advantage of the potential value these datasets hold. Hadoop and Spark, are two open source platforms that have been widely used for analyzing big sets of data effectively [7]. This paper also adopts these platforms and proposes a precipitation data processing system built on Cloudera. We consider the issue of finding zones of high, moderate and low precipitations in radar images such as that shown in Fig. 2 as a classification problem. We then employed Hadoop and Spark to analyze the large datasets of images. The system can be used as a replacement or complement to machine learning techniques for classification problems. The rest of this paper is organized as follows: Sect. 2 presents work related to the use of big data platforms in meteorology. Section 3 presents the data analytics of our system while Sect. 4 contains the conclusions and recommendations for future works.

2   Related Work

Recently, there has been a significant number of research work on the application of different Big Data analytics in the meteorology. Ibrahim *et al.* [9], Suggested the use of MapReduce on around 20 GB of whether historical data sets from 1929–2016 (NCDC, GSOD). The dataset files were stored in the Hadoop Distributed File System (HDFS), split and sent to different mappers. The mappers' output where a set of (key, value) pairs, with the station name and date as key, while the value consists of several parameters such as Wind, Precipitation, Temperature etc. The average, max and min of each month, year, and season for each parameter were calculated using the reducer script. In [10], Pandey *et al.* proposed the use of the word count algorithm in Hadoop on a file of text formats for weather forecasting. For data analytics, Riyaz *et al.* in [11], suggested the use of Hadoop MapReduce on a temperature dataset. The mapper function had to find the average temperature associated with place (key). Values such as average, max, min temperature were calculated using the reduce function. Jayanth *et al.* [13], analyzed weather using Spark and ipython for data analytics. Data was transformed into RDDs sequel to which the highest and average precipitation and temperature values for the top ten weather stations were calculated and displayed. In a similar work, Dagade *et al.* [12], computed the average temperature per year per station. An unstructed dataset was used, which required transforming the data into an understandable format using java scripts before uploaded into HDFS. Like these previous works, the objective of this study is to provide an analysis of precipitation data within the Cloudera QuickStart VM environment. Cloudera was chosen as it has Hadoop, HDFS, and Spark integrated.

3   Implementation

3.1   Data

24-Hour-Precipitation-Dataset. Data used for this study are 24-hour-radar images of the United State, from Jan 2012 to Feb 2019 - a total of 2,604 images. The data were sourced from the *National Centers for Environmental Prediction*, with a resolution of 400×320. Each image contains 15 different rainfall intensity level, a sample is shown in Fig. 2.

3.2   Weather Data Analysis: Hadoop MapReduce

Pre-processing was done on the images to structure them into key-value pairs. These pairs serve as input data, (see left side of Fig. 3), to the word count algorithm [10]. They keys are the year, while the value consists of corresponding rain intensities (Light, Moderate and Heavy) in pixel count values. Value extraction from pixels was done using "extcolors 0.1.2" python API.

The implementation is executed in two phases, which are - Map and Reduce. The map function reads each line and extracts the three classified values associating it with its relevant key. The output produced omits the description of

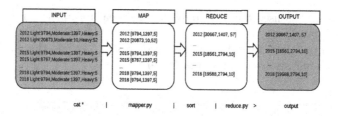

Fig. 3. MapReduce logical flow

the classification values and only displays the data representation, i.e. the rain intensity.

The reduce function reads the output from the map function, groups the keys and values and performs addition of each applicable classification value for each key. This produces an output for each key followed by the three classification values which are summed up for each matching key. The output is used to produce analytics describing the rainfall within the scope of the datasets used.

For our implementation of MapReduce, we made use of the Hadoop Streaming API. This API allows writing of map and reduce functions in several languages and utilizes Unix standard streams as the interface between Hadoop and written programs [14]. This enables us use Python (version 2.7) to read input data and write the corresponding results as output. The results of our analysis are displayed in Fig. 4

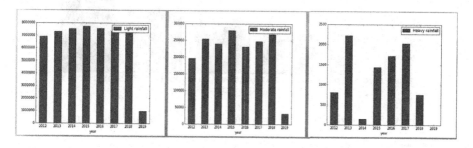

Fig. 4. MapReduce analytics (Daily data set)

3.3   Weather Data Analysis: Spark-Streaming

Analysis in Spark was performed using PySpark, streaming and applying a reduce function to each stream. Each line of the input are added to an RDD queue and streamed. Each queue entry is processed by applying a reducer function which adds all the values per line. To demonstrate the functionality, we used Spark to determine five days with the heaviest rainfall in our dataset. The daily rainfall dataset was used for this analysis, where each input line represents the rainfall for a day.

The execution flow for Spark is outlined in Fig. 5, while the results of our functionality analysis are displayed in Fig. 6

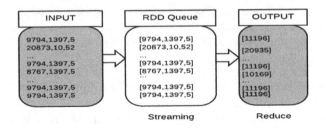

Fig. 5. Spark logical flow

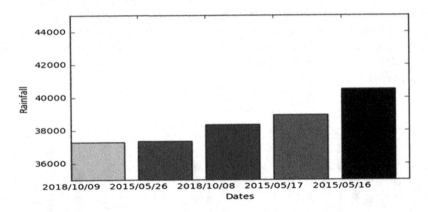

Fig. 6. 5 days with the heaviest rainfall according to Spark streaming

4   Conclusion and Future Work

In this work, the authors have demonstrated two approaches to the processing and analysis of unstructured meteorological image data. The application of Hadoop MapReduce and Spark was applied on a daily precipitation dataset. Using the Hadoop streaming API allowed for the specification of two custom functions, Map and Reduce, which can be written in any language with support for standard read/write of input and output data. Spark allowed for the image data to be analyzed in batches and in memory. We tested Hadoop MapReduce and Spark and both were able to accurately determine the precipitation based on the image dataset supplied. This result shows that big data analytics tools such as Hadoop MapReduce and Spark can be used as complementary or alternatives to Machine Learning tools. Future research might involve comparing the performance of both approaches Hadoop MapReduce and Spark and possibly benchmarking against known machine learning algorithms.

References

1. GmbH, J.: Joint Aviation Authorities Airline Transport Pilot's Licence Theoretical Knowledge Manual. Oxford Aviation Training (2001)
2. Ahrens, C.D.: Meteorology Today: An Introduction to Weather, Climate, and the Environment. Cengage Learning, Boston (2012)
3. Swails, B., Berlinger, J.: Tropical cyclone kenneth death toll rises to 38 in mozambique, officials say (2019)
4. Shi, E., Li, Q., Gu, D., Zhao, Z.: A method of weather radar echo extrapolation based on convolutional neural networks. In: Schoeffmann, K., et al. (eds.) MMM 2018. LNCS, vol. 10704, pp. 16–28. Springer, Cham (2018). https://doi.org/10.1007/978-3-319-73603-7_2
5. Kamilaris, A., Prenafeta-Boldú, F.X.: Deep learning in agriculture: a survey. Comput. Electron. Agric. **147**, 70–90 (2018)
6. Al-Jarrah, O.Y., Yoo, P.D., Muhaidat, S., Karagiannidis, G.K., Taha, K.: Efficient machine learning for big data: a review. Big Data Res. **2**(3), 87–93 (2015)
7. Dagade, V., Lagali, M., Avadhani, S., Kalekar, P.: Big data weather analytics using hadoop. Int. J. Emerg. Technol. Comput. Sci. Electron. (IJETCSE) ISSN, 0976–1353 (2015)
8. Chen, C.P., Zhang, C.-Y.: Data-intensive applications, challenges, techniques and technologies: a survey on big data. Inf. Sci. **275**, 314–347 (2014)
9. Ibrahim, G., et al.: Big data techniques: hadoop and mapreduce for weather forecasting. Int. J. Latest Trends Eng. Technol. 194–199 (2016)
10. Pandey, A., Agrawal, C., Agrawal, M.: A hadoop based weather prediction model for classification of weather data. In: 2017 Second International Conference on Electrical, Computer and Communication Technologies (ICECCT), pp. 1–5. IEEE (2017)
11. Riyaz, P., Varghese, S.M.: Leveraging map reduce with hadoop for weather data analytics. J. Comput. Eng. **17**(3), 6–12 (2015)
12. Oury, D.T.M., Singh, A.: Data analysis of weather data using hadoop technology. In: Satapathy, S.C., Bhateja, V., Das, S. (eds.) Smart Computing and Informatics. SIST, vol. 77, pp. 723–730. Springer, Singapore (2018). https://doi.org/10.1007/978-981-10-5544-7_71
13. Jayanthi, D., Sumathi, G.: Weather data analysis using spark-an in-memory computing framework. In: 2017 Innovations in Power and Advanced Computing Technologies (i-PACT), pp. 1–5. IEEE (2017)
14. White, T.: Hadoop: The Definitive Guide. O'Reilly Media, Inc., Newton (2012)

Classification of Plant Species by Similarity Using Automatic Learning

Zacrada Françoise Odile Trey[✉], Bi Tra Goore,
and Brou Marcellin Konan

Institut National Polytechnique Houphouët-Boigny,
Yamoussoukro, Côte d'Ivoire
mariefranceodiletrey@gmail.com,
bitra.goore@gmail.com, konanbroumarcellin@yahoo.fr

Abstract. The classification methods are diverse and variety from one field of study to another. Among botanists, plants classification is done manually. This task is difficult, and results are not satisfactory. However, artificial intelligence, which is a new field of computer science, advocates automatic classification methods. It uses well-trained algorithms facilitating the classification activity for very efficient results. However, depending on the classification criterion, some algorithms are more efficient than others. Through our article, we classify plants according to their type: trees, shrubs and herbaceous plants by comparing two types of learning meaning the supervised and unsupervised learning. For each type of learning, we use these corresponding algorithms which are K-Means algorithms and decision trees. Thus we developed two classification models with each of these algorithms. The performance indicators of these models revealed different figures. We have concluded that one of these algorithms is more effective than the other in grouping our plants by similarity.

Keywords: Automatic learning · Classification · Algorithm

1 Introduction

1.1 Context

Biodiversity conservation is based on a precise, science-based classification (i.e. a system for designating organisms). Without this classification, it will be unable to describe the multitude of species inhabiting tropical forests and compare them to the small number that live in these tropical countries. Also, without such classification, it would be impossible to identify plant species in our environment [1]. However, many of these species are either threatened with extinction or have already disappeared due to pollution and natural disasters, and others are still waiting to be discovered [2]. Plant species are important for nature and ecological balance, and many of them are raw materials for the chemical and wine industries for example... Therefore, their classification is of interest not only to botanists but also for other actors in different fields such as agronomists, environmental protectors, foresters, land managers and even amateurs or non-experts [3]. For a long time, this classification was done manually by

R. Zitouni et al. (Eds.): AFRICOMM 2019, LNICST 311, pp. 186–201, 2020.
https://doi.org/10.1007/978-3-030-41593-8_14

botanists with their own identification keys. Thus this process was slow and difficult. However, with the development of new computing tools such as Artificial Intelligence, several automatic classification methods have emerged. Artificial intelligence is defined as the set of means, theories, rules, techniques used to create machines' automatons, robots capable of simulating human behavior. These machines or artificial agents or non-human agents are effective, tireless and docile for performing repetitive tasks [4].

The main objective of this article is to reproduce all the facets of artificial intelligence in the field of botany through automatic learning by studying and training algorithms for making predictions on a large amount of botanical data. To achieve this, we firstly, analyzed the traditional classification of systematists. Secondly we used two types of learning, the clustering for unsupervised learning and decision trees for supervised learning to group plants into types, i.e. trees, shrubs, herbaceous plants. Finally, we compare the two classification methods to see which one has the best accuracy.

1.2 Motivation

For decades, the botanical field has remained in its traditional manual practices probably due to a lack of information and/or lack of computing skills by its specialists. In such way, for the morphological classification of their plants, a usual, flagship, popular activity, the botanists still work with dichotomous keys that are used by visual inspection of the systematist: a botanist, specialized in plant identification. The latest is quite used to this identification, which he could say, without consulting these keys, the type of plants. Would it be credible enough for novices who do not know anything about plant identification and who ask for its service? It sometimes happens that in countries such as Ivory Coast, these systematicians can be counted at their fingertips. How to transmit all these empirical knowledge to next generations?

In a context where new information and communication technologies are booming, it would be wise for the main actors of this technology, namely computer scientists, to be able to convey their knowledge. They must ensure that fields of study that do not yet demonstrate this technology can use it. Since the advent of IT in everyday practices has several advantages. Firstly, it helps saving time with the use of PLCs in manual activities making work easier and allowing results to be obtained in a short time. Then it promotes better results and automatic learning in this kind of human activity uses well-trained algorithms. However, it is their role to imitate human behavior, their results can far exceed those obtained manually. Therefore our article shows how to translate all this empirical knowledge of the systematist into algorithms. This will have the advantage of: (1) automating the classification of plants, (2) perennializing all its information and (3) allowing better results in a minimal time.

This system could therefore be used not only by experts such as the systematist but also by non-experts, such as florists, agronomists, etc.

2 Materials and Methods

2.1 State of the Art

Traditionally, botanists use identification keys to classify plants. These identifications generally concern the morphological characteristics of plants and are used manually. Authors have created a key that identifies sixteen genera in the *cyperraceas* family. To recognize the type of plant, they successively describe the characteristics of the leaves of these plants [5]. When these leaf descriptions fail to identify the plant, systematicians proceed to describe the flower of this species [6]. Others go as far as describing the fruits and even the roots. This is the case with cruciferous keys. They describe all the vegetative aspects of the plant, namely its leaves, roots, fruit and flowers [7]. For all these dichotomous keys, the operating mode remains a difficult activity. To compensate this lack, some actors are digitizing these keys. They created an automatic botanical document analysis tool, based on XML, corrected artifacts resulting from the digitization from written documents, performed a morpho-syntactic analysis for identification and finally an extraction of knowledge [8]. It is clear that this tool has not been validated by experts, which makes it unreliable. Raymond Boyd et al. have created a tool that includes a transdisciplinary database. They identified plant species by botanical nomenclature and names of these species in the *Sémé* language of Burkina Faso. Using XML, They made a semi-structured questionnaire describing the Semitic language. Then, they drew up a directory of scientific names of plants and made them correspond to their morphological representation, including a vocabulary of Semitic language [9]. Moreover, in the purpose of this idea perfection, scientists are setting up a key to determine plants by flower type. They also classify plants according to the criteria of the flower as well as identifying for each plant, the lengths and widths of the petals and sepals. Using the machine learning, they created four zones corresponding to these types of flowers, being able to be used from a computer. It is sufficient to harvest the plant, enter the different values of the petals and sepals into the system, and get automatically the result on the flower type. However, not all plants necessarily have flowers [10]. In addition, in their work, the vegetative characteristics of the plant, which are the roots, stem, leaf and flower are used. They obtained more than thirty descriptors per character. As a result, they ended up with many descriptors, to be entered which was tedious task. Nevertheless, they obtain a knowledge base of these plants. To classify plants by type, their system compares characteristics until a significant match rate is reached [11]. Sometimes the type of plant returned by the system does not correspond to reality. Other scientists have dealt with the recognition of weeds in a field. They used the leaf of the plant at its evolutionary stage. They identified the descriptors of shape, density and color. After segmentation, they pre-process the images of the leaves and apply neural networks on them to make the classification. They are able to develop an approach for the design and formation of deep convolutional neural networks for identification a large number of plant species [12]. However, this system encounters some difficulties due the use of this system, the harvested plant must have a size that conforms to the size of the images in the database, if necessary the result would be distorted; moreover, during segmentation, the removal of the stem from the leaf eliminates certain parts, which results in a defect in the extraction of the characteristics. The omission of segmentation or retention of the stem should also increase the accuracy of classification, as the regions of the stem removed by segmentation, will be retained. In this work, it determined the name of a plant from its leaf. The methodology adopted is as follows: on a given database of 126 plants, a segmentation of the images was carried out. For a better appreciation of the characteristics, an extraction of the texture, color and shape of the leaf is done. Finally, an Android-based plant leaf identification system is built [13]. However it must be noted that in its application, the name did not necessarily correspond to the plant; since semantics such as texture, color and shape do not give enough information. Therefore, the search for new descriptors to improve identification is in prospect.

2.2 Dataset

The classification of plants is a very important area. Several authors based their classification on the vegetative characteristics of the plant such as roots, leaves, flower and fruit. However, when all these characters are taken into account, it ends up with an infinite number of descriptors, which often skews the results. In recent years, other authors have focused their research on describing the flower. They identified different sizes of sepals and petals. For example, flowers do not appear in all plants throughout the year, Although roots, flowers and fruits are vegetative characteristics of plants, they are not present all year round, but the leaf and stem are still present [14]. Other authors have therefore based the classification of plants on the description of the plant leaf. However, leaves alone cannot identify the plant. And need to be combined with the leaf and stem to classify plants into trees, shrubs and herbaceous types, using botanical book databases such as flora of West Tropical Africa. These books contain all the plants with their morphological descriptions accepted by the botanist community in general, more precisely that of West Africa [15]. Minimum and maximum stem heights and the maximum and minimum leaf lengths were considered. The present dataset contains 412 elements from different plants. We evaluate our system with plants harvested in the forest.

2.3   Proposed Method

We propose an algorithm with four distinct steps from dataset development to classification. The details of the different steps are described in the following sections (Fig. 1):

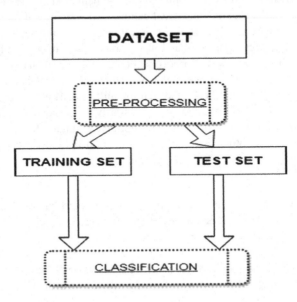

Fig. 1. Process for identifying type of plant

Elaboration of Dataset

To create our dataset, we acquire data from different sources and purge them. Figure 2 below shows how it works. According to our sources of acquisition of the different plants [15–17], we build a database. t the name of the plant with the maximum (**TMAX**) and minimum (**TMIN**) size of its stem in millimeters and the maximum length (**LMAX**) (**LMIN**) of its leaf in millimeters are reported. This is the redundant database as shown in Fig. 2.

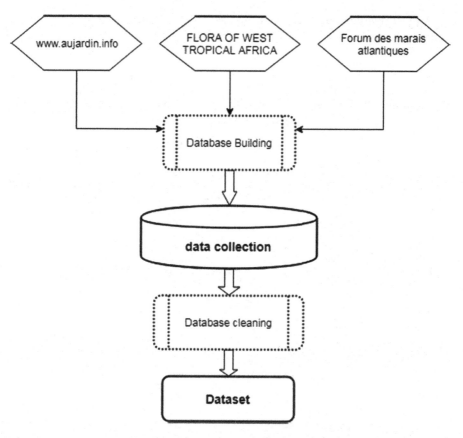

Fig. 2. Development of the dataset

Preprocessing

We remove redundant data from our database and put them all on the same scale (Table 1).

Table 1. Redundant data

PLANTES	TMAX	TMIN	LMAX	LMIN
Thomsonii	13716	13716	150	100
Xylopia Africana	12192	9140	160	90
Staudtii	45720	45720	160	90
Ruberscens	27432	27432	240	90
Eliotii	9144	9144	90	50
...	....	...	....	....
Sofa	....	....	....	....
Afzelii	....	....	....	....
Margaritaceus	....		....	....
Aucheri	1500	1500	5	4
UvariaScabrida	9144	9144	180	100

After cleaning this database, we obtain the dataset following (Fig. 3).

Index	TMIN	TMAX	LMIN	LMAX
0	1.37e+04	1.37e+04	100	150
1	9.14e+03	1.22e+04	90	160
2	4.57e+04	4.57e+04	90	160
3	2.74e+04	2.74e+04	90	240
4	2.74e+04	2.74e+04	130	130
5	9.14e+03	9.14e+03	50	90
6	2.44e+04	2.44e+04	60	130
7	1.83e+04	1.83e+04	150	150
8	914	2.44e+03	40	80
9	3.05e+03	3.05e+03	45	150
10	6.1e+03	6.1e+03	70	120
11	6.1e+03	6.1e+03	60	90
12	4.57e+03	4.57e+03	70	250
13	9.14e+03	9.14e+03	100	180

Fig. 3. DatasetDataPlant

Dataset Division

Once the processing is complete, we divide the dataset into training and test sets (Figs. 4 and 5).

	0	1
0	1500.00	3.50
1	20.00	10.00
2	36576.00	240.00
3	1000.00	2.00
4	1500.00	0.90
5	9144.00	180.00
6	10.00	2.50
7	1000.00	2.00
8	160.00	7.00
9	9144.00	250.00

Fig. 4. Training set

	0	1
0	2438.40	80.00
1	45.00	1.50
2	1200.00	8.00
3	1300.00	2.00
4	450.00	90.00
5	9144.00	500.00
6	130.00	5.00
7	27432.00	160.00
8	170.00	40.00
9	12192.00	180.00

Fig. 5. Test set

2.4   Classification

Automatic learning is subdivided into two types: supervised and unsupervised learning. This step of our model highlights the different classifiers capable of classifying our plants. We clarify both types of classification methods. Based on the characteristics extracted from our different plants, we analyze the supervised and unsupervised classification methods. As part of our work, it will be clustering and decision trees. We will see both classifiers, which more accurately identifies our plants.

K-Means

Clustering is an integral part of unsupervised learning. And this type of method dedicated to unsupervised classification refers to a corpus of methods whose objective is to establish or find an existing typology, characterizing a set of n observations, based on p characteristics, measured on each of the observations [18]. By typology, we mean that the observations, although collected during the same experiment, are not all from the same homogeneous population, but rather from K different populations. In unsupervised classification, the affiliation of observations to one of the K populations is not known. It is precisely this belonging that must be found from the available descriptors.

Let's Formalize the Problem

The purpose of unsupervised classification is to determine groups. These groups will be referred to as homogeneous and distinct clusters. To formalize this, we start by defining the inertia of our plant cloud. Given a set of plants represented by n points ($P1$, $P2$, ..., Pn), PG is referred to as the barycenter of the cloud of these points.

$$P_G = \frac{1}{n}\sum_{i=1}^{n} Pi \tag{1}$$

The total inertia is defined as follows.

$$IT = \sum_{i=1}^{n} d^2(P_i + P_G) = \sum_{i=1}^{n} d^2\|P_i + P_G\|^2 \tag{2}$$

where the chosen distance is the Euclidean distance. In reality, the point cloud is composed of K classes (cluster) of different points $C_1, C_2, ..., C_k$, each of these classes having for barycenter P G k, the total inertia is broken down as follows:

$$It = \sum_{i=1}^{n} \|P_i + P_G\|^2$$
$$= \sum_{k=1}^{K} = \sum_{k=1}^{K}\sum_{i\in Ck} \|P_i - P_{Ck} - P_G\|^2 = \sum_{k=1}^{K}\sum_{i\in Ck} \|P_i - P_{Ck}\|^2 \tag{3}$$
$$+ \|P_{Ck} - P_G\|^2 \text{(Hygens' theorem)}$$

$$IT = \sum_{k=1}^{K}\sum_{i=1}^{n} d^2(P_i - P_{Ck}) + \sum_{k=1}^{K} n_k(P_{Ck} - P_G) \tag{4}$$

where is the number of observations of class C k

$$I_W = \sum_{k=1}^{K}\sum_{i=1}^{n} d^2(P_i - P_{Ck}) \tag{5}$$

which is the sum of the distances between the points of a class and their center of gravity = intra-class inertia

$$I_B = \sum_{k=1}^{K} n_k(P_{Ck} - P_G) \tag{6}$$

This term measures how far apart the classes are from each other = intra-class inertia, so if there are K well-identified classes, it is theoretically possible to find them by trying all the possible groupings in k classes and choosing the one that minimizes intra-class inertia, which is the same as

$$I_T = I_w + I_B \qquad (7)$$

and that I T does not depend on classes. From a formal point of view, the optimal partition $C*_k$, of observations in K classes is therefore defined as follows:

$$C_k^* = arg\,min \sum\nolimits_{k=1}^{K} \sum\nolimits_{i=1}^{n} d^2(P_i - P_{Ck}) \qquad (8)$$

where C_k^* is the set of possible partitions of the n observations in k classes. To meet our classification objective, all that remains is to identify the optimal partition.

Determines the optimal partition that will be represented by the number of Ks of classes or clusters. The difficulty of any unsupervised classification method lies in the choice of the number of class K. In most cases, this number is unknown. Concerning the use of the K-means algorithm, it is possible to plot the curve of intra- class WSS inertia as a function of K (Fig. 6).

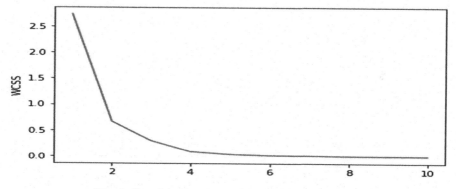

Fig. 6. Determination curve of the number K of classes

We try to identify the steps where we observe a break in this curve, synonymous with a strong degradation of inter-class inertia. This deterioration is the result of the strong heterogeneity of the two classes combined at the stage under consideration. It is therefore natural to consider a higher number of classes than the one for which the failure occurs, referred to as the elbow criterion, gives satisfactory results [19] (Figs. 7 and 8).

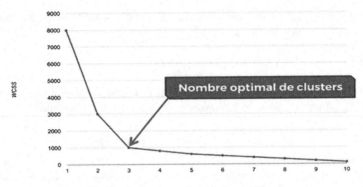

Fig. 7. Optimal number of classes K = 3

Let's Apply the Model to Our Plants to Be Classified

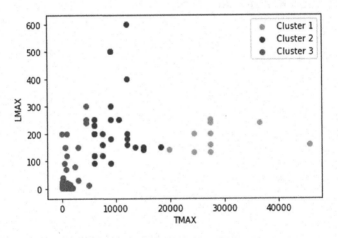

Fig. 8. Classified plants by K-Means

Model Performance

We evaluate the performance of our model. The table below lists the plants predicted from those observed (Table 2).

Table 2. Confusion matrix

		Predicted plants		
Plants observed	CLUSTERS	Tree	Shrub	Herb
	Tree	6	0	2
	Shrub	0	8	2
	Herb	2	0	7

In the following table, we calculate the basic indicators of the quality of prediction on the different clusters (Table 3).

Table 3. Performance indicators

	Precision	Recall	F-measure
Tree	0.857142	0.75	0.8
Shrub	0.8	1	0.88889
Herb	0.777778	0.7	0.736842

Decision Trees

The general purpose of a decision tree is to explain a value from a series of discrete or continuous variables. We are therefore in a very classical case of matrix X with m observations and n variables, associated with a vector Y to explain. The values of Y can be of two kinds: continuous, we speak of a regression tree; or if the values of Y are qualitative, we speak of a classification tree.

In our case, the values of Y are either tree, shrub or herbaceous plants, the values of Y are then qualitative. We are in the case of a classification decision tree. This inductive classification method has two advantages: it is quite efficient, non-parametric and linear. In principle, it will partition, by producing groups of plants, as homogeneous as possible from the point of view of the tree, shrub or herbaceous plants to be predicted, and taking into account a hierarchy of the predictive capacity of the variables stem size and leaf length considered [21].

Formalization of the Problem

The main principles for defining explicit explanatory rules are as follows: several iterations are necessary, at each iteration, the plants are divided. This division defines sub-populations represented by the "nodes" of the tree. Each node is associated with an output variable. The operation is repeated for each sub-population until no further separation is possible. Each leaf is characterized by a specific path through the tree called a rule. The set of rules for all sheets is the template (Fig. 9).

Let's Apply the Model to Our Plants to Be Classified

```
Rule 1:
If  TMAX == {10668,  12181.9,  12192,  13716,  15240,  18288,
19812, 2438.4, 24384, 27432, 3048, 36576, 4572, 45720, 6096,
7620, 9144};
Then result = 100% trees
Rule 2:
If TMAX == {10, 100, 1000, 120, 1200, 130, 1300, 140, 150,
1500, 160, 1600, 170, 20, 200, 2000, 230, 250, 30, 300, 3000,
350, 45, 450, 5000, 60, 600, 700, 800, 90, 900} AND
TMIN == {10, 100, 120, 130, 140, 150, 160, 20, 200, 230, 30,
300, 350, 400, 450, 50, 60, 600, 700, 800} AND
LMAXF == {1, 1.9, 11, 120, 17, 20, 25, 3.2, 30, 6.5, 70, 90}
```

```
Then result = 90% Grass and10% Shrub
Rule 3
If TMAX == {10, 100, 1000, 120, 1200, 130, 1300, 140, 150,
1500, 160, 1600, 170, 20, 200, 2000, 230, 250, 30, 300, 3000,
350, 45, 450, 5000, 60, 600, 700, 800, 90, 900} AND
TMIN == {10, 100, 120, 130, 140, 150, 160, 20, 200, 230, 30,
300, 350, 400, 450, 50, 60, 600, 700, 800} AND
LMAXF == {1.5, 10, 150, 2, 2.5, 200, 4, 4.5, 40, 5, 7}
Then result = 100% grass
Rule 4
If TMAX == {10, 100, 1000, 120, 1200, 130, 1300, 140, 150,
1500, 160, 1600, 170, 20, 200, 2000, 230, 250, 30, 300, 3000,
350, 45, 450, 5000, 60, 600, 700, 800, 90, 900} AND
TMIN == {1000, 1200, 1300, 1500, 1600, 2000, 3000, 5000}
Then result = 100% shrub
```

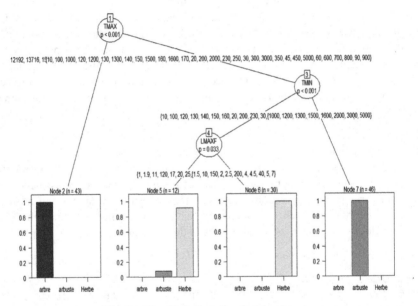

Fig. 9. Classified plants by decision trees

Model Performance

We evaluate the performance of our model. The table below lists the plants predicted from those observed (Table 4).

Table 4. Confusion matrix

	Predicted plants			
Plants observed	CLUSTERS	Tree	Shrub	Herb
	Tree	43	0	0
	Shrub	0	46	0
	herb	0	0	41

In the following table, we calculate the basic indicators of the quality of prediction on the different clusters (Table 5).

Table 5. Performance indicators

Clusters	Tree	Shrub	Herb
Sensitivity	1.0000	0,9787	1.0000
Specificity	1.0000	1.0000	0,9889

3 Discussion

We worked on both types of learning, supervised and unsupervised. The two classification methods were simulated with the same dataset called DataPlant; According to the criterion of the maximum leaf length and the maximum stem size of the plants, we obtain three classes of different plants, namely the tree, shrub and herb classes. We simulated the algorithms on the same computer. With the K-means algorithm, results are obtained after forty-five seconds, while with decision trees, results are obtained in only fifteen seconds. We tested the models with a base of harvested plants, and the results obtained are in accordance with the training results. However, for the K-Means, the total accuracy of the model is 81.16% with a margin of error of 18.83% and for the decision trees, we have an accuracy of 99.24% with a margin of error of 0.76%. We conclude that the decision trees are more appropriate in this type of classification. This table summarizes the comparison of the algorithms (Table 6):

Table 6. Algorithm comparison

	Precision	Margin of error	Execution time (seconds)
K-means	0.8116	0.1883	45
Decision trees	0.9924	0.76	15

4 Conclusion

We have shown that the classification of plant species can be done automatically. We used automatic learning, which is an area of artificial intelligence. It aims to use algorithms to reproduce all activities that are repetitive and require large amounts of data. We are based on the stem and leaf characteristics of the plant; because these characteristics are common to all plants, whatever their stage of evolution. We used K-Means algorithms and decision trees to classify plants by three types, trees, shrubs and grasses. We found that decision trees classify plants with better accuracy than any K-means algorithms. We hope to further our research by using other classification methods.

References

1. Picouet, D., et al.: les règles de la taxonimie: nommer les espèces (2018)
2. Kaya, A., et al.: Analysis of transfer learning for deep neural network based plant classification models. Comput. Electron. Agric. (2019)
3. Saleem, G., et al.: Automated analysis of visual leaf shape features for plant classification. Comput. Electron. Agric. (2019)
4. Coulon, A.: supplément à l'intelligence artificielle, la Lettre 111, Printemps (2018)
5. Paquette, D., et al.: Clés des 16 genres de Cypéraceaes, Flora Quebeca, 19 Septembre 2016
6. Paquette, D., et al.: Clés des verges d'or, Flora Québéca (2016)
7. Sabourin, A., et al.: clé des crucifères., flora Québéca, mars 2018
8. Guillaume, R., de La Clergerie, É.V.: Analyse automatique de documents botaniques: le projet Biotim. In: Proceedings of TIA 2005: Journées Terminologie; Intelligence Artificielle, Rouen, France, April 2005
9. Boyd, R., et al.: Une base de données informatisée transdisciplinaire de la flore chez les sémé du burkina faso: un outil pour l'étude du lien nature-société (2014)
10. Pegliasco, G.: Classer une fleur selon des critères observables: Initiation au Machine Learning avec Python - La pratique
11. Piernot, T., et al.: Flora Bellissima, un nouvel outil pour découvrir la flore, mars 2014
12. Dyrmann, M., et al.: Plants species classification using deep convolutional neural network (2016). https://doi.org/10.1016/j.biosystemseng.2016.08.024
13. Zhao, Z.-Q., et al.: ApLeaf: an efficient android-based plant leaf identification system. Neurocomputing (2014)
14. Tippannavar, S., et al.: A machine learning system for recognition of vegetable plant and classification of abnormality using leaf texture analysis. Int. J. Sci. Eng. Res. 8(6), 1558–1563 (2017)
15. Hutchinson, J., Dalziel, J.M., Keay, R.W.J., Hepper, N.: Flora of West Tropical Africa (2014)
16. Forum des Marais Atlantiques 2017, Herbier Numérique, Flore en zonz humide, Région nouvelles d'Aquitaine, 93 p. http://www.forum-zones-humides.org
17. Schoonderwoerd, K.M., et al.: Zygotic dormancy underlies prolonged seed development in Franklinia alatamaha (Theaceae): a most unusual case of reproductive phenology in angiosperms. Bot. J. Linn. Soc. 181(1), 70–83 (2016)

18. Dundar, M., Kou, Q., Zhang, B., He, Y., Rajwa, B.: Simplicity of Kmeans versus deepness of deep learning: a case of unsupervised feature learning with limited data. In: 2015 IEEE 14th International Conference on Machine Learning and Applications (ICMLA), pp. 883–888 (2015)
19. Bholowalia, P., Kumar, A.: EBK-means: a clustering technique based on elbow method and k-means in WSN. Int. J. Comput. Appl. **105** (2014)
20. Beraud, P.: MSFT, 5 August 2014
21. Biernat, E., et al.: Data science: fondamentaux et études de cas, EYROLLES (2015)

Mobile Health Applications Future Trends and Challenges

Teddy Ivan Ibrahim Bessin[(✉)], Alain Wilfried P. Ouédraogo,
and Ferdinand Guinko

Institut Burkinabè des Arts et Métiers, Université Joseph KI-ZERBO,
Ouagadougou, Burkina Faso
bess_ivan@hotmail.fr, wilfriedalaino@gmail.com, tonguimferdinand@guinko.net

Abstract. Digital technologies are now a big part of the healthcare industry. With the rapid evolution of information and telecommunication technologies, mobile phones offers amazing opportunities to improve healthcare system, in the way that physicians, patients and other health system actors are more interconnected than it is in the traditional healthcare system. The goal of this study is to present the current and future trends in the field of mobile health (mhealth) and also to present the challenges in the use of mhealth apps.

Keywords: mhealth · Mobile health future trends · mhealth opportunities

1 Introduction

Mobile health can be defined as *a medical and public health practice supported by mobile devices, such as mobile phones, patient monitors, personal digital assistants, and other wireless devices.* Digital technologies has become an integral part of the health sector. With the rapid evolution of information and telecommunication technologies, mobile phone offers tremendous opportunities to improve the healthcare system. In [1] they estimate that 500 million patients would use a mobile health apps to help them manage their disease now. These apps are used as tools for personal electronic records, disease management, clinical alerts and reminders [2]. Our work consisted on the realization of a state of art on the theme: *Mobile Health Applications future trends and challenges* and its aim was to determine future trends and challenges in the field of mobile health applications. For this, we first present the current state of these applications that are oriented towards the monitoring of patients suffering of chronical diseases. Then we present, in a short term line future those technologies and application in use, trends, their impact on health systems, and how much they improve patient's lives. Finally, we present the challenges facing mobile solutions such as usability, privacy, security, authentication, as well as those related to the processing of

R. Zitouni et al. (Eds.): AFRICOMM 2019, LNICST 311, pp. 202–211, 2020.
https://doi.org/10.1007/978-3-030-41593-8_15

large data generated by this plethora of applications commonly called Big Data. All these elements mentioned above were the subject of our study. This paper is organized as follow: Section 2 presents the current state of mobile health; Sect. 3 the future trends of mobile health apps; Sect. 4 the challenges and the last section concludes our paper.

2   Current State of Mobile Health Applications

In this section we describe the current state of mobile health applications. We present the use of smartphones in the field of health and how people can use them to manage their disease. According to the World Health Organisation Chronic diseases are long-term conditions that generally progress slowly. Responsible for 63% of deaths, chronic diseases (heart disease, stroke, cancer, chronic respiratory diseases, diabetes ...) are the leading cause of death in the world. Of the 36 million people who died of chronic disease in 2008, 29% were under 60 and half were women [3]. According to [4] the mobile health is define as *medical and public health practice supported by mobile devices, such as mobile phones, patient monitoring devices, personal digital assistants, and other wireless devices.* There is an estimated 500 million patients who potentially use mHealth applications to support chronic health and self-care [1]. They have their advantages such their simplicity, and their low cost; they also provide an immensely user-friendly service and are have a potential to enhance the speed and accuracy of healthcare delivery.

Medication adherence and compliance can be defined as the *act of (the patient) conforming to the recommendations made by the provider with respect to timing, dosage, and frequency of medication taking.* To improve medication adherence the following strategies are used: reminder strategy, educational strategy and behavioral strategy [5]. Varkey et al. [6] found that medication adherence apps are available to patients having smartphones however, most of the current medication adherence apps do not track the important health parameters for diabetes management, according to the DSMES guidelines such as FBS, HbA1c, weight loss, exercise, carb intake, stress management and BMI.

Nowadays there are many kind of mobiles health applications which are used as tools for remote data collection, to access patients records, to access health information databases, for census taking, and for electronic health records creation and storage. We can find theses type of applications in the Google/Apple market. Health informatics emerged as a separate discipline which lead the improving of accuracy, timeless and reliability of decision making in the healthcare field by the involvement of computers and communication technologies used to acquire, store, analyse, communicate, display medical and health information [7]. In the case of hearth failure self care the features of mobile applications vary widely from the medication management, weight and symptom assessment, mobile messaging on hearth failure self-management and hearth failure education. All these features might help patients to improve their skills on health failure self-care management system. The Internet of Things (IoT) is a concept reflecting a connected a set of people, anytime, anyplace, any service and any network and its gaining more and more importance in the field of health care domain. The wearable sensors are ideal for monitoring a patient's health without the interruption of his daily activities [6]. There are many mobile health applications architecture which integrate the use of wearable device such as smart watch, smart clothes, etc.

In Fig. 1 Deshkar et al. [8] present a new Internet of Thing (IoT)-based platform to support self-management of diabetes.

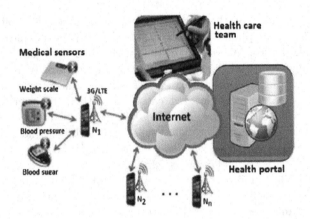

Fig. 1. Architecture of the smart phone based e-Health system [8]

Kitsiou et al. [9] present Icardia in Fig. 2 an innovative platform designed to support remote monitoring and health coaching of cardiac rehabilitation patients.

In their architecture they used a fitbit wearable sensor devices, a smartphone equiped with android, iOS, windows OS and cloud services; they tried to add SMS based features and tried also to subscribe to the fitbit cloud-based server API to get data from patient and integrate them in their web-based application. Another study shows that looking down to the phone is equivalent to placing a 60 pound weight on one's neck. The continue use of the computers and smartphones without a survey to maintain straight posture causes many backs diseases such as low back pain, kyphosis and pain in the neck because the tilt the head down to check Facebook or write a message on your smartphone leads to a stress of the spine [10]. To avoid these complications there are several posture monitoring systems. There is some posture monitoring systems based on the weight information, based on the tilt angle information or on the spine curvature information which use many sensing technologies that are able to provide this information to posture monitoring system in order to elaborate decision about the person posture.

To summerize, there are many mobile health applications which can help patient to improve their life style and their wellness or can help doctor to better provide healthcare even if the patient is not near from him. Given the role

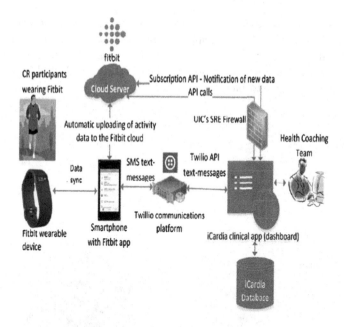

Fig. 2. iCardia platform components and architecture [9]

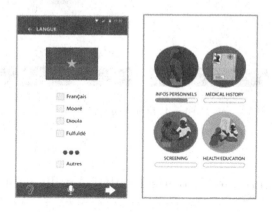

Fig. 3. PANDA *Pregnancy and Newborn Diagnostic Assessment* [11]

of mobile health applications in improving health status of patients and the support they could provide to health systems in developing countries, or other development countries like Burkina Faso have taken initiatives to appropriate these technologies. As example they use PANDA, as showed in Fig. 3, that is a system enabling doctors, midwives and community health workers to work together across traditional boundaries to provide antenatal care to vulnerable populations and to help prevent maternal and newborn mortality [11].

During breast cancer screening campaign, they trained all women who came to be screened for the use of the dearMamma application which provide reliable medical information about breast cancer for the poorest women around the world – especially for illiterate women who have been totally neglected by the health- or pharma-industry due to lack of spending capacity DearMamma as shown in Fig. 4.

Fig. 4. DearMamma

3   Future Trends of Mobile Health Applications

The proliferation of mobile technologies has paved the way for the widespread use of mobile health devices (mHealth). This in turn generates a large amount of data, mostly large data that can be used for a variety of purposes. In addition, these Big Data are closely linked to the Internet of Things (IoT) offering new applications for your individual eHealth and mobile health technologies. Also with the likely arrival of 5G technology, it is obvious that it will have a cat-alyzing effect on health as well as on many other areas [12]. The global usage of mobile health applications is increasing rapidly and so is the voluminous data sets generated from these and other smart connected devices leading to com-plex, voluminous and multi-dimensional mobile health data that are collected and stored globally on explosive levels. This game-changing trend is largely pro-pelled by the unprecedented global usage of the Internet connected devices, and the massive amounts of smart phone data generated by services and applications linked to these devices. As a consequence, there is major push on how to better manage, optimise and analyze this volume of data. Also, and more importantly how to convert these into meaningful information that can benefit patients, clinicians and other stakeholders. The recent developments from major corporations like Apple (HealthKit), Google (DeepMind), Microsoft towards developing smarter mobile healthcare systems are evident of these trends [13]. The adoption of the Cloud and Internet of Things (IoT) model in the field can bring multiple opportunities to medical informatics and experts believe that it can significantly improve health services and participate in its continuous and systematic innovation in a Metadata environment such as Industry 4.0 applications. Indeed, this model aims to deliver performance improvements in health applications while reducing the time required to complete stakeholder requests, optimizing the storage of large patient data, and providing realtime extraction mechanisms for these applications [14]. Regarding the 5G, it must be said that its impact on mobile health applications will include these elements namely continuous monitoring, which allows support for the continuous monitoring and treatment of sensory devices. Then, predictive analysis from where a continuous monitoring will feed the development of new data flows. There is the impact on business models hence the transition from fee-for-service, volume-based, and outcome-based payment delivery models could be significant following 5G activation. In addition, we have remote diagnosis and imaging through this 5G technology. Finally, the last point called improving the state of the art will be an important piece in the proliferation of data. The consolidation of the latter with predictive analysis as well as the autonomous training will allow doctors and researchers to access aggregated information and accumulated knowledge on treatment trends.

With the rapid evolution of information and communication technologies, the internet of things, smart cities increase the possibilities of mobile health applications, thus enabling the development of the concept of smart health, which is defined as the provision of health services in the preference to use context-aware network and sensing infrastructure of the identified smart cities. To explain this concept of smart health Al-Azzam et al. [18] take the example of a cyclist who wears a bracelet with built-in accelerometers whose main objective is to monitor an accident. The body sensor network helps to detect the fall of the individual and sends a notification to the city's infrastructure. As soon as the system receives a notification, the traffic conditions are evaluated and an ambulance is sent using the best selected route. Capossele et al. [19] illustrated in Fig. 5 a platform model that enables the development of shealth apps to collect, combine and analyze a variety of data provided by citizens and patients, social feeds and urban sensors. This model makes possible the reutilization of infrastructure and application interfaces already existing with mobile health applications that make them a full part of smart cities and so improve people's living conditions. In Fig. 6 they described the stakeholders required to make shealth apps development practical, the benefits they might gain from being part of the s-health ecosystem, and the barriers they face.

- AP: Asset providers use the common s-health platform to share existing infrastructures;
- AD: App developers create applications for Users, using assets (devices and data) provided by AP;
- UP: Use case providers (UP) are those providing use cases and business cases and incentives for new apps to be developed;
- PR: Policy makers and regulators (PR) can leverage the transparency embedded in the s-health platform contract layer to assess compliance;
- AU: Users (AU) are those consuming s-health apps for a given perceived benefit.

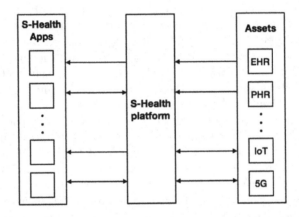

Fig. 5. S-health schema [19]

4   Challenges of Mobile Health Applications

Mobile health applications are good opportunities for developing countries. They can help them improve their health care system and provide more care to those who need it. But to develop a health system that takes into account the mobile health aspect, we have to deal with certain challenges. These challenges are related to a lack of ICT infrastructures, resources, security and privacy issues.

About the lack of infrastructures it mainly consist of a lack of coverage and quality by the telecommunication operators who are the main provider of internet. This is the cause of a low internet connection rate which is not negligible in the process of creating and using these mobile health apps. Internet is expensive in many developing countries and that consists in a real barrier to the mHealth implementation so that those countries people are not able to access health information.

The resource problems are mainly financial's, as health structures often fails to mobilize enough resources to acquire the infrastructure needed to computerize all or part of their health system.

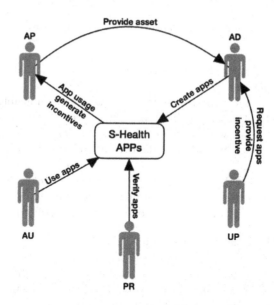

Fig. 6. S-health stakeholders interaction flow [19]

Albabtain et al. [15] shows a serious problem which is the low education and few health literacy skills in some countries of the developing world. This lack of education required are also important hurdles in the effective use of mHealth applications

According to [2] there is evidence indicating that the technology itself can also be part of the problem despite the benefits of their using; in fact, neglecting the complications and challenges of the use of emerging technology in the healthcare field may be dangerous and may have irreparable results. Tayebeh et al. describe in their study 6 kinds of challenges which are the user-related which correspond to users of system, infrastructure which are related to standard regulation, process which might be considered in every component of system, management related to weak quality control and legislation, resources related to hardware and software and training challenges related to the lack of user training and instruction. Other challenges are the security and privacy issues. Papageorgiou et al. [16] in their study found that some applications need for permissions to access certain features like the list of contacts or the dial phone number directory whereas the using of these applications did not show any functionality justifying such requests. They also used MobSF to evaluate the security of apps and found that many apps did not connect using https protocol which can cause several security and privacy issues. Also 45% of the apps tried to determine if the device was rooted which is a feature irrelevant to their goals. The usability of the mobile health apps is another key challenges that can act on it frequency and the use adoption. Teng et al. [17] evaluated in their study a set of health apps authentication and determine the burdens placed on the patients and providers and they conclude that:

- Username/password authentication approaches are not ideal for mHealth apps in acute care settings;
- Combining SMS with one-time-password (OTPs) significantly reduces the burdens on patients and providers but introduces the requirement that all patients have cellular service on a device and creates the significant potential that a patient's authentication credentials might accidentally be sent to the wrong person.
- The QR-code + OTP method preserves the key usability improvements of SMS + OPT authentication, but eliminates the requirement for cellular service and the potential of sending credentials to the wrong person.

We can cite the internet connection as another challenge to the use of the mobile health applications. In most of the cases, health apps needs to send collected data on the patient to a remote server for processing and/or visualisation by the professional health care purposes. A problem can occur if the patient's mobile devices doesn't have access to internet.

5 Conclusion

Mobile health is a medical and public health practice supported by mobile devices. There are many mobile health applications that help patients to improve their life style and their wellness or that help doctors to better provide healthcare even if the patient is not near from him. The IOT wearable devices are frequently use in the mobile health application for the patients monitoring and is very helpful in the decision making process by the doctor. The next 5G technology will come with the possibility of continuous monitoring which will increase the possibility in the field of IOT and mobile health apps. Despite the benefits in the use of the mobile health applications there is some challenges that if it is neglecting it will be dangerous and have irreparable results. These are the security, privacy, usability, internet connexion challenges that can make the use of the mhealth application burdens for the patients or healthcare provider. This first work consisted mainly on the state of the art on mobile health applications. The next step would be to work on the implementation of a mobile health application that would be suitable for developing countries like Burkina in view of the difficulties related to the Internet connection and the high rate of illiteracy.

References

1. Athilingam, P., Jenkins, B.: Mobile phone apps to support heart failure self-care management: integrative review. JMIR Cardio 2, e10057 (2018)
2. Baniasadi, T., Niakan Kalhori, S.R., Ayyoubzadeh, S.M., Zakerabasali, S., Pourmohamadkhan, M.: Study of challenges to utilise mobile-based health care monitoring systems: a descriptive literature review. J. Telemed. Telecare 24, 661–668 (2018)

3. https://www.who.int/topics/chronic_diseases/fr/
4. Bassi, A., John, O., Praveen, D., Maulik, P.K., Panda, R., Jha, V.: Current status and future directions of mHealth interventions for health system strengthening in India: systematic review (2018)
5. Bhattacharya, S., Kumar, A., Kaushal, V., Singh, A.: Applications of m-Health and e-Health in public health sector: the challenges and opportunities (2018)
6. Varkey, M.R., Wu, G., Leung, B., Luu, S., Lu, K.: Medication adherence mobile apps and diabetes self-management education/support guidelines, March 2019
7. Bessin, T.I.I., Ferdinand, G., Sta, H.B.: Reutilization and adaptation of a mobile architecture for diabetes self-management (2018)
8. Deshkar, S., Thanseeh, R.A., Menon, V.G.: A review on IoT based m-Health systems for diabetes, January 2017
9. Kitsiou, S., et al.: Development of an innovative mHealth platform for remote physical activity monitoring and health coaching of cardiac rehabilitation patients (2017)
10. Tlili, F., Haddad, R., Ouakrim, Y., Bouallegue, R., Mezghani, N.: A review on posture monitoring systems (2018)
11. https://pandatelemedicine.wordpress.com/the-panda-system/ , Juillet 2019
12. Istepanian, R.S.H., Alanzi, T.M.: m-Health 2.0: new perspectives on mobile health, machine learning and big data analytics, June 2018
13. Elhoseny, M., Abdelaziz, A., Salama, A.S., Riad, A.M.: A hybrid model of Internet of Things and cloud computing to manage big data in health services applications, December 2018
14. Teece, D.J.: 5G mobile: impact on the health care sector, October 2017
15. Albabtain, A.F., AlMulhim, D.A., Yunus, F., Househ, M.S.: The role of mobile health in the developing world: a review of current knowledge and future trends (2014)
16. Papageorgiou, A., Strigkos, M., Politou, E., Alepis, E., Solanas, A., Patsakis, C.: Security and privacy analysis of mobile health applications: the alarming state of practice, January 2018
17. Teng, Z., et al.: Authentication and usability in mHealth apps, Novembre 2018
18. Al-Azzam, M.K., Alazzam, M.B.: Smart city and smart-health framework, challenges and opportunities (2019)
19. Capossele, A., Conti, M., Gaglione, A., Lazzeretti, R., Missier, P., Nati, M.: Leveraging blockchain to enable smart-health applications (2018)

AmonAI: A Students Academic Performances Prediction System

Iffanice B. Houndayi, Vinasetan Ratheil Houndji[✉], Pierre Jérôme Zohou, and Eugène C. Ezin

Institut de Formation et de Recherche en Informatique (IFRI),
Université d'Abomey-Calavi (UAC), Abomey-Calavi, Benin
`ratheil.houndji@uac.bj`

Abstract. This paper presents a system, called `AmonAI`, that predicts the academic performances of students in the LMD system. The approach used allows to establish, for each of the teaching units of a given semester, some estimates of the students results. To achieve this, various machine learning techniques were used. In order to choose the best model for each teaching unit, we have tested 9 different algorithms offered by the Python Scikit-learn library to make predictions. The experiments were performed on data collected over two years at "Institut de Formation et de Recherche en Informatique (IFRI)" of University of Abomey-Calavi, Benin. The results obtained on the test data reveal that, on five of the nine teaching units for which the work was conducted, we obtain an F2-score of at least 75% for the classification and an RMSE of less than or equal to 2.93 for the regression. The solution therefore provides relatively good results with regard to the dataset used.

Keywords: Students performances prediction · Machine learning · Classification · Regression · Teaching unit · LMD

1 Introduction

The increasing use of ICTs in the different socio-economic fields has contributed to the generation of a large amount of data. The analysis of these data by humans can be a difficult task. Thus, several disciplines such as machine learning are involved in extracting knowledge or highlighting interesting structures from these data in order to solve problems or improve existing solutions. When one is interested in the field of education, from all the interactions and data produced, a large amount of information containing hidden patterns is also generated. To ensure that students are properly trained, it is important that they receive adequate support to improve and succeed in their studies. Unfortunately, several conditions (like huge number of students) make more difficult to monitor students; a situation that decreases their chances of success. This work is part of an initiative to reduce the failure rate of students. It will then dive into the application of machine learning techniques on the available data to make

© ICST Institute for Computer Sciences, Social Informatics and Telecommunications Engineering 2020
Published by Springer Nature Switzerland AG 2020. All Rights Reserved
R. Zitouni et al. (Eds.): AFRICOMM 2019, LNICST 311, pp. 212–218, 2020.
https://doi.org/10.1007/978-3-030-41593-8_16

the prediction of academic performances of the students in the LMD system. This paper presents a system that allows to anticipate their results in order to reduce their failure as much as possible (by taking appropriate decision). The system makes the prediction of the students academic performances through classification and regression in each teaching unit of a given semester and provide visualizations based on these predictions. We have developed a prototype for the "Institut de Formation et de Recherche en Informatique (IFRI)" of University of Abomey-Calavi, Benin. One of the challenge of this work is that such university schools do not store many social data (for example the distance between the student's house and the school, the fact that the student has an internet connection, etc.) that can be very useful here. On the other hand, our experiments show that any machine learning algorithm tested does not clearly dominates all others. Thus our system tests several machine learning algorithms (9 in this paper) to select the best one for each teaching unit.

This paper is organized as follows: Sect. 2 gives an overview of the related works; Sect. 3 presents our solution; Sect. 4 provides some experimental results got after applying our solution to available data and Sect. 5 concludes and gives possible directions for future works.

2   Related Works

Machine learning is nowadays widely used and its use is widespread in many fields, such as education, where obtaining a high success rate is a major challenge. Several researches were carried out in the sense of the prediction of the academic performances. In addition, these researches show that the use of machine learning in the field of predicting academic performance leads to good results.

A review on predicting students performance using Data Mining techniques was conducted at the School of Computer Science at Universiti Sains Malaysia [1]. It shows that the attributes frequently used by researchers are: the cumulative grade point average (CGPA), which is the most important input variable, internal evaluation (lab work, class queries, presence), student demographics (gender, age, family history and disability), external assessments (final exam score for a particular subject), extracurricular activities, secondary studies, social interaction, and psychometric factor (rarely used because it is based on qualitative data). A study conducted in April 2017 by Ali Daud et al. deals with the prediction of student performance (in terms of dropout: degree completed or dropped) using advanced learning techniques [3]. This research paper presents the prediction methods used, which use four different types of attributes, namely: family expenses, family income, student personal information and family assets. Another study carried out at the Tampere University in June 2017 by Murat Pojon addresses the theme of the use of machine learning to predict the performance of students, whose specific objective in this case is to measure the improvement made by feature engineering according to the performance of algorithms [2]. It focuses on linear regression, decision trees, and naive Bayes to make prediction of classification type. Better prediction results were obtained when feature engineering was applied. But the combination of method selection and feature engineering approaches provided the best results. Similar works have been done by other researchers including in the University of Minho in 2008 by Paulo Cortez and Alice Silva where the subject of academic prediction has been applied to high school students (specifically predict students results in mathematics and Portuguese) [4]. The results show that the students performances are strongly affected by their previous results. Interested readers may refer to [5–7] to see some other related works.

An important remark is that there is no algorithm that is suitable for any type of data. The method used is strongly conditioned by the structure and the content of the data. Since we do not have the wide range of features used in the previous works (extra-scholar, social data, etc.), we propose an adapted and contextualized solution to the data available at IFRI, UAC.

3   Our Solution

Our system, called AmonAI[1], predicts academic performances through a web platform. It allows to estimate students performances of a given semester by making predictions of the students results in each teaching unit of the concerned semester. These predictions are of two kinds, classification and regression. Classification means that the system predicts whether a student validates or not a teaching unit while regression means that students grades results in each teaching unit are anticipated.

The system of AmonAI is based on multiple classes. It contains the classes **User, Advanced User, Report, Semester** and **Analysis**. We present below the two important classes **Semester** and **Analysis**:

– the class **Semester** is used to record data for a semester. It is linked to the User class, which means that a Semester object has an **author** property of type **User**. When a semester is added with the training files (sample of previous semester data which will be used for inputs and sample of the current semester data which will be used for outputs/outcomes), it is possible for a user to generate the predictors of this semester, which will be used to generate the report of an analysis related to the concerned semester;
– the class **Analysis**, also linked to the class **User**, is used to configure the information relating to the analysis that the user wishes to perform. He/She specifies in particular the type of the analysis (classification or regression analysis), the file of the analysis, and the semester to which this analysis is related.

For the prediction phase, depending on the analysis to be performed by the user, an analysis file is specified. Then if the structure of this file matches with the one of the sample of previous semester data, a pre-processing is done in order to clearly identify the input variables that will be used for the prediction. Depending on the type of analysis, the predictors of the semester in which the

---

[1] Amon (in Fongbé) is a prediction of the oracle Fà, AI stands for Artificial Intelligence.

analysis is related will make a prediction of performance for each student in the analysis file according to each semester teaching unit. The predicted outcomes for each teaching unit are **validated/non-validated** and a **score between 0 and 20** for respectively a binary classification analysis and a regression analysis.

Algorithm 1. Algorithm describing the performances prediction phase

---

Input: An instance a of the Analysis class
Output: The performances predictions of all the students in the analysis file of a

```
1  begin
2      if structure(a.analysisFile) = structure(a.basisSemester.trainingFilePreviousSem)
       then
3          students ← preprocessing(a.analysisFile);
4          if a.type = "Classification" then
5              predictors ← a.basisSemester.classificationPredictors;
6          else
7              predictors ← a.basisSemester.regressionPredictors;
8          end
9          predictions ← [ ];
10         listTeachingUnits ← a.basisSemester.listTeachingUnits;
11         for i ← 0 to length(students) − 1 do
12             prediction_student ← [ ];
13             for j ← 0 to length(listTeachingUnits) − 1 do
14                 ŷ ← predictors[j].predict(students[i]);
15                 prediction_student[j] ← ŷ;
16             end
17             predictions[i] ← prediction_student;
18         end
19         return predictions;
20     else
21         return ("Error! Analysis should be reconfigured");
22     end
23  end
```

---

4 Experimental Results

4.1 Data and Algorithms Used

For the experiments, we have used the IFRI's data. At IFRI the cycle for bachelor degree consists of three (03) academic years, each with two semesters. The courses taught concern several teaching units subdivided in subjects (for example Mathematical Logic, C language, etc.). This work took into account the available data, which concerned those of the first year of bachelor in IT security and software engineering collected over two years (2016–2017 and 2017–2018). The prediction task was therefore performed on the second semester of the first year (not having relevant data to do so for the first semester) compared to which nine (09) of the ten (10) teaching units were taken into account (the teaching unit of Discipline being the one that has been isolated). Thus, as a basis for training phase, data on marks in first semester subjects and social data such as age and gender have been used. Finally, after pre-processing and isolation of irrelevant information, the data was collected in a dataset (with 258 instances) then separated into two parts using the 70/30 train-test split: 180 instances for the training and 78 instances for the tests.

Unlike in the previous studies we do not have lot of extra school data. We will so focus on applying multiple techniques in terms of algorithms. Thereby, before getting the best models for each teaching unit, the following algorithms were tested: Support Vector Machines (SVM), Decision Trees, Random Forest, Ridge regression (used specifically for regression), Logistic Regression (used specifically for classification), AdaBoost, Gradient Boosting Machine (GBM), k-Nearest Neigbors (KNN) and Feed Forward Neural Network (Multi-layer Perceptron: MLP).

4.2   Algorithms Evaluation

For the selection and evaluation of models, the "Training-Validation-Test" approach was used. The k-fold cross-validation method was performed on the training dataset for the selection of models and parameters. Thus, for the effective evaluation of the models, unknown data not having intervened in the training and validation phases were used: as previously mentioned a sample of 78 instances was used to make the tests.

With regard to classification, the null hypothesis is fixed to the fact that a student does not validate a teaching unit[2]. In order to detect as much as possible the cases of students who might not validate a teaching unit, it is preferable in this context to make a type II error, that is, to accept the null hypothesis whereas it's wrong. In this case, as an evaluation metric we have used the **F2-score** [8]. For regression, the metric used for the evaluation is the Root Mean Square Error (RMSE). Tables 1 and 2 show respectively the performance results (F2-scores and RMSEs) of the various algorithms after cross-validation and hyper-parameters tuning about the classification and regression tasks for each teaching unit.

Table 1. Summary of algorithms performances for classification (results rounded to 10^{-2} - best algorithms scores per teaching unit in bold - best scores per algorithm underlined)

F2-scores									
Algorithms	Teaching units (TUs)								
	TU1	TU2	TU3	TU4	TU5	TU6	TU7	TU8	TU9
Support Vector Machines	0,88	**0,87**	0,76	0,76	0,55	0,57	**0,60**	0,65	0,62
Decision Tree	0,85	0,70	0,65	0,68	0,28	0,40	0,57	0,68	0,47
Random Forest	0,81	0,83	0,74	0,72	0,51	**0,65**	0,53	**0,75**	0,54
Logistic Regression	0,80	0,80	**0,77**	**0,79**	0,53	0,59	0,57	0,68	**0,65**
AdaBoost	0,73	0,80	0,66	0,62	**0,57**	0,26	0,58	0,62	0,40
Gradient Boosting	0,91	0,83	0,54	0,13	0,53	0,34	0,38	0,1	0,41
KNN	0,83	0,79	0,44	0,56	0,47	0,38	0,31	0,40	0,40
Feed forward neural network	**0,92**	0,83	0,57	0,51	0,29	0,52	0,38	0,66	0,47

---

[2] The positive class is then "Non-validated".

Table 2. Summary of algorithms performances for regression (results rounded to 10^{-2} - minimum algorithms errors per teaching unit in **bold** - minimum errors per algorithm underlined)

RMSEs Algorithms	Teaching units (TUs)								
	TU1	TU2	TU3	TU4	TU5	TU6	TU7	TU8	TU9
Support Vector Machines	1,97	2,62	2,70	2,31	2,63	**2,89**	2,56	**2,93**	2,91
Decision Tree	2,41	3,10	4,34	2,90	2,73	3,81	3,73	3,51	3,44
Random Forest	**1,92**	**2,60**	2,51	2,23	2,58	2,91	**2,50**	3,04	2,85
Ridge Regression	2,11	2,90	3,04	**2,10**	**2,41**	2,92	2,71	3,28	2,84
AdaBoost	2,01	2,75	2,65	2,31	2,62	3,17	3,19	3,06	2,82
Gradient Boosting	2,02	2,69	**2,49**	2,37	2,74	2,93	2,65	3,10	**2,81**
KNN	2,30	2,76	2,52	2,46	2,85	3,01	2,62	3,51	2,94
Feed forward neural network	2,09	3,17	3,19	2,18	2,63	3,46	3,38	3,49	2,86

5 Conclusion and Perspectives

We have presented AmonAI, a system based on machine learning techniques that predicts students results in each teaching unit of a given semester. We have tested 9 different algorithms in order to choose the best one for each teaching unit. For the evaluation of the different algorithms which were tested, the metrics F2-score and RMSE were respectively used for classification and regression tasks. The different predictions are globally good with regard to our dataset. On 5 of 9 teaching units, the F2-score is $\geq 75\%$ (classification) and the RMSE is ≤ 2.93 (regression) in all the teaching units.

For future works, it would be interesting to obtain a larger sample for training the algorithms (including other academic and extra-school data) because they contain several key aspects that were not considered in this work. In the same way, it would be important to perform more advanced pre-processing on the data. Finally, we would like to add a system of recommendations that will exploit the results from the predictive analysis to make suggestions.

References

1. Shahiri, A.M., Husain, W., Rashid, N.A.: A review on predicting student's performance using data mining techniques. School of Computer Sciences, Universiti Sains Malaysia (2015)
2. Pojon, M.: Using machine learning to predict student performance. University of Tampere (2017)
3. Daud, A., Aljohani, N.R., Abbasi, R.A., Lytras, M.D., Abbas, F., Alowibdi, J.S.: Predicting student performance using advanced learning analytics. In: Proceedings of the 26th International Conference on World Wide Web Companion, pp. 415–421 (2017)
4. Cortez, P., Silva, A.: Using data mining to predict secondary school student performance. University of Minho (2008)

5. Meier, Y., Xu, J., Atan, O., van der Schaar, M.: Predicting grades. IEEE Trans. Signal Process. **64**(4), 959–972 (2016)
6. Agrawal, H., Mavani, H.: Student performance prediction using machine learning. Int. J. Eng. Res. Technol. **4**(03), 111–113 (2015)
7. Github: Student Performance Prediction. https://github.com/sachanganesh/student-performance-prediction. Accessed 9 Jan 2019
8. Clusteval: Integrative Clustering Evaluation Framework F2-Score. https://clusteval.sdu.dk/1/clustering_quality_measures/5. Accessed 7 Nov 2018

Factors Influencing the Adoption of m-Government: Perspectives from a Namibian Marginalised Community

Karin Frohlich[1(✉)], Marko Nieminen[1], and Antti Pinomaa[2]

[1] Alto University, Espoo, Finland
karin.frohlich@aalto.fi
[2] Lapperanta-Lahti University of Technology, Lappeenranta, Finland

Abstract. Mobile-government (m-Government) services adoption is being advanced as an alternative solution for addressing challenges faced by electronic-government (e-Government) adoption in marginalised communities. However, factors of m-Government need to be understood if it is to be adopted by marginalised communities. There are suggestions that many contextual factors affect to the adoption of m-Government services. In this study, factors of m-Government in Oniipa, a marginalised rural community in Namibia are researched. Results show that security, technology trust, ICT supporting infrastructure, usage experience, costs, awareness, skills for accessing m-Government, language literacy, training, perceived ease of use, perceived usefulness, social influence, perceived empathy and compatibility are critical factors of m-Government services adoption. The study findings shall be used to propel m-Government adoption in a Fusion Grid project that aims to address infrastructural challenges faced by marginal communities when adopting e-Government. Similarly, policy makers can draw lessons on m-Government adoption from this study.

Keywords: m-Government · e-Government · Rural areas · Marginalised communities · Information and communication technologies (ICT) · Government

1 Introduction

As governments move towards improving service delivery through electronic government (e-Government), the adoption of e-Government services has gone well for others while progressing at a slow rate in some regions [1]. The literature suggests that the rural dwellers who are more likely to be less educated are the least adopters of e-Government [2]. From an economic point of view, study in [3] suggested that e-Government is more suited for urban settlements that are characterised by a dense population something that makes internet distribution cheaper when compared to "sparsely populated rural areas". The rapid growth of mobile phone usage has seen mobile-government (m-Government) services being fronted as a suitable alternative for advancing government services in Africa, especially in marginalised areas [3–5]. Marginalised rural areas are often characterised by a poor Information and Communication Technology (ICT) supporting

© ICST Institute for Computer Sciences, Social Informatics and Telecommunications Engineering 2020
Published by Springer Nature Switzerland AG 2020. All Rights Reserved
R. Zitouni et al. (Eds.): AFRICOMM 2019, LNICST 311, pp. 219–236, 2020.
https://doi.org/10.1007/978-3-030-41593-8_17

infrastructure, sparse population, less educated and old population that is usually less economically active [3–6]. However, m-Government awareness and ownership of a mobile phone does not guarantee that the citizens will use m-Government [7]. Hence, the willingness to adopt m-Government by citizens in marginalised areas need to be investigated if m-Government is to be successful. This is important given the fact that the adoption of m-Government is still in its infancy phase something that can be explained by the dominance of e-Government research when compared to m-Government research [1, 3, 8]. In addition, research on m-Government has been focused on economically developed countries [3] that may present unique adoption characteristics when compared to economically less developed countries [2]. This is critical given that culture does have an effect on factors of m-Government [9] something that limits the transferability of findings from one context to another without further confirmation. All these arguments motivate the need to investigate factors of m-Government within the context. This study focuses on factors of m-Government adoption in a marginalised rural community in Namibia. Findings from this study can be used as a point of reference when formulating policies for m-Government adoption in Namibia and other countries that may exhibit similar characteristics to the referenced case.

2   Literature

2.1   Mobile Phone Adoption

The growth in use of mobile phones world over is said to be happening at a faster "rate than that of any other technology ever adopted" [10]. The International Telecommunications Union [11] states that the number of mobile phone subscriptions is bigger than the world population. For example, the mobile phone subscription is believed to be within the region of 170% to 190% in the Kingdom of Saudi Arabia [1]. Of late, the Asian-Pacific (57% of global subscribers) and Africa (10% of global subscribers) are among the leading continents that are experiencing a fast adoption rate of mobile phones. It should be noted that Africa has the least number of mobile phone users when compared to all the other continents. Nevertheless, the adoption of mobile phones shows to be extending to rural areas world over. For example, 93.7% of the respondents from the rural Zhejiang province of China had mobile phones with 32.8% owning a 3rd generation phone [3]. This trend might also be a reflective of developments in mobile phone adoption in rural Africa. Emerging results shows that Africa is experiencing a phenomenal growth rate in mobile phone subscription. For example, mobile phone adopters increased by 91% between 2010 and 2016 in Tanzania [4]. Similarly, the International Telecommunications Union (ITU) [11] showed that mobile phone subscribers increased from 0,32 per 100 inhabitants in the year 2000 to 69,72 per 100 inhabitants at the end of 2017 in Tanzania. Within the Southern region of Africa, Namibia is among the leading countries that are experiencing a fast adoption rate of mobile phones. In the year 2000, Namibia had 4,32 per 100 inhabitants a figure that increasing to 105,79 per 100 inhabitants at the end of 2017 [11]. This is in comparison to South Africa's 156,03 per 100 inhabitants at the end of 2017, up from 18,24 in the year 2000. Similarly, Botswana had 12,85 per 100 inhabitants owning a mobile phone in 2000 that increased to 141,41 at the end of 2017. However, Namibia's other neighbouring countries such as Angola (44,73 per 100), Zambia (78,61 per 100) and Zimbabwe (85,25 per 100) had less than 100 mobile phone subscribers per 100 inhabitants at the end of 2017 [11]. The growth in mobile phone usage in Namibia is attributed to an improved telecommunication regulation that is paving way for private sector investment in ICTs, an area that was previously dominated by the public sector [12].

Another interesting statistic is a finding that, at the end of March 2019, 56.8% of the world population had access to the Internet [13]. Though showing a constant growth, Africa remains the least Internet adopter with a penetration rate of 37.3% [13]. It has been suggested that Africa's growth in Internet access is largely attributed to a growth in mobile phone adoption [12]. This has been found true with reference to Ethiopia, Kenya, Namibia, Nigeria, Rwanda, South Africa and Tanzania. Statistics released by ITU [11] indicate that the dominant use of mobile phones to access the Internet is largely attributed to a constant drop in fixed Internet connection. Access to the Internet is critical as it facilitate the access to some of the m-Government applications [4].

2.2   m-Government and e-Government Challenges and Opportunities

m-Government relates to the use of mobile phones such as tablets, notepads, feature phones to facilitate the deployment of government services and information to citizens [1, 3]. There is a general consensus in the literature that m-Government is not a replacement of e-Government. Instead, m-Government aims to complement e-Government [1, 14]. As such, m-Government is often seen as a component of e-Government. The literature goes on to suggest at least three different factors that are influential in motivating m-Government adoption. These factors vary according to the context and objectives of the m-Government adopter. For example, the adoption of m-Government can be motivated by a need to address challenges faced by e-Government in its attempt to extend services and information delivery to remote and underserved rural areas. [3] reports of a pilot study that aimed to promote government services and information delivery using short message service (SMS) in the Madhya Pradesh government of India. This Madhya Pradesh government project was used in rural areas that had no Internet access. [3] adds that rural China is characterised by a scattered population whose main economic activity is farming. Such a populace cannot afford a computer, Internet access and has low literacy rates to an extent that e-Government websites are considered less attractive [3]. Similarly, [2] found that e-Government is less attractive to rural dwellers. Namibian rural areas share these characteristics where most of the rural communities "are scattered in low densities on farms" [15, p. 4]. In addition, these rural areas have a poor ICT supporting infrastructure such as no access to the national electricity grid, no access to tap water, a poor road network and poor

ICT skills [16, 17]. As such, m-Government through simple technologies like SMSs is expected to play a critical role in service and information delivery in rural areas.

Secondly, the adoption of m-Government can be motivated by a need to take advantage of the wide use of mobile phones by the citizens [1, 4, 14]. In light of a high mobile phone adoption rate discussed in the previous section, it is imperative that governments implement m-Government solutions and benefit from a wide mobile phone usage. This is the most common reason for m-Government adoption in the literature. For example, study in [18] reports of how some African countries have taken advantage of a growing mobile phone adoption and used SMSs to enhance information delivery to rural farmers. This led to improved agricultural yields and profits. In addition, [1] noted that the Saudi Arabian government took advantage of a growing mobile phone usage by its citizens and deployed m-Government through mobile applications. Examples of such applications include the "Health Mobile, tracking of Higher Education Information, Riyadh and Madinah Education, Appointments and Document Tracking and Employee Inquiry" [1]. Similarly, the government of Jordan sought to take advantage of a high mobile phone adoption rate that exceeded the population size reaching 103% in 2010 [14]. The government of Jordan developed a mobile portal with 27 electronic services for its m-Government. In addition, the government of Jordan made use of SMSs to address ICT infrastructural challenges that limited the accessibility of Internet driven mobile applications in some regions. The SMS function played two critical roles of pushing communication (e.g. sending awareness messages) and pulling SMS from the populace. The option of pulling SMSs allowed citizens to send messages to government departments at a fee [14]. In addition, [4] suggested that the decision to adopt m-Government by the Tanzanian government was motivated by the wide use of mobile phones. The m-Government services offered by the Tanzanian government include the mobile government service payment platform, national examination results SMS facility, general SMS pushing platform and a USSD government menu that allow citizens to use a code (*152*00#) to access a menu with different government services. The Namibian government has also shown interest in taking advantage of a booming mobile phone usage by its citizen and adopted m-Government. This is reflected by the use of SMSs to push communication to citizens. For example, the Ministry of Finance send messages to Namibian citizens with the aims of communicating reminders or making awareness campaigns on tax. In addition, the Ministry of Home Affairs use the SMS service to inform the citizens of the outcome for any services that citizens would have applied for.

Lastly, m-Government can be adopted in order to enhance government service and information delivery to citizens [8]. Thus, even though e-Government is performing well, a government may also decide to implement m-Government in order to enhance service delivery. For instance, the Prime Minister of the UAE echoed that "the government of the future works 24/7 and 365 days a year. A successful government is one that goes to the people and does not wait for them to come to it" [Emirates 24|7, 2015a in 8]. Hence, the government took advantage of a good ICT infrastructure to promote m-Government with the aims of improving service delivery.

2.3   Factors of m-Government Adoption

The literature suggests different factors that influence m-Government adoption by citizens. A literature review by [4] found security and privacy/trust, infrastructure, usability, accessibility, personal initiatives and characteristics, and costs as critical factors influencing m-Government adoption. In addition, [1] adopted the Technology Adoption Model (TAM) and used a qualitative research methodology to investigate factors of m-Government. Their study found trustworthiness, usage experience, awareness and security as factors for m-Government adoption. Enjoyment was the only factors that was found not important to m-Government adoption [1]. [7] conducted an exploratory survey in order to establish factors of m-Government adoption by citizens. Their study went on to identify the availability of mobile phones, awareness, the skills for accessing m-Government services, "the ability to read and write in a language used in the mobile phone", costs, training, trust in m-Government and anxiety as important factors of m-Government. While their study confirmed some of the factors identified in the literature, [7] also identified unique factors such as training, skills for accessing m-Government, anxiety and the availability of mobile phones. Another study by [3] investigated factors of m-Government adoption by rural dwellers of the Zhejiang province in China. [3] acknowledged that technological and environmental factors are important in influencing m-Government. As such, they proposed a model of m-Government that was based on the TAM and social environmental factors. Data collection and analysis found perceived ease of use (PEOU), perceived long-term usefulness and social influence having a significant direct influence on the Intent to use m-Government. In addition, a perceived near-term usefulness, image, integrity and benevolence were seen as having an indirect influence towards m-Government adoption. In addition, a study by [19] found social influence, perceived trust, cost of services, perceived usefulness and ease of use important to m-Government adoption. Furthermore, a study by [9] on the impact of culture on m-Government made interesting findings. Thus, the PEOU, security and reliability were found critical to m-Government adoption in Bangladeshi and the USA. However, [9] noted that the perceived empathy in m-Government use was an important factor to participants from Bangladesh while those from the USA found empathy not critical. In addition, USA participants valued compatibility with perceived enjoyment seen as having an indirect effect on m-Government use. Interestingly, participants from Bangladesh did not find compatibility and enjoyment influential to their decision to use m-Government.

Table 1 summarise factors of m-Government that were found in the literature. Similar factors were consolidated under a given new name while other factors were splitted where necessary. Focus was on factors that had a direct effect on factors of m-Government. In addition, preference was given to factors that had supporting empirical evidence. Hence, factors of m-Government that were arrived at through literature review, for instance those in [4], were not considered in this study.

Table 1. Factors of m-Government adoption.

The identified factor	Description	Source
Security	Users perception that m-Government platforms provide the needed security to personal data influences adoption. Anxiety as a result of anticipated risks was considered an element of security	[1, 4, 7, 9]
Technology trust	Given that m-Government is still a new phenomenon, it is possible that citizens may have uncertainties regarding the capability of the technology to deliver the aspired services. In addition, trustworthiness goes hand in hand with citizen's perspective on m-Government reliability. As such, trust in technology will positively promote m-Government use	[1, 4, 7, 9, 19]
ICT supporting infrastructure	The provision of ICT infrastructure such as the telecommunication network and access to electricity promotes the adoption of m-Government	[3, 4]
Usage experience	Experience in related technologies may promote m-Government adoption. For example, experience in using mobile phones to acquire a service promotes m-Government adoption	[1]
Costs	The cost of accessing m-Government determines the willingness of citizens to adopt the technology. The lower the cost the better chances of m-Government adoption	[4, 7, 19]
Awareness	Awareness of m-Government initiatives may create a basis for adoption	[1, 7]
Availability of mobile phones	The availability or ownership of mobile phones enhances chances of m-Government adoption. However, it should be noted that ownership of a mobile phone does not guarantee m-Government	[7]
Skills for accessing m-Government	Within the context of developing countries, having the skills to operate mobile phones when accessing and using m-Government is important	[7]
Language literacy	This relates to the ability to read and write in a language used in the mobile phone	[7]
Training	Training to use m-Government services has been found important in other developing countries	[7]
Perceived ease of use	The extent to which citizens can easily navigate around the system promotes m-Government adoption. Thus, this measures the extent to which m-Government is considered easy to use or is free from error. This is important for rural dwellers who are often less skilled	[3, 4, 8, 9]
Perceived usefulness	This factor expresses the benefits that citizens expect to derive from using m-Government. Citizens are more likely to adopt m-Government if they can foresee themselves yielding a lot of benefits	[3, 19]

(continued)

Table 1. (*continued*)

The identified factor	Description	Source
Social influence	Social influence involves peer pressure from those within the adopter's environment and the perception that, adopting m-Government would enhance one's social standing or image within their society	[3, 19]
Perceived empathy	A feeling that someone cares about customers/citizens when accessing government services through m-Government can enhance adoption. Thus, the lack of physical interaction implies that the belief that someone will sincerely and promptly respond to services requested via m-Government enhances chances of adoption	[9]
Compatibility	Compatibility reflects the extent to which citizens find m-Government to be consistent with their beliefs or habits or customs or expectations or ways of doing things	[9]

3   Methodology

This study is part of an ongoing community network project, the Fusion Grid, that aims to address infrastructural concerns in order to enhance e-Government use by citizens based in a selected marginalised rural community in Namibia. The e-Government challenges faced by citizens who are based in rural areas includes a lack of electricity, limited ICT skills, low incomes and poor connectivity as discussed in the literature review. It is in this regard that the Fusion Grid project aims to make an initial provision for ICT supporting infrastructure with solar powered technology [20, 21]. These technologies aim at being less complex, simply plug and play that suits rural communities that are characterized by less skilled individuals. Fusion Grid provides a solar powered mobile network 4th generation long-term evolution (4G LTE) base station that delivers mobile network connectivity to the targeted rural community. Thus, the three main pillars of the research project are electricity provision (solar PV-based power system integrated with energy storage; Lithium-ion batteries, and power electronics), connectivity (4G LTE mobile network base station), and digital services (electronic learning (eLearning), mobile pay, and m-Government). Despite the highly technological characteristic of the initial Fusion Grid application, it needs to be considered as a prototype [6] for further elaboration with the end-users, the members of the community. Selected Namibian Offices/Ministries/Agencies (OMAs) were engaged in the experiment for delivering m-Government services. As part of the project initiation, it was important to understand factors that influence m-Government adoption. Data was gathered during a baseline survey. Quantitative and qualitative data was gathered by use of a questionnaire. Descriptive statistics and qualitative data analysis techniques were used to analyse data. It should be noted that qualitative data was only gathered to assess factors of m-Government adoption.

3.1 The Targeted Community: Oniipa Town Council (OTC)

Oniipa town council (OTC) is located in Oshikoto region (province), north of Namibia. OTC has a population of approximately 30 000, and attained a town council status on the 3rd of April 2015. According to the Namibian Local Authorities Act, a town council is an urban settlement that can rely on its own financial resources to pay for some of its operations. The donor agents and the central government are expected to contribute additional funding for the operation of a town council. It is important to realise that the growth of Namibian urban settlements where partly influenced by the developments in the colonial era. OTC is on the north of the Red Cordon Fence that was erected during the colonial era. During the apartheid rule by South Africa, the Red Cordon Fence divided Namibia into two, the north, dominated by villages (Bantustans) and the south dominated by urban settlements. This implied that the Bantustans, like OTC, were to be administered by Traditional Authorities with little or no government support while the southern part of Namibia was under the then homeland government. This partly explain why the Oshikoto region, home to OTC, is among the top three Namibian regions with a big proportion of rural areas that have the poorest people (Namibia Statistics Agency 2012). The level of poverty and poor infrastructure in Namibian rural areas make these regions less attractive for business investment especially those in the ICT sector. Small-scale farming is the major economic activity in the Oshikoto region.

4   Results

A total of 150 hard copies of the questionnaire were distributed in OTC, and 105 completed ones were returned. The following sections present demographics results, and goes on to outlay findings on factors of m-Government adoption.

4.1   Gender and Age Distribution

Females by far contributed a significant proportion of the respondents. Of the 105 respondents that took part in the study, 67% were females while 33% were males. In terms of age distribution, the majority of respondents were more than 36 years old. In fact, those above 40 years old contributed 42% of the total respondents as shown in Fig. 1. Rural areas are often characterised by an aged population [6].

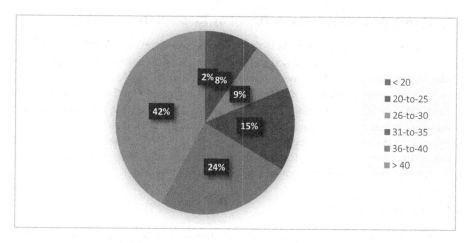

Fig. 1. Age distribution of the respondents.

4.2   Level of Education

Those with a certificate and metric (high school) as the highest qualification were represented by nearly 50% of the respondents. Exactly 14% had no educational qualifications. A fair share of the respondents had a diploma (22%) as the highest qualification followed by a small proportion of respondents with a degree and post graduate degree. This huge proportion of respondents with an educational qualification in a rural setting can be explained by the fact that the majority of the respondents came from Oniipa Town Council, with few of these coming from the adjacent rural areas (Fig. 2).

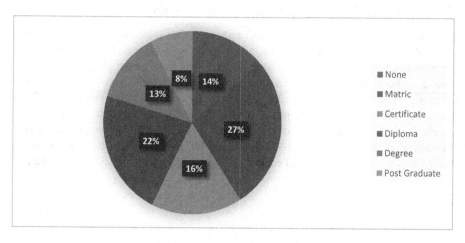

Fig. 2. Level of education across the respondents.

4.3   Household Electronic Goods Owned by Respondents

Respondents were asked to indicate if they own or have access to selected house hold electronic goods. Only 38% indicated that they have access to lights. Interestingly, 31% of the respondents showed to have a television set at home, while 14% indicated that they have an electric cooker. In addition, only 25% indicated that they own an electric iron. Similar small proportions of the respondents indicated that they have an air conditioner at home (6%), a fan (13%) and a refrigerator (15%). It should be noted that temperature ranges vary between 3 and 31 °C in OTC. Nevertheless, these results could be explained by a lack of access to electricity as only 36% of the respondents indicated that they have access to the national electricity grid.

4.4   Ownership of ICTs

Respondents were asked to indicate if they own or have access to selected ICTs. The radio (90%) was found to be the most popular ICT gadget owned by respondents. This was followed by mobile phones that are owned by 77% of the respondents. However, only 59% indicated that they own a smart phone. Nevertheless, 31% of the respondents indicated that they own a television set as indicated in the previous section. Furthermore, 30% of the respondents indicated that they have access to the Internet. Another 30% indicated that they own a computer. It is interesting to note that the mobile phone penetration in OTC is comparable to that of rural Zhejiang province of China as reported in [3]. However, results from this study confirms that Internet access remains low in the rural areas. This could be explained by a lack of lightweight Base Station solutions, and accordingly no business case for mobile network operators to extend the coverage to each corner and village of rural populated countries as is the case in Namibia.

4.5   Important ICTs and Electronic Household Goods

Respondents were asked to rate the importance of nine selected ICTs and electronic household goods. These included mobile phone, lights television, air conditioner, refrigerator, computer, radio, tablet and a cooking stove. For every item, respondents were to indicate its importance in their livelihoods. Figure 3 shows the ICTs and electronic household goods that were considered important by respondents from OTC. Access or owning lights, mobile phones and a refrigerator are the most important ICTs and electronic household goods for respondents. It is interesting to note that ownership of a mobile phone is among the most important ICTs. In particular to ICTs, respondents showed less interest in tablets and computers. This finding can be explained by the fact that, being low income earners, members from the rural areas may not fancy ICTs they feel are luxurious. A basic mobile phone may be adequate for such a populace.

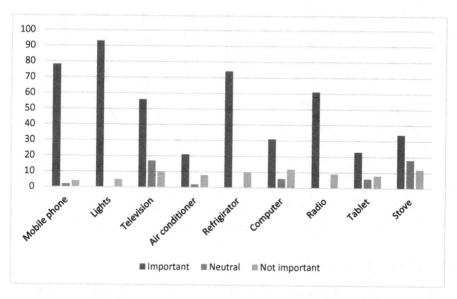

Fig. 3. Important ICTs and electronic household goods.

4.6 Important Services

Respondents were asked to rate the importance of selected services to their community. Nine services that were listed include: access to electricity, Internet access, health access, education, clean water supply, having sanitation, access to government services having a better job and security. Figure 4 summarise the study finding on important services. It is interesting to note that access to electricity; clean water and health are the most important services to respondents. Internet access is considered the least important service. Of the nine evaluated services, access to government services is rated the sixth most important service. Electricity and water access are the basic needs for any community. However, the low interest in Internet may be explained by the fact that, rural dwellers are not aware of the benefits associated with the Internet. Alomari (2011) in [1] suggested that it is important to promote awareness of technologies in use such that citizens would be interested in adopting them.

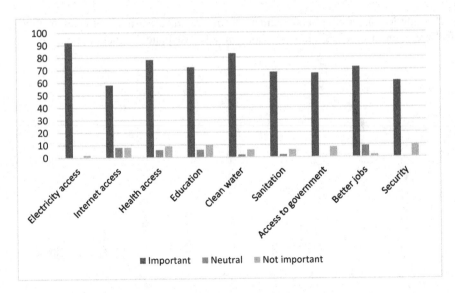

Fig. 4. Important services.

4.7 Factors of m-Government Adoption

Findings on factors of m-Government adoption are presented in this section. The findings are in particular to the identified factors of m-Government adoption presented in Table 1. Presentation of findings is based on quantitative data. However, relevant supporting qualitative data on each factor is also presented if available.

Security. Respondents were asked to indicate the importance of security and privacy in m-Government. The majority of respondents (56%) indicated that security is an important factor in their decision to adopt m-Government. Similarly, the literature shows that security is important for m-Government adoption [1, 9]. Security is important as it promote privacy, data integrity and availability.

Technology Trust. To establish if trust was an important factor of m-Government adoption, respondents were asked to indicate if they would prefer to go to the governmental office, instead of using mobile phone to access governmental services. Approximately 46% of the respondents agreed that they rather walk into a government office instead of using m-Government. However, 50% of the respondents suggested that they would prefer to use m-Government. These findings suggest that technology trust is yet to reach inspiring levels to an extent of facilitating the access of government services using mobile phones. Hence, promoting trust among citizens can go a long way in enhancing m-Government adoption.

ICT Supporting Infrastructure. Respondents were asked to indicate if it was important to have access to mobile network for m-Government to be adopted. 76% of the respondents indicated that ICT supporting infrastructure is important for m-Government adoption. To some extent, this percentage is supported by the 77% who indicated that they own a mobile phone. However, 22% of the respondents indicated that they do not know while the remaining 2% did not consider mobile network access important. The importance of ICT supporting infrastructure was emphasised by comments made by some of the respondents. For instance, one of the respondents indicated that rural areas "lack infrastructure". She went on to explain that rural areas "don't have the MTC [Namibia's leading mobile network service provider] towers close. They don't have access to Internet you understand." These findings are supported by the literature that shows that rural areas are characterised by a poor ICT infrastructure [3].

Usage Experience. Data was gathered to establish if the experience gained in using the Internet or other mobile phone services could be considered as an important factor in influencing the decision to adopt m-Government. 63% of the respondents agreed that they could use their experience with other mobile phone services to know how to use m-Government services. The difference in m-Government adoption between economically advanced communities when compared to less economically advanced communities has always been down to differences in the level of adoption and use of other Internet and computing services [1]. Accordingly, the population's experience with other mobile phone services may promote m-Government adoption.

Costs. The literature suggest that rural communities find accessing m-Government services expensive [4, 7, 19]. A high cost of accessing m-Government services discourage adoption. When asked if buying mobile phone credit was expensive, 72% of the respondents indicated that mobile phone credit was expensive. A follow-up question was asked in order to find out if the respondents thought that using mobile phones to access government services would be too expensive for many people. 69% percent of the respondents agreed that accessing m-Government services would be expensive. Only 16% thought it would not be expensive. Rural dwellers have limited sources for generating an income. Hence, it is expected that they would find m-Government expensive. However, one would expect that using m-Government is less expensive when this factor is being considered in light of perceived benefits such as cutting travelling costs. In a way, this finding on costs suggest a lack of awareness of benefits associated with m-Government.

Awareness. Data was gathered to establish the impact of m-Government awareness on adoption. Respondents were asked if they could consider using m-Government services if they were familiar with a government department using such a facility. 63% of the respondents indicated that they would use m-Government. Only 24% indicated that they would not use m-Government even if they were familiar with a Ministry that uses the technology. These findings strongly suggest that the awareness of government departments that use m-Government could positively influence adoption. Alomari (2011) in [1] stated that "a lack of awareness is one factor that prevented Jordanian citizens from adopting e-Government" (p. 59).

Skills for Accessing m-Government. Respondents were asked to indicate if they would adopt m-Government if they have the necessary skills to access and use m-Government services. [7] found that having skills to operate a mobile phone and accessing m-Government plays a critical role in influencing adoption. 54% of the respondents indicated that they had the skills to operate a mobile phone something they could use in m-Government adoption. However, 54% is just above half. Hence, policy implementers need to look into acquainting m-Government potential adopters with ICT skills if they are to adopt the technology. [5] noted that citizens' ICT skills were critical to m-Government acceptance.

Language Literacy. Namibia is a multilingual country with at least two dominant Indio-European languages namely English and Afrikaans that are widely used in urban areas. While English is the official language, it is common that the rural populace mainly use native languages when communicating. Hence, the ability to read and write in a language used in the mobile phone has the potential to enhance m-Government adoption [7]. A strong interest (76%) in using local language when displaying content of m-Government suggest that respondents were particular about language literacy. This goes on to suggest that the Fusion Grid project may consider developing mobile applications that are oriented in local languages in order to maximise m-Government adoption.

Training. Data was gathered to establish the importance of m-Government services user training prior to adoption. For instance, respondents were asked if they would only consider accessing government services using mobile phones after getting explanations on how to use it from someone. 59% of the respondents indicated that they would need someone to explain to them how to use m-Government before using it. Only 23% indicated that they would not need any explaining from anyone prior to m-Government adoption and use. These findings were corroborated by a finding that 50% of the respondents indicated that they would need advice from someone prior to using their mobile phone to access government services. Only 27% of the respondents indicated that they would not need any advice from anyone for them to adopt m-Government. Hence, m-Government training is critical when targeting rural areas.

Perceived Ease of Use. The literature suggest that the usability of m-Government plays a pivotal role in its adoption [3, 4, 9, 19]. To evaluate the perceived ease of use, respondents were asked if they felt that their mobile phones were user friendly. Fifty four percent of the respondents indicated that their mobile phones were user friendly. However, 30% of the respondents thought their phones were not user friendly. In addition, respondents were asked if they felt it would be complicated to use their mobile phones to access m-Government. Sixty three percent of the respondents indicated that using their mobile phone to access government services would be more complicated for them. Only 27% of the respondents indicated that using their mobile phones to access government services would not be complicated. Similarly, 55% of the respondents indicated that using mobile phone to access government service was not clear to them and sounded difficult. Only 31% of the respondents indicated that they understood how to use m-Government and it was not difficult. These findings can be explained by respondent's keen interest to be afforded training prior to adopting m-Government. Accordingly, perceived ease of use is an important factor of m-Government adoption.

Perceived Usefulness. The literature suggests that understanding perceived advantages associated with m-Government will likely promote adoption [3, 19]. To some extent, it can be argued that respondents are aware of the potential benefits of using m-Government. For instance, 71% of the respondents indicated that using m-Government would make it easy for them. Only 13% thought using m-Government would not make life easy for them. Respondents weighed in with comments that suggest they were well informed with m-Government usefulness. One of the respondents indicated that using m-Government allows her to *"apply for services online than to going to the office and join the queues"*. Another respondent who seemed enthusiastic about m-Government also indicated that she would benefit from being able to *"pay for the municipality bills, apply for death, birth, ID card/certificate"*. In addition, another respondent weighed in by stating that *"it can [would] be nice to pay bills like electricity and water online"*. However, findings from a follow-up question appears to contradict the view that respondents are well informed of m-Government's usefulness. When asked if the respondents were informed about why mobile phones should be used for accessing government services, only 34% of the respondents indicated that they consider themselves to be well informed. Surprisingly, the majority (43%) of the respondents suggested that they were not informed on why m-Government should be used. The remaining 23% were undecided. These findings support the perception that the targeted population require training on m-Government for them to understand its importance.

Social Influence. The literature suggest that social influence is one of the most important factors promoting m-Government adoption [3, 19]. As such, respondents were asked for questions with the aims of evaluating the potential effect of social influence on m-Government adoption. Firstly, respondents were asked if they would adopt m-Government because their friends are using it. Fifty five percent of the respondents indicated that they would adopt m-Government if their friends were using it. Only 38% of the respondents indicated that they would not adopt m-Government because of their friends, while 7% were undecided. These findings suggest that social influence does have an effect on m-Government adoption. In addition, respondents were asked if they would wait to see others use mobile phones to access government services before trying out the technology. Fifty four percent of the respondents agreed to waiting and see others use the technology first. Only 27% of the respondents indicated that they would not wait for others to adopt m-Government while 19% were undecided. Again, these findings emphasise the role of social influence though a close call given that close to 50% of the respondents suggest otherwise. Nevertheless, it can be argued that the respondents from rural OTC portray cultural characteristics of a collectivism where no one is keen on taking an independent initiative. Instead, they prefer to assume collectivism when solving problems as suggested by Hofstede [9]. However, when asked if the decision to adopt m-Government was entirely a respondent's own decision without the influence of anyone else, 53% of the respondents agreed to this. Only 19% of the respondents indicated otherwise while 27% were undecided. These findings suggest that, while group opinion was important, respondents would still need to make their own final decision on m-Government. Factors such as anticipated costs and previous experience may influence the final decision. This reasoning is supported by the fact that, only 31% of the respondents went on to indicate that they would quit using m-Government services because a friend or family member has a negative opinion over it. Forty nine percent of the respondents indicated that they would not stop using m-Government services due to negative comments from friends and family. The remaining 20% was undecided.

Perceived Empathy. [9] found that respondents from Bangladesh valued empathy in m-Government adoption. Similarly, respondents in this study appear to be motivated by perceived empathy when adopting m-Government. Eighty percent of the respondents indicated that they would be motivated by quick response in m-Government. In addition, 78% of the respondents also suggested that the ability to track the status of service application motivates them into adopting m-Government. One of the respondents stated that *"I'm a bit concerned about backlog, because umm sometimes you might fill it on the app, or online, and then you, they might never show up to, go to the verification process. Unless, maybe if that app or form has a time limit. That would be great"*. These findings suggest that the perceived empathy would positively motivate m-Government adoption.

Compatibility. There are suggestions that the extent to which m-Government is consistent with available technology, beliefs and practices positively influence adoption [9]. Data was gathered to establish the importance of compatibility in m-Government adoption. To evaluate the effect of technology compatibility, respondents were asked if they were of the opinion that their mobile phones were good enough for providing government services. Fifty percent of the respondents indicated that their mobile phones were compatible with m-Government. Approximately 37% indicated that their mobile phones were not compatible with m-Government while the remaining 13% was undecided. Even though 50% of the respondents indicated that their mobile phones are compatible with m-Government, the remaining 50% calls for a closer consideration before implementing m-Government. In addition, respondents were asked if using mobile phones to access Internet services was consistent with their life style. Fifty percent of the respondents indicated that using mobile phones to access Internet services was compatible with their life style. Only 27% of the respondents thought this was not compatible with their lifestyle while 23% were undecided. Again, these findings suggest understanding the lifestyle of respondents may help enhance m-Government adoption.

5 Conclusion

m-Government is a recent phenomenon whose introduction was motivated by a need to enhance government services in rural areas or take advantage of the growing use of mobile phones. While governments are contemplating the adoption of m-Government, factors influencing m-Government remain debatable. Accordingly, this study investigated important factors that influence m-Government adoption by a rural populace based in OTC. Besides identifying factors of m-Government adoption, this study explored the dynamics within which these factors occur with reference to OTC. The factors that were found important include m-Government security, technology trust, ICT supporting infrastructure, usage experience, costs, awareness, skills for accessing m-Government, language literacy, training, perceived ease of use, perceived usefulness, social influence, perceived empathy and compatibility. These factors are critical for initiating a community network of this study project dubbed the Fusion Grid. In addition, it is also believed that policy implementers of e-Government can learn on important factors of adoption from this study.

References

1. Alotaibi, R., Houghton, L., Sandhu, K.: Exploring the potential factors influencing the adoption of M-government services in Saudi Arabia: a qualitative analysis. Int. J. Bus. Manag. **11**(8), 56–71 (2016)
2. Nam, T., Sayogo, D.S.: Who uses e-government?: examining the digital divide in e-government use. In: Proceedings of the 5th International Conference on Theory and Practice of Electronic Governance, pp. 27–36. ACM (2011)
3. Liu, Y., Li, H., Kostakos, V., Goncalves, J., Hosio, S., Hu, F.: An empirical investigation of mobile government adoption in rural China: a case study in Zhejiang province. Gov. Inf. Q. **31**(3), 432–442 (2014)
4. Ishengoma, F., Mselle, L., Mongi, H.: Critical success factors for m-Government adoption in Tanzania: a conceptual framework. Electron. J. Inf. Syst. Dev. Ctries. **85**(1), e12064 (2018)
5. Ochara, M., Mawela, T.: Enabling social sustainability of e-participation through mobile technology. Inf. Technol. Dev. **21**(2), 205–228 (2015)
6. Winschiers-Theophilus, H., et al.: Moving away from Erindi-Roukambe: transferability of a rural community-based co-design. In: Proceedings of the 12th International Conference on Social Implications of Computers in Developing Countries, May, Ocho Rios, Jamaica (2013)
7. Rana, N., Janssen, M., Sahu, G.P., Baabdullah, A., Dwivedi, Y.: Citizens' perception about m-government services: results from an exploratory survey. In: Proceedings of the 52nd Hawaii International Conference on System Sciences (2019)
8. Ahmad, S.Z., Khalid, K.: The adoption of M-government services from the user's perspectives: empirical evidence from the United Arab Emirates. Int. J. Inf. Manag. **37**(5), 367–379 (2017)
9. Shareef, M.A., Kumar, V., Dwivedi, Y.K., Kumar, U.: Service delivery through mobile-government (mGov): driving factors and cultural impacts. Inf. Syst. Front. **18**(2), 315–332 (2016)
10. Maoneke, P.B., Shava, F.B., Gamundani, A.M., Bere-Chitauro, M., Nhamu, I.: ICTs use and cyberspace risks faced by adolescents in Namibia. In: Proceedings of the Second African Conference for Human Computer Interaction: Thriving Communities, p. 11. ACM (2018)
11. ITU: ITU releases 2018 global and regional ICT estimates (2019). https://www.itu.int/en/mediacentre/Pages/2018-PR40.aspx
12. Stork, C., Calandro, E., Gillwald, A.: Internet going mobile: internet access and use in 11 African Countries. Info **15**(5), 34–51 (2013)
13. Internet World Stats: Internet world stats. Usage and population statistics (2019). https://www.internetworldstats.com/stats.htm
14. Abu-Shanab, E., Haider, S.: Major factors influencing the adoption of m-government in Jordan. Electron. Gov. Int. J. **11**(4), 223–240 (2015)
15. Namibia Statistics Agency: Profile of Namibia. Facts, figures, and other fundamental information (2013). https://cms.my.na/assets/documents/p19dpmrmdp1bqf19s2u8pisc1l4b1.pdf
16. Gumbo, S., Jere, N., Terzoli, A.: A qualitative analysis to determine the readiness of rural communities to adopt ICTs: a Siyakhula living lab case study. In: Proceedings of the IST-Africa 2012 (2012)
17. Pade-Khene, C., Mallinson, B., Sewry, D.: Sustainable rural ICT project management practice for developing countries: investigating the Dwesa and RUMEP projects. Inf. Technol. Dev. **17**(3), 187–212 (2011)
18. Vark, C.V.: Empowering farmers through SMS (2012). http://www.guardian.co.uk/global-development-professionals-network/2012/nov/27/farmersmobile-phones-sms-agriculture

19. Almarashdeh, I., Alsmadi, M.K.: How to make them use it? Citizens acceptance of M-government. Appl. Comput. Inform. **13**(2), 194–199 (2017)
20. Demidov, I., Lana, A., Pinomaa, A., Pyrhönen, O., Partanen, J.: Techno-economic analysis of network configuration of PV-based off-grid distribution system. In: Proceedings of 25th International Conference on Electricity Distribution, Madrid, 3–6 June 2019, pp. 1–5 (2019)
21. Nardelli, P.H.J., et al.: Energy internet via packetized management: enabling technologies and deployment challenges. IEEE Access **7**, 16909–16924 (2019)
22. Namibia Statistics Agency: Poverty dynamics in Namibia: a comparative study using the 1993/94, 2003/04 and the 2009/10 NHIES surveys (2012). https://cms.my.na/assets/documents/p19dnar71kanl1vfo14gu5rpbkq1.pdf

Recent Approaches to Drift Effects in Credit Rating Models

Rachael Chikoore[1], Okuthe P. Kogeda[2(✉)], and S. O. Ojo[1]

[1] Department of Computer Science, Faculty of Information Communication Technology, Tshwane University of Technology, Private Bag X680, Pretoria 0001, South Africa
maichicco@gmail.com, OjoSO@tut.ac.za
[2] Department of Computer Science and Informatics, Faculty of Natural and Agricultural Sciences, University of the Free State, P. O. Box 339, Bloemfontein 9300, South Africa
kogedapo@ufs.ac.za

Abstract. Credit Rating is the valuation of the credit worthiness of the borrowing entity, which gives an indication of the borrower's current credit position and the probability of default. A credit rating model must be very accurate in doing its predictions because critical decisions are made based on the classification that would have been made for the prospective borrower. Different changes occur in the environment that would have been used to come up with the initial model, which might not be applicable to the current sample population and this might have an effect on the prediction accuracy. Changes to the data stream, economic climate, social and cultural environment may cause a drift. Drift shows that there is a change in probability distribution of the concept under study. Population drift is an example of concept drift. Having a static credit rating model will bring challenges in future predictions, hence, there is the need for designing a dynamic credit rating system that caters for the changes that might occur to the initial population sample in order to maintain the prediction accuracy of the model. In this paper, a detailed literature study was conducted exploring recent solution approaches to drift effect in credit rating models. A comprehensive recent solutions is presented in this paper that could be a source of information of interested researchers.

Keywords: Credit rating · Drift effect · Concept drift · Population drift · Prediction · Approaches · Credit rating models · Probability distribution

1 Introduction

It is very common for researchers and model designers to assume that the probabilities of class membership, which are conditional on the feature vectors do not change. When model data changes over time, it can result in poor and degrading predictive performance in predictive models that assume a static relationship between input and output variables. This problem of the changing underlying relationships in the data is called concept drift in the field of machine learning.

The reality is that both population drift and concept drift occur and can affect the prediction accuracy of any given model. It is highly likely that there is a change in

R. Zitouni et al. (Eds.): AFRICOMM 2019, LNICST 311, pp. 237–253, 2020.
https://doi.org/10.1007/978-3-030-41593-8_18

population in a credit scoring model. The population may change responding to the change in the economic environment and other social changes that could affect an individual. There is a very thin line that separates population drift from concept drift. Population drift shows that there is a change in probability distribution of the concept under study yet concept drift is said to have occurred to this change in distribution and also other related changes hence concept drift is the broader change in the model environment.

Evolving data means that data distribution changes over time. This can happen in different ways, for example, Feature drift in which the distribution of input data X changes, p(X), Real concept drift in which the relationship between input X and target y changes, p(y|X) and Changing prior distribution, for example, of the target p(y) when the arrival of new information occurs [1].

This paper aims at analyzing the different approaches to managing drift and its effects in credit rating. A detailed literature review was undertaken unearthing a number of recent solution approaches to drift effect in credit ratings.

The remainder of this paper is organized as follows: In Sect. 2, we provide the general credit rating approaches. In Sect. 3, we give the statistical approaches. In Sect. 4, we outline the data mining approaches. In Sect. 5, we explain the hybrid/ensemble approaches. In Sect. 6, we provide the general approaches to handling drift. In Sect. 7, we give the drift effects and proposed solutions. In Sect. 8, we provide the credit scoring models application areas and in Sect. 9, we conclude the paper.

2   General Credit Rating Approaches

Credit rating in different countries is managed by credit rating bureaus. The most common rating is using a range of values and the letters of the alphabet. Scoring can be done for a new applicant in order to estimate the credit risk. Behavioral scoring is based on the client's previous or current credit standing, it is believed that the way an individual handles the previous or the current loan might have a direct link on their future behavior. Collection scoring is used to categorize the clients into groups, depending on their behavior. Fraud detection classifies the applicants according to the probability that an applicant is guilty [2].

Credit rating classifies the methods of coming up with a rating into two categories, Statistical methods and Data mining methods. Examples of statistical methods include but not limited to simple Ordinary Least Square (OLS) and ordered probit model. Examples of data mining methods include but not limited to Decision trees, Multi Class Support Vector Machines and Multi Class Proxial Support Vector Machines (PSVM) [3].

3   Statistical Approaches

Statistical methods are usually used for feature selection and the most common and effective classifiers that have been used in credit scoring are Artificial Neural Networks (ANN) and Support Vector Machine (SVM) [4]. Linear Discriminate Analysis (LDA) is an example of a statistic approach which was first proposed by Fisher as a classification method. It uses a Linear Discriminate Function (LDF) which passes through the centroids of the two classes to classify customers. It is a commonly used approach but its disadvantage is that it requires linear relationships between depended and independent variables and its assumption is that input variables follow a normal distribution. Logistic Regression (LR) does not require normal distributed input variables. It has the ability to predict default probability of an applicant and pick on the variables related to his behavior. Multivariate Adaptive Regression Splines (MARS) is a non-linear and non-parametric regression method and is excellent in dealing with high dimensional data. It does not presume that there is a linear association amongst the dependent and independent variables. It has a short training time and also has a strong intelligibility.

4 Data Mining Approaches

A comparison on the most commonly used data mining methods in credit rating was done. The research aimed at bringing awareness to researchers on the various approaches that can be applied in credit scoring [5]. Data mining methods have been widely used due to their ability in discovering practical knowledge from the database and transforming it into meaningful information. Data mining approach to credit rating was classified as ranging from Neural Networks, Bayesian Classifier, Logic regression, K-Nearest Neighbor, Decision tree, Survival analysis, Fuzzy rule based system, Support Vector machine and also Hybrid methods. The research concluded that the Support Vector machine approach was commonly used.

Paleologo et al. [6] did a comparative study on the accuracy of classification models in order to reduce the credit risk. They used data mining of the enterprise software to come up with four classification models. The four models were decision tree, logic regression, neural networks and support vector machines. The conclusion indicated that the support vector machine models performed better than the decision tree, logic regression and neural network model.

Zhong and Li [7] gave a summary of the different approaches that are used in credit scoring and introduced a new approach called ensemble learning model. The main focus of their study was to show that it is important to move away from the static approach to credit scoring towards a dynamic approach. They summed up the approaches to credit scoring into Statistical models, Artificial Intelligence (AI) models, Hybrid models and also Ensemble methods.

Bayesian classifiers are white box in nature. They predict that a given sample belongs to a certain class. They are believed to be highly accurate when used in prediction. Decision trees use the recursive partitioning approach to prediction. The virtual subdivisions are done on customer data to make the homogeneity of default risk in the subset greater than the original set. Division continues until the new subsets meet the specifications of the end node. C4.5 and CART are the most popular approaches used in credit scoring. Markov models perform predictions based on past trends. It uses historical data to predict the distribution of population at any given time.

Apart from Statistical methods, Artificial intelligence methods such as Artificial Neural Networks (ANN), Genetic Algorithms (GA) and Support Vector Machines (SVM) have been use in credit scoring. ANN comprises a large number of nodes which are linked and they receive signals from the pre-layer and output them into the next layer. The feed–forward network with Back Propagation (BP) is widely used for credit scoring. ANN possess a strong learning ability and does not make assumptions on the relationship between input variables. ANNs' major disadvantage is their black box nature hence they are difficult to understand and also it is difficult to design the network for experimental purposes because of its complexity and also long training time and demand for large training samples.

SVM is easy to implement on small samples and does not limit the data distribution. Many researches that did work around the implementation of SVM in credit scoring concluded that it was a superior approach to ANN in the aspect of classification accuracy, however, SVM is also black box in nature hence it is complicated to implement on large data. GA simulate natural selection of Darwinian biological evolution theory in order to search for an optimal solution. It is self-adaptive, globally optimal and robust, because it is evolutionary in nature, it does not need to understand the inherent nature of the problem, be it linear or non-linear, continuous or discrete.

KNN is a clustering method that learns by analogy. It searches the pattern space for training samples that are closest to the unknown sample. Hsieh *et al.* [8] built a new classifier called Clustering Launched Classification (CLC) and concluded that it was more effective than the SVM approach. Case Based reasoning is another approach that can be used in credit scoring and it works in such a way that it compares each case to see if there is an identical one, if not, the search continues until an identical case is found.

5   Hybrid/Ensemble Approaches

Hybrid models have become very common in credit scoring. A hybrid is a combination of different approaches in order to come up with one model. Simple hybrid models are made from performing three steps namely, feature selection, determination of model parameters and then classification. The hybrid models can also be built from a class wise classifier. In this approach samples of data are clustered in order to decide the number of labels before they are classified. Ensemble classification is another approach that can be used in credit scoring. It works by first producing several classifiers to obtain classification results trained on different samples.

The difference between Ensemble classification and hybrid approaches is that the Hybrid approach uses one classifier for learning while Ensemble learning produces various classifiers with different parameters. There is a difference between credit scoring and behavioural scoring, the difference being that, the latter is a dynamic approach to credit scoring. Zhong and Li [7] recommended that it is important to incorporate economic conditions to credit scoring since they have an effect on the evolution criterion of credit institutions. They suggested that, when the economic conditions are in a depression, evolution criteria should be lenient to increase the revenue for credit institutions.

6 General Approaches to Handling Drift

Credit rating models that are able to adapt to changes in population samples due to unexpected changes in the economic conditions are the most favourable ones. Drift can be classified into two categories namely abrupt and gradual drifts. When the drift is abrupt, distribution changes at different time points normally referred to as change points. When moving from one change point to the other, the distribution is static. When the drift is gradual, the distribution changes at each time step. A general approach to handle population drift would be to re-estimate the parameters of the classifier at different intervals using a current section of the available data. Unfortunately this approach is not so accurate because population drifts occur at unpredictable times [2].

Another approach that is common is to rebuild the classifier using current data after observing a major degradation in the prediction accuracy. Rebuilding can be a good approach if the population drift does not occur soon after rebuilding, if this occurs, it means all the predictions done between the drift period and the next rebuilding will be inaccurate. Another challenge to this approach is the time factor; it is time consuming to start gathering new data for new clients in order to use it for the rebuilding process.

Forgarty [9] investigated how genetic algorithms can be used in credit scoring. Genetic algorithms work in a way that is similar to the way biological genes are passed from one generation to the next. He noted that one of the key challenges faced in maintaining scoring systems include population drift which happens to be a process by which scores deteriorate over a certain given period. As data grows in this bid data era, most organizations do not have enough resources to curb the population drift problem hence do not commit enough resources to mitigate this situation. The common approach that has been used to deal with population drift is the use of sophisticated semi-automated prediction tools, which operate in the background to ensure that the models meet minimal standards of efficiency. These tools include genetic algorithms. The concept behind genetic algorithms is beneficial because it enables the production of robust and effective model offspring from a given set of surviving genes thereby curbing the population drift challenge.

In order for Forgarty [9] to prove that genetic algorithms can be used to facilitate scoring system maintenance functions, he created a proprietary genetic algorithm that could facilitate the credit scoring function. The genetic algorithm that is implemented in scoring models is based on Darwin's survival of the fittest principle hence in this case, better scoring models must live longer as compared to poor performers. The genes represent the data attributes or independent variable, chromosomes are composed of genes and represent a model. The evolutionary process starts by breeding the first population of randomly selected models and evaluating the worthiness of each model, then new generation models are bred by cloning, mating and mutating with the best evolved model being the final solution.

The proprietary genetic algorithm model was applied to the datasets on 25 models developed in a traditional manner using logistic regression using data of a large finance company. The genetic algorithm outperformed the traditionally built models thus indicating that they are suitable for model redevelopment maintenance functions. In

72% of the trials, the genetic algorithms performed better than the traditional techniques, 16% of the trials, genetic algorithms and the traditional ones performed the same then 12% of the trials failed due to data over fitting. There was never a situation when the traditional ones outperformed the genetic algorithms. The genetic algorithms are best used for maintaining credit score systems in order to curb population drift but are not very popular because they require high processing power and also it is difficult to come up with a genetic model for all class of problems and data in credit scoring scenarios. Forgaty [9] suggested the use of neural networks and support vector machines as other methods that could solve problems in credit scoring.

7 Drift Effects and Proposed Solutions

Hand and Adams [10] explained the problems that arise when inferential statements are made about a population based on a non-random population sample. One example that they concentrated on was the issue of reject reference, a situation that arises when a score card is built only from previously accepted customers. In credit scoring, it is of paramount importance to keep evaluating the existing scorecards to maintain the prediction accuracy. Usually performance degrades due to changes in applicant population, economic climate and also the competitive environment. If there is a bias in the selection, the resulting situation will be favouring a new scorecard as compared to the existing one. When a new scorecard is favoured, unnecessary costs might be incurred in an effort to phase out the old score card. More costs like the cost of new software and retraining of staff are incurred.

Kelly *et al.* [11] performed a study on a UK dataset of 92958 unsecured personal loans with a 24 month term from 1993 to 1997. They used two classifications to categorize the clients. A client with at least three months in arrears was classified as bad and good was for opposite scenario. They observed that there was need for a waiting period of about 2 years after the granting of the loan for a client to be classified in their accurate class. This misclassification is evidence enough to show that there is some shifting of classification conditions that occurs to a model overtime. In most cases the change in the posterior distribution of the class membership is the one that affects classification accuracy.

Kadwe and Suryawanshi [12] in their review on concept drift did an analysis on how concept drift occurs and how it affects the performance and accuracy of the model. The general current trend is the handling of large streams of data and this data can change over a certain period of time and this is what is being referred to as concept drift. Concept drift occurs when the concept about which data is being collected changes from time to time. There is that need to incorporate a model that can detect the changes so that when there is a change in concept it will be easily noticed and dealt with. There is no way one can detect that a change has occurred unless the change has been detected and also the level of the change has been noted. It is against this background that there exist different kinds of concept drift. The relation between the input data and target variable makes concept change take different forms. Concept drift between time point $t0$ and time point $t1$ can be defined using Eq. (1) as:

$$\exists X: pt0(X, y) \neq pt1(X, y) \tag{1}$$

Where pt0 denotes the joint distribution at time t0 between the set of input variables X and the target variable y. There are three ways in which concept drift may occur and these are prior probabilities of classes, p(y) may change over time, class-conditional probability distributions, p(X, y) might change and also posterior probabilities p(y|X) might change hence concept drift can then be grouped in terms of reason of change and also the rate at which the change has taken place. When the class labels are different from point to point, that is referred to as a real drift but when the concept does not change but there is a change in data distribution, it is called a virtual drift. Drifts can be sudden, incremental and also gradual. When it is a sudden drift, there is a sharp change between the old data and the current data. When it is incremental, the change will be happening sequentially over a given time and when it is gradual, there could be sudden change in some cases but the concept might go back to the previous trend then have a sharp change again. A lot of real world applications are subject to drift issues and these range from monitoring systems, personal assistance systems, Decision support systems and also artificial Intelligence Systems.

Knotek and Pereira [13] did a survey on concept drift. When instances are no longer from the same distribution, it is an indication that concept drift would have occurred. As indicted by other authors, Knotek and Pereira [13] mentioned that concept drift can occur in different ways and these are sudden, gradual, incremental and reoccurring and suggested some of the main approaches to handling it. They suggested the following approaches: instance selection, instance weighing, ensemble learning and statistical methods.

Instance selection mainly deals with the identification of instances that are applicable to the current concept. In general there will be a window that moves over recently arrived instances, as new examples arrive they are placed into the beginning of the window, the same number of examples are removed from the end of the window, and the learner is reapplied. The learnt concepts are used for prediction only in the immediate future. In some cases the window size can be changed and in some cases it can be fixed.

In Instance weighting, the main concept lies behind forgetting. The new training examples are regarded as of higher priority than the older ones and their priority is reduced as time lapses. A gradual forgetting function or a kernel function can be used to calculate the weights. SVM and neural networks have been used for this purpose.

Ensemble learning keeps a set of concept descriptions and the predictions are combined using voting or the most relevant description is selected. In most cases the weight is a function of the previous performance and shows the future capability of the base learner. When accuracy of the model takes precedence as compared to the time taken to run and update the ensemble, an ensemble is a very good solution to solving concept drift. Statistical methods usually calculate a statistic that picks the similarity between two example sets of a multivariate data. The value of the statistic is then compared to the expected value under the null hypothesis that both sets are sampled from the same distribution. The resulting value can be seen as a measure of the extent to which concept drift would have occurred. There is no concrete approach to solving concept drift problems. Any given solution depends on the problem domain and also nature of the data that is being used, if the data is artificial, the model may behave differently when exposed to real world problems.

Sun *et al.* [14] did a concept drift adaptation framework by exploiting historical knowledge. They came up with a new model that could adapt to changes in the concept. They named the ensemble Diversity and Transfer based Ensemble Learning (DTEL). They did experiments with 15 synthetic data streams and also with 4 real life situations and observed that the results given by DTEL were better than the existing approaches to adapt to concept drift changes. Assuming that some new data has just arrived, DTEL uses each preserved historical model as the starting model and further trains it with the new data through transfer learning. In general, there are two research questions that one has to answer during the design of an ensemble method for incremental learning with concept drift. These two questions are, which previously trained models are we going to maintain for use in future and also which approach is going to be adopted to exploit the maintained models to enable future learning with concept drift?

DTEL makes use of a decision tree as the base learner and a diversity-based strategy for maintaining historical models. When there is the introduction of new data, the preserved models are exploited as the stating points for training the new models, then the recently acquired models are joined to form the new ensemble. This approach becomes very effective in curbing population drift challenges and hence improves on the prediction accuracy.

Zliobaite *et al.* [15] did an analysis of the current approaches that are being used in adaptive learning with an effort to make it more applicable in real life situations. They appreciated that there is a growing amount of data that is continuously being exchanged and requires real time processing and mining so that it becomes meaningful. The fact that data evolves over time is reason enough to make a predicting model flexible and to adjust accordingly so that it does not give false predictions as the data evolves. Zliobaite *et al.* [15] identified six areas which need to be addressed when one wants to build a meaningful adaptive model and these are, making adaptive systems scalable, dealing with realistic data, improving usability and trust, integrating expert knowledge, taking into account various application needs, and moving from adaptive algorithms towards adaptive tools. Making adaptive systems scalable can be achieved by making sure that data is processed as it arrives or it can be handled at the hardware side where its main application areas are in cloud computing, grid computing and mobile applications. Scaling up can also be achieved by dedicating the training process to different processors so that the task is not only managed on one machine. The building of new incremental algorithms and the conversion of current learning algorithms so that they will be able to work in incremental online mode, building techniques that allow learning algorithms to work in changing hardware environments, coming up with approaches that would be able to run data mining algorithms in resource aware devices and also developing algorithms that are able to return an estimate of the correct solution, depending on the amount of processing they were able to perform would be a good way to achieve scalability.

There is a difference between dealing with a synthetic data stream and dealing with a real data set. Usually the general assumption is that data comes in an orderly way and it would have already been pre-processed such that feedback is instantaneously available after performing each prediction and before the arrival of new data. Real data usually comes from complex environments and is usually noisy, redundant and sometimes has missing values hence it is very important to dedicate much time to pre-processing when dealing with real data in order to achieve high levels of prediction accuracy. Improving usability and trust can be done by making sure that the process of setting parameters that determine that the prediction is made easy for the user or better still to make the parameters self-adjusting to suit the change in environment. When one is building an adaptive system, there is that need for them to merge their proposed model with the knowledge that has already been unearthed by the experts in this field. A lot of research work has been conducted but some of the work is not being used to solve real life problems. Adaptive learning models can be used in different application areas and it is of paramount importance to note that there is no software tool that has been developed so far to solve adaptive learning problems in different application areas using one solution. Coming up with such a software solution is quite a challenge because it requires the synchronization of different data sources, data formats, size and also arrival frequency so that they become easy to process. Zliobaite et al. [15] appreciated that adaptive learning has come to help solve real life problems but a lot still needs to be done to increase its use.

Krempl and Hofer [16] did a study on population drift. They highlighted that it is of paramount importance to study the different categories of drift because many adaptive classification methods make assumptions concerning the drift type. They highlighted that drift can affect the Posterior distribution $P(Y|X)$, the feature distribution $P(X)$ and the class Prior distribution $P(Y)$ where X is the explanatory variables or features and Y is the binary response. They also defined verification latency as the time interval between classification and verification of the prediction. Drift mining needs to be done on prediction systems in order to come up with ways to handle the drift to improve on accuracy. There is that need to identify and track sub-populations in un-labelled data over time in order to observe the drift pattern. Krempl and Hofer's [16] work helps in understanding how the population drift comes into play to degrade the prediction accuracy.

A new Dynamic Credit Scoring Model Based on Clustering Ensemble was developed to solve the problem that could not predict customer credit dynamically as well as population drifts in customer credit scoring [17]. Firstly, the training set samples were clustered into multiple subareas, then the entire observation period was fractionized into several fractional periods. Finally, customer credit scoring sub classifiers were established using cost-sensitive support vector machine. The empirical results showed that the dynamic model that they proposed not only had lower misclassification rate than static model, but also could predict the bad customers as early as possible.

Adams et al. [18] suggested a new streaming technology might be adapted to handle drift without an explicit drift model. A data stream comprises data sets that arrive at high frequency generated by a process that is subject to unknown changes, these changes are generally referred to as drift. Credit card transaction data is a very good example of a data stream. The nature of streaming data requires algorithms that are efficient and also adaptive in order for them to handle the high frequency and the drift also. A number of different approaches for streaming classifications have been proposed and these are data selection approaches with standard classifications and ensemble methods.

Adams *et al.* [18] mainly concentrated on modifying standard classifiers to incorporate forgetting factors, which are parameters that control the contribution of old data to parameter estimation. They used the main concept from the adaptive filter theory, so that the forgetting factor is automatically turned on. They concluded that adaptive forgetting methods have some advantage of reducing performance degradation between classifier rebuilds.

Nikolaidis *et al.* [19] concentrated on how population drift affects behavioural scoring. They gave examples of different data sources that can be used to start behavioural scoring. The examples that they gave are, delinquency history, usage history, static information such as age and demographic data, payment history, collections activity, type of credit and bureau data. The data set that they used was from Greece. The country's economic situation had been affected since 2009. Data used in behavioural scoring is dynamic in nature because it evolves over time yet most scoring models are static in nature hence there is that need to study the relationship between the two. The measure that they used in their experiment is the probability of default (PD) where their default definition was either good or bad using a performance window of 12 to 24 months and an outcome window of 12 months.

An entity that was being awarded the good status is the one that had 0–1 months in arrears, 2–3 months in arrears was indeterminate and 4 or more months in arrears was classified as bad. They concluded that behavioural scoring is a little bit affected by population drift and in situations where the population is good, it becomes better but when the population is bad, it becomes worse.

Whittaker *et al.* [20] used the Kalman filtering algorithm to come up with a technique for monitoring the performance of a client credit scorecard over a period of time. In their new approach, they allowed systematic updates on the scorecard after comparing the new applicant information to the previous ones. The Kalman filtering algorithm in this instance was used to cater for scorecard degradations, which can occur due to different factors which include but not limited to population drifts and changes in the economic conditions.

They adapted the Kalman filter so that it can be used as a diagnostic tool to monitor credit scorecards. Whenever there is a new applicant, the filter adaptively estimates a value so that current observations are given higher weight. The updated scorecard can be observed over time and suggestions can be made if there is need to rebuild the scorecard. The data that they used was that of a commercial company's mortgage portfolio which contained records on about 180 000 applicants and used about 30 variables from the application form. After the implementation of the dynamic scorecard, there was clear evidence that it properly and accurately scored new clients as compared to its baseline counterparts.

Pavlidis *et al.* [2] developed an adaptive and sequential approach for logistic regression, which caters for any type of population drift storing any previously captured data. Their main idea was to incorporate new data upon arrival into the system.

They defined a weighted likelihood function that regularly removes the effects of past data on current parameter estimates. The previously used information is forgotten and this produces an online algorithm that can cater for the changes in the population. The proposed method was evaluated on artificial data sets that show gradual and abrupt drift changes. The proposed method was also done on static artificial data sets. The performance of the proposed method, Adaptive Online Logistic Regression (AOLR) proved that it works better than the general logistic classifiers. The results proved that, updating the classifier as data becomes available gives an improvement as opposed to just re-estimating the classifier parameters.

There is an aspect related to population drift that Pavlidis *et al.* [2] did not consider, which is the delay between the observation of the predictor variables and the corresponding class label. This aspect can be generally solved by a survival analysis model, which changes over time as more data becomes available. A combination of the adaptive online logistic regression and the survival analysis model would make a great enhancement in solving the population drift problem.

Romanyuk [21] developed a credit scoring model based on contour subspaces. In his approach, he suggested the separation of a client's personal data and credit terms so that there is the creation of a contour subspace for credit scoring. Banks must take cognisant of the fact that the creditworthiness of a borrowing entity can change and must allow a platform to adjust the credit terms so that credit risk is effectively managed. Proper adjustments to the changes that occur can improve on the number of applicants that are more credit worthy. In his proposed model, credit terms form a contour subspace for each creditworthiness value to such an extent that when this model is being used, it must give assistance in making a decision on whether to grant a loan or not.

The decision can be reached through the visualization of a contour subspace of credit terms for an applicant in relation with an individual creditworthiness, giving choices on credit terms from this contour subspace and manage credit terms online in association with the changes in creditworthiness valuation. In general credit scoring, the applicants' personal data is combined with credit attributes in order to decide whether to grant a loan or not. Romanyuk's [21] model distinguishes the applicant's creditworthiness from the riskiness of the credit terms through the use of contour subspaces. This approach makes future decisions become less hectic because the bank does not need to go through the complete recalculation process when the same applicant applies for a different credit type. Whenever a client's credit worthiness changes, there should be a change also in the loan rate. Assuming that there is an increase in creditworthiness, the bank must respond by decreasing the loan rate, if creditworthiness remains constant then the bank must maintain the same loan rate, if creditworthiness decreases then the bank should ideally increase the loan rate. The introduction of contour spaces enables the bank to manage the dynamism in credit worthiness.

Babu and Satish [22] came up with a model based on the application of K-Nearest Neighbor (K-NN). They used the K-NN method to perform an approximating of good or bad risk likelihoods for an applicant. In order for one to be classified good and bad, it is based on the k most similar points in the training samples. The similarity of points accessed by the appropriate distance metric. They gave the advantages of using K-NN credit scoring as the automatic updating of the design set, providing a reason for refusal of credit by exploiting the information about class separation in the data provided by the regression weights and also it is less prone to declining credit on the basis of one characteristic regardless of all other attributes as compared to its linear or logistic regression counterparts.

Barakat [23] proposed the inclusion of context awareness in an effort to adapt classification models to different changes that might occur. Most changes occur to the data due to changes in the environment. There is need to study, understand and analyse the contextual issues in order to unearth the causes of the drift. Information regarding contextual issues helps in deciding on the relevant data to train and also to detect the changes that would have occurred in the model.

Identifying the appropriate training data size is one approach that can be used to manage drifts but this can bring a dilemma between stability and plasticity. A smaller window will easily capture the changes in the data hence detecting the drift easily but might be too small to bring stability in the concept description of the observed data. Barakat [23] proposed the incorporation of a context learning model that makes use of historical data to pick on the variables that have an effect on the concept of interest. The proposal suggested the use of drift detection mechanisms. It is more advantageous to implement drift detection algorithms since there will be no need to revisit the model or data that existed before the detection. The learner is designed in such a way that it has multiple levels and each model will be representing a different concept. Once the same concept resurfaces, the previously learned concept is the one that is run hence there is no need to continue giving reference to the previously trained data. Understanding the concept drift and handling it helps in maintaining the prediction model accuracy by adapting to the changes that would have occurred.

Bifet et al. [24] presented on handling concept drift and highlighted that, the fact that data continues to evolve over time is the reason why models suffer changes in data distribution normally referred to as concept drift. When a learning model is built, there is need to make sure that the model adapts to the changing environment in order to maintain model prediction accuracy. The adaptation of the model has to occur in a timeous and accurate manner. For a system to be able to handle concept drift, it has to be possessing some desirable properties like prompt detection and adaptation to the drift, be able to differentiate between drift and noise because in machine learning, noise can also affect the prediction accuracy. The adaptation must occur in such a way that it does not have much effect on the system resources like time and memory. Different adaptive learning strategies can be used in order to manage concept drift. The strategies can be grouped as single classifiers or ensembles. Single classifiers can make use of detectors, which can detect the changes they can implement the forgetting approach in which the old data is forgotten and retraining occurs using new data. In the ensemble approach, the strategy can be contextual based on or it can be in the form of a dynamic ensemble. In the contextual approach, many models are switched according to the observed incoming data. In dynamic ensemble, many models are built and the models are dynamically combined.

The best approach to use in different circumstances depends on the nature of change that would have occurred to the data. Changes can be categorized in terms of speed that it can be a gradual change or a sudden change. The other category is in terms of occurrence, whether it is always a new change or a reoccurrence. Sudden changes are best solved using single classifiers either by detection of by forgetting in which fixed windows are used with instance weighting. Gradual drift can be solved using dynamic ensembles, which have the implementation of adaptive fission rules. Reoccurring drift is best solved using contextual ensembles.

Drifts can occur due to different circumstances hence the sources of change can vary from adversarial in which there is an input to the learning model that is sent intentionally to cause an error in the model. Changes can also be caused by a change in interest, change in population or even a change in model complexity. These changes can be predictable, unpredictable or identifiable hence there is that need to keep the model up to date, detect the change whenever it happens and explain the change in order to deal with it in the case of reoccurrence.

Žliobaitė et al. [1] in their overview of concept drift applications did an analysis of the major applications that are usually affected by concept drift. They defined concept drift as the change that occurs in personal interests, population or adversary activities. The change is given the term concept drift in machine learning, data mining and predictive analysis but it has a different names in other area of study. When the change occurs in pattern recognition, it is referred to as covariate shift or data set shift, when it occurs in signal processing, it is referred to as non-stationarity. There is a difference in data source between the training data and the application data. Usually there is a wrong assumption when it comes to model building, test data source is different from train data source and this causes a deviation in the model accuracy for as long as data is distributed in streams rather than in static form evolution will always occur. There is no single solution that can solve the concept drift problem because it occurs in different scenarios.

Žliobaitė et al. [1] identified the main categories that are in use which suffer concept drift. The major application areas were identified as monitoring and control applications which mainly concentrate on detection and taking corrective action, information management which mainly deals with recommender systems [35] and personalized learning and also analytics and diagnostics, which deals with predictive analytics like evaluation of credit worthiness.

Garcia et al. [25] suggested an approach to handling concept drift in situations where there is both abrupt and slow gradual changes. They named their proposed solution as the Early Drift Detection Method (EDDM). The solution was based on taking into consideration the distance between two erroneous classifications instead of just concentrating on the number of errors as suggested by other researchers that designed the general detection methods. Their experimental results showed that it was also worth considering the distance between the errors in order to detect drift occurrence earlier, however, their work is not enough to use to model a dynamic credit scoring model because of the existing technological change which introduces a lot of dynamism.

Klinkenberg and Joachims [26] proposed a method of handling concept drift in Support Vector Machines (SVM). The proposal was based on keeping a window on the training data. Once a change has occurred, the window size must automatically adjust in order to reduce the estimated generalization error. The major strength of this proposal is on giving the correct window size per given scenario. SVM is based on structural risk minimization principle hence it basically learns linear decision rules explained by weight and a vector. In many common machine learning problems, researchers use a fixed window size but this approach's major drawback is that it makes a lot of assumptions on the rate of concept drift. A fixed window would work perfectly fine if concept drift will never occur or occurs after a very long period of time.

Klinkenberg and Joachims [26] proved that there is a direct relationship between the training window size and the rate at which a model responds to concept drift hence they suggested an algorithm that automatically adjusts the training window to suit the change. The choice of a training window must be done with caution because it must not be too big or too small. A training window must not be too big, otherwise it will keep including some old data hence giving a false prediction. The window must also not be too small in order to train the model widely to improve accuracy. In their experimental set up, they used four data management approaches which are full memory, no memory, fixed size window and adaptive window size. In the full memory approach, there is no forgetting, all previously used examples are considered, the no memory approach bases its data on the most recently used batch, there is no reference to the older versions. Fixed window size uses an unchanging window size for three batches and the adaptive window size implements the proposed window adjustment algorithm.

For as long as there was no concept drift, the full memory and adaptive window size performed almost the same. When concept drift occurred, the other three non-adaptive methods underperformed hence the adaptive method is the only one that produced accurate results. For as long as there is the occurrence of concept drift, it is more advantageous to make the window adjustable.

Hofer and Krempl [27] supported the fact that scoring data suffers changes over time hence there is that need to predict and monitor these changes in order to achieve the highest level of prediction accuracy. The main goal is to establish when the change would have occurred and act accordingly. Change can be revealed through change detection algorithms or change diagnosis which can be based on spatio-temporal density estimation, velocity density estimation or post analysis of changes in the distribution. There is need for an appreciation of the general distribution pattern so that when changes occur, it will be easily detected. Hofer and Krempl [27] suggested the use of un-labelled data to detect class priori changes. They also suggested the use of temporal goodness of fit and also the implementation of a controlled adaptation process. All these approaches help in monitoring and controlling drift in order to maintain prediction accuracy.

Tsymbal [28] explained the subject of concept drift in detail. When there is a change in the hidden context, it can cause a big change in the target concept. Models need to be set correctly in order to be able to distinguish between noise and concept drift. If an algorithm over reacts to noise, it might regard it as concept drift and also making it less reactive, it might react too slowly to concept drift when it occurs and it will not be efficient. Many concept drift handling approaches are based on updating the model when new data arrives but this approach is very costly because data can arrive at very fast unmanageable rates. In some systems, the data needs to be labelled based on user feedback and this can be very time consuming. The best approach to handling drift is to detect and adapt to the change. Tsymbal [28] also highlighted the major approaches to concept drift handling as instance selection, instance weighting and ensemble learning.

Ang *et al.* [29] analysed the existence of drift in distributed computing environment in which peer machines learn from each other in order to classify different concepts. When a change has occurred in one peer, the other peer must be able to detect the change and react accordingly in order to learn the correct model and produce correct classification results. Ang *et al.* [29] developed an ensemble approach that they referred to as Predictive and Parameter Insensitive Ensemble (PINE). PINE is an approach which enables drift to be handled in two ways namely the reactive and the proactive approach. In the reactive approach, drift would have occurred and it is detected and corrective action is taken. In the proactive, upcoming events are assessed and warning signs and adaptation approaches are communicated across the network to other peers.

Ang *et al.* [29] did a comparison of the performance of the Ensemble of Proactive Models (PEM), the Ensemble of Reactive Models (REM) and PINE. They concluded that PINE being a combination of the proactive and the reactive approaches performed better in detecting and managing drift in situations where the drift was occurring at different times for different peers. This study was done for distributed computing but it is very relevant in detecting drift in data streams scenarios such as credit scoring hence the ensemble approach can be used to detect and manage drifts in such cases.

Zliobaite *et al.* [30] produced a framework that can be used for active learning on changing data streams. They produced this framework as further work to the initial work on Massive Online (MOA) system. Bifet *et al.* [32] under normal circumstance active learning strategies concentrate on queuing the most unlikely instances, which are usually found on the decision boundary. This implies that whenever a change occurs away from the decision boundary it is most likely unidentified hence there is no adaptation. The major goal in coming up with adaptive learning strategies is to maximize prediction accuracy as time lapses but at the same time managing resources such as labelling costs and time. The software framework that they produced is suitable for use in active learning classifications on data streams. The platform can be used by researchers to do experiments on data stream learning benchmarks for active learning. Credit scoring [31, 33, 34] is ever challenging research area with a number of researchers providing solutions.

8   Credit Scoring Models Application Areas

When used in Financial Institutions credit scoring models are used in loan applications to make credit decisions for loan applications, set credit limits, manage existing accounts and forecast the profitability of consumers and customers.

When used in the insurance industry, they are used to decide on the applications of new insurance policies and the renewal of existing polices. They can also be used in Real Estate where landlords can make use of credit scores to determine whether potential tenants are likely to pay their rent on time. In Human Resources, some employers make use of credit history and credit scores to decide whether to hire a potential employee, especially for posts where employees need to handle huge sums of money.

9   Conclusion

The design of a dynamic credit scoring model that caters for the drift problem is of paramount importance in improving the prediction and the rating accuracy. Most of the models that have been implemented do not consider the drift problem. Some models do consider drift and adapt to it by revisiting the model and making adjustments to it but this process has proven to be costly in terms of time and other resources hence designing a model that can detect a change and automatically adapt to it is recommended.

References

1. Žliobaitė, I., Pechenizkiy, M., Gama, J.: An overview of concept drift applications. In: Japkowicz, N., Stefanowski, J. (eds.) Big Data Analysis: New Algorithms for a New Society. SBD, vol. 16, pp. 91–114. Springer, Cham (2016). https://doi.org/10.1007/978-3-319-26989-4_4
2. Pavlidis, N.G., Tasoulis, D.K., Adams, N.M., Hand, D.J.: Adaptive consumer credit classification. J. Oper. Res. Soc. **63**(12), 1645–1654 (2012)
3. Huang, S., Day, M.: A comparative study of data mining techniques for credit scoring in banking. In: IEEE IRI, San Francisco, California, USA, 14–16 August 2013 (2013)
4. Huang, Z., et al.: Credit rating analysis with support vector machines and neural networks: a market comparative study. Decis. Support Syst. **37**(4), 543–558 (2004)
5. Keramati, A., Yousefi, N.: A proposed classification of data mining techniques in credit scoring. In: Proceedings of the International Conference on Industrial Engineering and Operations Management (2011)
6. Paleologo, G., Elisseeff, A., Antonini, G.: Subagging for credit scoring models. J. Oper. Res. **201**(2), 490–499 (2010)
7. Li, X.L., Zhong, Y.: An overview of personal credit scoring: techniques and future work. Int. J. Intell. Sci. **2**(04), 181 (2012)
8. Luo, S.T., Cheng, B.W., Hsieh, C.H.: Prediction model building with clustering-launched classification and support vector machines in credit scoring. Expert Syst. Appl. **36**(4), 7562–7566 (2009)
9. Fogarty, D.J.: Using genetic algorithms for credit scoring system maintenance functions. Int. J. Artif. Intell. Appl. **3**(6), 1 (2012)
10. Hand, D.J., Adams, N.M.: Selection bias in credit scorecard evaluation. J. Oper. Res. Soc. **65**(3), 408–415 (2014)
11. Kelly, M.G., Hand, D.J., Adams, N.M.: The impact of changing populations on classifier performance. In: Proceedings of the Fifth ACM SIGKDD International Conference on Knowledge Discovery and Data Mining, pp. 367–371. ACM, August 1999
12. Kadwe, Y., Suryawanshi, V.: A review on concept drift. IOSR J. Comput. Eng. **17**, 20–26 (2015)
13. Knotek, J., Pereira, W.: Survey on Concept Drift. Faculty of Economics, University of Porto, Portugal. https://is.muni.cz/el/1433/podzim2011/PA164/um/drift_detection_methods.pdf
14. Sun, Y., Tang, K., Zhu, Z., Yao, X.: Concept drift adaptation by exploiting historical knowledge. IEEE Trans. Neural Netw. Learn. Syst. **29**, 4822–4832 (2018)
15. Zliobaite, I., et al.: Next challenges for adaptive learning systems. ACM SIGKDD Explorations Newsl **14**(1), 48–55 (2012)
16. Krempl, G., Hofer, V.: Classification in presence of drift and latency. In: 2011 IEEE 11th International Conference on Data Mining Workshops (ICDMW), pp. 596–603. IEEE, December 2011

17. Wei, G., Mingshu, C.: A new dynamic credit scoring model based on clustering ensemble. In: 3rd International Conference on Computer Science and Network Technology (2013)
18. Adams, N.M., Tasoulis, D.K., Anagnostopoulos, C., Hand, D.J.: Temporally-adaptive linear classification for handling population drift in credit scoring. In: Lechevallier, Y., Saporta, G. (eds.) Proceedings of COMPSTAT'2010, pp. 167–176. Physica-Verlag HD, Heidelberg (2010). https://doi.org/10.1007/978-3-7908-2604-3_15
19. Nikolaidis, D., Doumpos, M., Zopounidis, C.: Exploring population drift on consumer credit behavioral scoring. In: Grigoroudis, E., Doumpos, M. (eds.) Operational Research in Business and Economics. SPBE, pp. 145–165. Springer, Cham (2017). https://doi.org/10.1007/978-3-319-33003-7_7
20. Whittaker, J., Whitehead, C., Somers, M.: A dynamic scorecard for monitoring baseline performance with application to tracking a mortgage portfolio. J. Oper. Res. Soc. **58**(7), 911–921 (2007)
21. Romanyuk, K.: A dynamic credit scoring model based on contour subspaces. In: Proceedings of SAI Intelligent Systems Conference (IntelliSys). IntelliSys (2016)
22. Babu, R., Satish, A.R.: Improved of k-nearest neighbor techniques in credit scoring. Int. J. Dev. Comput. Sci. Technol. **1**(2), 1–4 (2013)
23. Barakat, L., Pavlidis, N., Crone, S.: A context-aware approach for handling concept drift in classification (Doctoral dissertation, Lancaster University) (2018)
24. Bifet, A., Gama, J., Pechenizkiy, M., Liobait, I.: Handling concept drift: importance challenges & solutions. Tutorial. In: Proceedings of the Pacific-Asia Conference on Knowledge Discovery and Data Mining (2011)
25. Baena-Garcia, M., del Campo-Ávila, J., Fidalgo, R., Bifet, A., Gavalda, R., Morales-Bueno, R.: Early drift detection method. In: Fourth International Workshop on Knowledge Discovery from Data Streams, vol. 6, pp. 77–86, September 2006
26. Klinkenberg, R., Joachims, T.: Detecting concept drift with support vector machines. In: ICML, pp. 487–494, June 2000
27. Hofer, V., Krempl, G.: Predicting and Monitoring Changes in Scoring Data (2015)
28. Tsymbal, A.: The problem of concept drift: definitions and related work, vol. 106, no. 2. Computer Science Department, Trinity College Dublin (2004)
29. Ang, H.H., Gopalkrishnan, V., Zliobaite, I., Pechenizkiy, M., Hoi, S.C.: Predictive handling of asynchronous concept drifts in distributed environments. IEEE Trans. Knowl. Data Eng. **25**(10), 2343–2355 (2013)
30. Zliobaite, I., Bifet, A., Holmes, G., Pfahringer, B.: MOA concept drift active learning strategies for streaming data. In: Proceedings of the Second Workshop on Applications of Pattern Analysis, pp. 48–55, October 2011
31. Bhatia, S., Sharma, P., Burman, R., Hazari, S., Hande, R.: Credit scoring using machine learning techniques. Int. J. Comput. Appl. **161**(11), 1 (2017)
32. Bifet, A., Holmes, G., Kirkby, R., Pfahringer, B.: MOA: massive online analysis. J. Mach. Learn. Res. **11**, 1601–1604 (2010)
33. Kogeda, O.P., Vumane, N.N.: A model augmenting credit risk management in the banking industry. Int. J. Technol. Diffus. (IJTD) **8**(4), 47–66 (2017)
34. Chikoore, R., Kogeda, O.P.: A credit rating model for Zimbabwe. In: Proceedings of the Southern Africa Telecommunication Networks and Applications Conference (SATNAC), Fancourt, George, Western Cape, South Africa, 4–7 September 2016, pp. 88–89 (2016)
35. Bhebe, W., Kogeda, O.P.: Shilling attack detection in collaborative recommender systems using a meta learning strategy. In: Proceedings of the IEEE International Conference on Emerging Trends in Networks and Computer Communications, ETNCC 2015, Windhoek Country Club Resort, Namibia, 17–20 May 2015, pp. 56–61 (2015)

Author Index

Printed in the United States
By Bookmasters